Life
on the
Road

*The Gospel Basis for a
Messianic Lifestyle*

Athol Gill

HERALD PRESS
Scottdale, Pennsylvania
Waterloo, Ontario

Library of Congress Cataloging-in-Publication Data

Gill, Athol.
    Life on the road : the Gospel basis for a messianic lifestyle /
Athol Gill.
        p. cm.
    Includes bibliographical references and index.
    ISBN 0-8361-3588-1
    1. Christian life—Biblical teaching. 2. Bible. N.T. Gospels—
Criticism, interpretation, etc.   I. Title.
BS2555.6.C48G55 1992
226'.06—dc20   92-15251
                                                        CIP

The paper used in this publication is recycled and meets the minimum requirements of American National Standard for Information Sciences—
Permanence of Paper for Printed Library Materials, ANSI Z39.48-1984.

Some Scripture is the author's own rendering (AG), and most quotations
are from the *New Revised Standard Version Bible*, copyright 1989, by the
Division of Christian Education of the National Council of the Churches of
Christ in the USA, and are used by permission.

Life on the Road was published in 1989 by Lancer Books, Anzea Publishers,
Homebush West, Australia, and is reissued here by permission.

LIFE ON THE ROAD
Copyright © 1989 by Anzea Publishers, and © 1992 by Herald Press,
    Scottdale, Pa. 15683. Published simultaneously in Canada
    by Herald Press, Waterloo, Ont. N2L 6H7. All rights reserved
Library of Congress Catalog Number: 92-15251
International Standard Book Number: 0-8361-3588-1
Printed in the United States of America
Book design by Jim Butti
Cover art by Kathy Cline Miller

01 00 99 98 97 96 95 94 93 92 10 9 8 7 6 5 4 3 2 1

To
Judith,
Jonathan, and Kirsten

Contents

Abbreviations

Parentheses in the text enclose authors' names, title keywords when necessary, and page numbers. These books are identified in the bibliography.

Standard abbreviations inside parentheses are used for the books of the Bible, Old Testament Apocrypha, Pseudepigrapha, and New Testament Apocrypha. Each is composed of the first letters of the book's name.

Foreword by Donald B. Kraybill

Over the centuries layers of theological interpretation have shrouded our image of Jesus. These masks that cover the face of Jesus have often been constructed for good reasons as Christians in many religious traditions around the world have sought to translate Jesus into their cultural context. Indeed, the recent accent on contextualizing the gospel has underscored the necessity of constructing different masks of Jesus for different cultural settings. Such masks are helpful to link the message of the gospel to the particularities of a social context—to the forces of nation, tribe, ethnicity, and culture that shape a people. But as helpful and essential as they may be, such masks may also distort and camouflage.

In other cases theological masks have domesticated Jesus: they have tamed him to fit the mold of our pious religious desires. Such masks have contextualized Jesus, but not in an honest fashion. These masks of piety have given Jesus a gentle smile of blessing that endorses everything. This tolerant Jesus blesses nationalism, militarism, economic exploitation, greed, and luxuriant lifestyles. This Jesus overlooks the poor and homeless, the marginal social outcasts. Whatever the reason for their construction, the masks that we have placed on Jesus, often with good intentions, have nevertheless blurred his true complexion.

In creative exegetical fashion, Athol Gill pulls the masks of theological distortion from the face of Jesus. In a stimulating style, Gill takes us back to the original sources in the synoptic Gospels and introduces us to a Jesus who without his many masks often surprises, yes, even startles us. By peeling off the many layers of old masks, Gill's creative work reveals a new Jesus that may disrupt our expectations and assumptions. And yet in many ways the familiar themes persist: the call to discipleship, the cost of following, the need for community on the journey, and the sources of prayer.

Gill's work is important for several reasons. First, he doesn't strip off the masks of theological interpretation in a reckless fashion. Trained in critical methods of scriptural exegesis, he knows the theological issues that have shaped the life of the church and brings a responsible and mature spirit to his work. Moreover, he writes not only as an academic but also as an active churchman conversant with the issues of faith in the concrete context of community. The most helpful contribution of *Life on the Road* is its application to modern life. It is a creative biblical study, but it is more than that. After mining the biblical material, Gill takes the new insights and lets them address the questions of our day. His findings and his unmasked Jesus are no longer biblical trivia; they speak to our situation today with eloquence and power.

Gill's efforts may make us uncomfortable. The unmasked Jesus challenges many of the value assumptions of modern North American culture. But this is not a flaming radical call for social revolution. A tone of warm and reverent spirituality threads its way through these pages. Here are words of grace, resources for prayer, and support from brothers and sisters in the community of faith for the journey on the road.

The motif of a journey which structures the book is a fitting metaphor for the pilgrimage of faith. In his gospel, Mark often talks of being "on the way" with Jesus. They are unexpected turns and twists, surprises, risks, and detours on the journey of faith. Christian faith is indeed a process: there are phases, stages, a history, and a destination. Gill's good work provides a resourceful map—a manual for life on the road. And his lively style makes it a pleasurable read.

—*Donald B. Kraybill*
Elizabethtown College
Elizabethtown, Pennsylvania
June 1, 1992

Foreword by Bruce Wilson

C. S. Lewis said that when we try to picture God, most of us don't get beyond seeing a bright blur. Though few would deny the spiritual nature of human beings, we are sensate bodily creatures in a sensate matter-energy universe which, with all the advances of modern science, is more a mystery than it ever was, even though that mystery has been pushed wider and deeper into the cosmos than previously.

The mystery of the cosmos beckons to consciousness the greater mystery of the Creator of the cosmos. Does the Creator care for creatures? Why did the Creator create us? Can we ever see the Creator as anything more than a bright blur in our imaginations?

At the heart of the Christian faith is the discovery that the mysterious Creator revealed himself in sensate form as the human being Jesus of Nazareth. If we want to picture God, then we must picture Jesus Christ; that is the Christian way.

Athol Gill's *Life on the Road* explores the evidence of the biblical Gospels to recreate for those of us living at the end of the second millennium of the Christian era an authentic understanding of Jesus, what he taught, who he was, and what he did. This task must be undertaken for every generation because, earthen vessels that we are, each generation of Christians tends to fall into the trap of seeing Christ in its own image. To rediscover the freshness and vitality of Jesus of Nazareth, and therefore of the Christian faith itself, we always need to go back to the primary source in the Gospels.

For me what is remarkable about *Life on the Road* is not Gill's exercise of the modern crafts of New Testament scholarship, though he has them aplenty and uses them well. Rather, it is his ability to employ the scholarly tools of trade, albeit unobtrusively, to create, not academic theories or theological abstraction, but a picture of Jesus which challenges readers to live authentically.

Life on the Road is not a book for the spiritually squeamish. Nor is it a book for those who want Jesus to legitimate their lives in quiet suburbia or the comforting practices of bourgeois Western churches. Neither is it a book for those who are happy to let God remain just a bright blur out there somewhere so that they can comfortably get on with their own lives regardless. For Jesus, as *Life on the Road* disarmingly re-presents him, is just the sort of person you might expect to turn the world upside down. He is the wild man of God, not the tame spiritual elixir of pleasant Sunday mornings or the arch-supporter of conservative causes.

Gill's relationship with third-world Christians liberates him from the spectacles of Western academic scholarship. Here is insight into Jesus which will shake to the boots most Western readers' complacent and comformingly enculturated notions of discipleship.

There is humorous irony in Gill's careful use of the crafts of academic New Testament scholarship. Instead of a Jesus presented for scholarly opinion and debate, we see a Jesus who questions almost everything the bourgeois church values, including the usual way of studying the Gospels. Academic tools of trade are used to offer us a picture of Jesus as the Savior of our souls and of our culture—not for debate in universities, theological colleges, and seminaries.

Life on the Road is a book out of temper with the conservative times of its publication. Yet it is also a book which will challenge the complacency of our era with the spiritual depth and radicalism of Jesus of Nazareth. If God is just a bright blur, irrelevant to life in this decade, it is because we are dodging his incarnation in Jesus Christ and living with comfortable abstractions. Athol Gill's book challenges us to return to the wellsprings of the Christian faith as we enter the third millennium of the Christian era.

—*Bruce Wilson,*
Anglican Bishop of Bathurst, Australia

Learning to Read the Road Maps

The Journey Thus Far

One of my earliest recollections of life is of the morning my mother first took me to the Methodist Sunday school in the small country town where I was born. Dressed in brown shorts, shirt, and sandals, my face was aglow. I had been scrubbed clean the night before, ready to start out on a new adventure in life. We sat on small chairs in a circle and listened to a story, and my feet were barely touching the floor.

The story that day was about four fishermen and a man called Jesus. What a day it was and what a story! After the story the teacher brought out some crayons and a picture to color. It showed two men in water up to their knees trying to catch fish with a net. And there was a man walking along the shore watching them. He was taller than they were and, for some reason or other, when he called to them they dropped the net on the sandy beach and went off somewhere with him. I'm not sure if we were ever told where they went, but I didn't need to know. It would have been exciting wherever it was. The man with a long robe and a beard had captured another young boy's heart.

I kept going to Sunday school, but eventually they stopped telling me the stories of Jesus. They took me back into the Old Testament where there were some more good stories, especially the ones about David and his merry men. They took me into the life of the early church and the adventures of Paul and Barnabas and others. As time went on, they introduced us to Romans and Ephesians and a lot of rather heady stuff. Not long after I finished high school, I was invited to join a student group at a Baptist church in the city, and we spent months piecing together a jigsaw of texts from

Ezekiel, Daniel, Revelation, and other books of the Bible. A trainee architectural draftsman put it all together on a chart, and we were able to work out where we were on the time line of history!

Well, that was all quite interesting. But what had happened to that tall man on the seashore? My teachers kept on speaking about someone who had the same name, but somehow it all seemed different. Sometimes he was more like a philosopher than I could remember him, and once in a while he even seemed a little like a policeman. Whatever he was, he seemed a long distance away, and a lot of what he said didn't seem important any more. Certainly the adventure and the excitement had gone out of it, and I was left with the distinct impression that the stories about the tall stranger and his fishermen friends were for children only.

Some of this was probably just part of the normal experience of growing up in church, but some of it was perhaps not all that innocent. It was part of the process of the cultural captivity of Jesus, a process which continued right through my initial training in theological college. I learned some great things there, and if I had been more attentive I might have learned a lot more. But I certainly would never have learned that the life and ministry of Jesus was supposed to have had a profound influence on the way I lived. His death, yes. Perhaps some of his teaching, though we were never quite sure what we were going to do with all those idealistic sayings in the Sermon on the Mount. No, the Jesus whom we studied definitely belonged in the past, and we were determined to leave him in Galilee.

One of the nearby theological colleges seemed to have solved the problem with a pithy little saying of theirs: "The Gospels are descriptive, Paul is prescriptive." It sounded good, but the problem is that such a theology is a betrayal of the gospel and the Gospels. Almost 60 percent of the New Testament was reduced to the realm of history, and the other 40 percent made to sound like the work of an English philosopher-theologian giving a series of lectures on theology and ethics. In the whole process, Paul was as distorted as Jesus was neglected, and the Christian faith was reduced to a lifeless set of ideas and ideals.

What had happened to the stranger from Nazareth? He had not been forgotten; rather he had been left back in Galilee where he belonged. Paul, the drawing-room theologian, had become our guide. I say "the drawing-room theologian" because I am sure that the Paul we were studying never did anything that would have resulted in him being thrown into prison. Yet I do remember having to write an essay on the question "Where was Paul in prison when he wrote Philippians?" How strange that they did not force us to reflect on "Why was Paul in prison when he wrote Philippians?"

We were given the strong impression that if we followed Paul today, we would never be thrown into prison because we would always be recognizing the authority of the state and keeping the law! Perhaps if we were in a communist country, it might be different, but not in Australia! While all this was happening, the man with the beard and a long robe refused to go away. He was still there in the background, even though he looked quite uncomfortable in our company.

Jesus started to come to life at a later stage in my studies when I was reintroduced to the Gospels and was assured that they were not just children's stories: the people who wrote them were, in fact, preaching the gospel through the Gospels. Jesus was decidedly respectable now, more at home in the halls of London and Zurich than in the dusty streets of Nazareth and Managua, but the stories about him were coming to life again, and there was something to get excited about. Christianity was real and was related to life—related to real life, not just to ideas about life.

There still seemed to be a difference, however, for Jesus now seemed to work with precision and to think with the absolute logic of a Swiss reformer. Although I don't recall anyone ever speaking about the tall stranger in those terms (any more than they had earlier spoken of him as an English gentleman), I am sure that is how I had come to see him. Jesus was at home in the university setting, holding his own in debate—even in the debates of the radical 1960s, he was always one step ahead! Those were exciting times, and this approach to faith was certainly a big improvement over earlier days. For all its limitations, it had truly brought the Gospels back into my life in a way I had not known since the early days of Sunday school.

The problem now, however, was that while Jesus seemed at home in his new setting, his friends looked out of place. The tax collectors would probably have managed to find a spot on the Faculty of Commerce, but what about the fishermen? And the lepers, and prostitutes, and notorious sinners? And where were the poor, the oppressed, the outcasts, and the marginalized going to take their lectures?

Gradually, the stranger from Galilee began to introduce me to his friends among the little people of Australian society. When I learned to watch and listen, Jesus' friends showed me many things about him that I had missed or taken for granted or not fully understood. That he was born in a stable and crucified on a rubbish dump, raised in a despised town of Nazareth and killed among the criminals. That he began his mission on the margins of society and spent most of his time on the other side of the tracks. When I started to view history from this new perspective, suddenly many of his friends seemed at home as well. Gradually I came to see that his strangeness was not so much one of time but of perspective. He simply saw things differently. He had different interests and different priorities. Above all, he was calling us to follow him and to live differently.

Contacts with Christians and with churches of the third world have helped me to see a little more clearly some of the areas where my cultural captivity has deep political roots and far-reaching economic consequences. They have shown me just how politically convenient it was for me to leave Jesus in the Galilee of my boyhood. Had his Nazareth experience continued with me, I would certainly have had to make far-reaching changes in the way I was living and in the nature of the church and the society for which I was working. Life and liberation are both processes, however, and the journey continues.

Such is my own pilgrimage of faith. It is not intended as a criticism of my teachers of New Testament in Australia, England, and Switzerland (though on some things they were probably as captured by their culture as I was by mine). They encouraged me in my journey even when they must have entertained serious doubts as to whether I would make it to the next stage. They will recognize my indebtedness to them on every page that follows, even when our conclusions are vastly different.

Pausing to Read the Maps Again

The road leads on and the journey continues. Before we plunge into the future again, we may need to pause and get our directions straight. We will at least want to be heading in the right direction. Some of us, however, may have difficulty in reading maps, particularly the old maps that we have. The significance of the signs and symbols they use may be as strange to us as the terrain through which we have to travel. Some of us may need to relearn some of the basic facts again; the times have changed, and we have probably already made many mistakes and developed many bad habits in deciphering the directions. A few hints will help us stay on track.

We must bear in mind at the outset that one of the more remarkable things about the early church was the way they remembered and reinterpreted the stories of Jesus. After Easter, as Christianity was spreading throughout the Roman Empire, the early Christians continued to tell the stories of the way Jesus called his disciples to follow him through Palestine. People who lived in small communities scattered throughout the Mediterranean world remembered and reinterpreted these stories as the call of Christ to them. Many had never seen the Sea of Galilee and knew nothing about tax collecting, much less about fishing; yet they saw in these stories definitive examples of the way God works in the world.

In the crowded marketplaces and out on the lonely hillsides, the gospel was preached through the Gospel stories, and people were invited to make a gospel response, to leave what they were doing, and to follow Jesus. As they recounted the stories, Jesus encountered them, calling them to faith, bringing them together as his people, and sending them out to continue his mission in the world. The stories gave direction to their lives.

Still later, when the Gospels were written, this process of

remembering and reinterpreting continued as the Evangelists sought to draw out the significance of the stories for the
churches to whom they were writing. They sought to set the
directions and prepare the maps, outlining the road they
wanted their churches to travel (to build on our imagery).
The Gospels were never allowed to become mere recitations
of events in the life of Jesus and his friends, biblical maps of
the journeys of olden times, destined to collect dust in the ar-
chives of Christian history. The maps were continually re-
drawn as the terrain varied and the road wound its way into
settings and situations as yet unexplored.

The early scrolls on which the Gospels were written did
not have chapter divisions, verses, or headings to indicate
their contents. Even punctuation was rarely used in those
days. When the Evangelists purchased their twenty-foot roll
of papyrus from the city market and ruled it into columns,
they wrote the story in unbroken form. There usually were
20-24 letters to the line, with no punctuation and no gaps between the words.

For us, it is a strange way of writing; imagine, a whole
Gospel, and not one footnote! But for them, it was the natural
way to do things, and their readers knew exactly what they
were doing. If the Evangelists wanted to tell a story from a
particular perspective, if they wanted their readers to learn a
particular lesson from a story or group of stories, they simply
arranged the material in such a way as to emphasize those
features in their presentations. It was as simple as that. They
knew how to use the maps.

In some ways the Gospel presentations are like an art gal-
lery. If you take a certain picture, put it in a certain frame,
hang it in a certain position in a certain room with the light
coming from a certain angle, you will accentuate certain features in that picture. However, if you take the same picture,
put it in a different frame, hang it in a different room with the
light coming from a different angle, then you will accentuate
a different feature. So, if we want to know what the Evangelists are really trying to say at a certain point in the journey,
we will have to pay close attention to the context in which
they place the various stories and sayings.

Look, for example, at the way Mark arranges the central section of his Gospel and places it between two miracle stories. Both stories recount healings of blind men, but they are quite different, and the sequence is certainly no accident—not even of history. Having told us about the blindness of the disciples in the earlier stories (Mark 8:17-21), Mark introduces his section on the meaning of discipleship with the healing of the blind man of Bethsaida (8:22-26) and concludes it with the healing of blind Bartimaeus of Jericho (10:46-52). At Bethsaida, Jesus spits on the blind man's eyes and lays hands on him. The man can make out human shapes, although they are like trees walking about. Only after a second attempt at healing is he able to see clearly. How hard it is to open the eyes of the blind! Apart from the grace and power of God, it is impossible; yet all things are possible with God (8:22-26)!

How hard Jesus has to work to teach the disciples the meaning of discipleship. He clearly tells them that he is to suffer and die (Mark 8:31; 9:31; 10:32-33) and that this is the way of discipleship (8:34—9:1; 9:35-50; 10:38-45). Yet they repeatedly misunderstand what he is saying (8:33; 9:9-11, 31-32; 10:13-16, 38-40), and he has to tell them all over again. But when grace and power have worked in the life of blind Bartimaeus, at the end of the story, he can see again. He follows Jesus on the way to Jerusalem, the way to suffering, death, and resurrection (10:46-52)! That is the way it is to be, says Mark, not only for Bartimaeus but for everyone whose eyes are opened to the meaning of life by Jesus—whoever they are, wherever they live. It is Gospel truth!

Let us look at Matthew's account of Jesus' stilling of the storm (Matt. 8:18-27). He begins to recount the stilling of the storm (cf. Mark 4:35) and then inserts two discipleship sayings (Matt. 8:19-22)—sayings which occur in quite a different context in Luke (Luke 9:57-61)—before finally telling the rest of the story about the storm on the lake (Matt. 8:23-27). He recasts the story of the storm in such a way that it describes what happens time and again when we are following Jesus. He has transformed a miracle story into a powerful sermon on discipleship; thus he describes Jesus leading his followers into the church and rescuing them when they are in danger of going down. To follow Jesus is a costly and risky business, says Matthew, but Jesus may be trusted to care for his people in times of difficulty and danger.

Or we might observe the new setting for the call of Simon in the Gospel of Luke. In Mark, the call of the fishermen (Mark 1:16-20) is placed immediately after Jesus' initial proclamation of the kingdom of God as an illustration of the meaning of repentance and faith (1:14-15). In Luke, however, the call focuses upon Simon and takes place considerably later in the ministry of Jesus, which has been underway for some time (Luke 4:14-44). Most importantly, Simon already knows all about Jesus because of the healing of his mother-in-law (4:38-39), and he has ample opportunity to count the cost before leaving everything to follow Jesus (5:1-11). His decision is therefore well considered, deliberate, and radical! A model discipleship decision, according to Luke's presentation (14:28-33).

The settings and the context of the various sayings and stories are of fundamental importance in interpreting the message of the Evangelists. However, it is ultimately the picture itself which conveys the heart of the message. We must therefore pay attention to the details. If an Evangelist paints in the crowd, for instance, or certain of the opponents of Jesus, or even his disciples, it is because of what they add to the message. They are not there by accident; they all contribute to the message which he is seeking to convey to his church.

So, for example, when Jesus teaches about the meaning of discipleship for the first time, Mark deliberately says that Jesus called to him and the crowd, as well as to his disciples, and told them, "If any want to become my followers, let them deny themselves and take up their cross and follow me" (Mark 8:34). This teaching is of fundamental importance for everyone; all are to live this way, says Mark, not just the church leaders.

Throughout the chapters that follow, however, the teaching is addressed only to the disciples because the issues which Mark singles out for special attention are those relating particularly to leaders: the abuse of power, privilege, and possessions (Mark 9:33—10:31). Jesus takes three disciples with him up the mountain so that they might receive divine confirmation of his message (9:2-8). It is, significantly, the three who, in Mark, are having most difficulty in accepting his message about the suffering Son of Man and the need for disciples to follow in the way of the cross. In Mark 8:31—9:1, Jesus rebukes Peter for his negative response to his teaching about the suffering Son of Man. In 10:35-45 James and John ask for positions of glory in the coming kingdom!

Let us look again at Matthew's account of the stilling of the storm and notice how carefully the Evangelist goes about his work. In Mark's story, Jesus is already in the boat and the disciples take him across to the other side of the lake. Other boats are also with him (Mark 4:36). The other boats are not there in Matthew's picture, since for him the boat is intended as a symbol for the church (as in much early religious art). Jesus is not yet in the boat. He leads the way in and the disciples "follow" him into the boat, into the church (Matt. 8:23).

In Mark's picture, we can see Jesus sleeping on a cushion in the back of the boat (Mark 4:38). However, the cushion is not there in Matthew's picture (Matt. 8:24), for he has just taught that "the Son of Man has nowhere to lay his head" (8:20)! In Mark's picture, Jesus speaks to the wind and the sea first (Mark 4:39); he is describing the stilling of a storm. But in Matthew, Jesus speaks to his troubled disciples before he calms the storm (Matt. 8:26) because his is a picture about discipleship. We could go on and on looking at this scene. Since we will return to it later as we consider the cost of life on the road, those few details will suffice to illustrate how carefully the Evangelists work on their pictures. It is no wonder the church has always taught that they are inspired! It is no wonder that we have to pay careful attention to what we are reading!

Careful attention must be paid to stories which include quotations from the Old Testament, for on almost every occasion the Evangelists have made significant changes to the wording. These changes provide important keys for the interpretation of the message.

Mark, for example, begins his Gospel by asserting that what is taking place is in accordance with what was written by Isaiah the prophet (Mark 1:2-3). The opening verse of the citation, in fact, combines words from Exodus 23:20 and Malachi 3:1, while the dominant portion of the quotation derives from Isaiah 40:3. In this way Mark is highlighting that in Jesus the three great points of salvation history have found their fulfillment: the Exodus, the return from the exile in Babylon, and the coming of the day of the Lord.

The passage in Isaiah 40:3 says, "A voice cries out: 'In the wilderness prepare the way of the Lord, make straight in the desert a highway for our God.' " Mark adapts this so that the voice now cries in the wilderness—not in Babylon, as in Isaiah. The way of the Lord is prepared in the lives of people—not by a route through the wilderness, as in Isaiah. And the Lord is Jesus—not "our God," as in Isaiah. It now fits exactly the role which John the Baptist plays in Mark as the one who prepares for the way of discipleship manifested in Jesus Christ.

Mark makes the wilderness the location of divine revelation: "John the baptizer appeared in the wilderness" (Mark 1:4). He then describes how "people from the whole Judean countryside and all the people of Jerusalem were going out" to John to be baptized by him in the Jordan River (1:5). The Old Testament expectation was that in the day of the Lord, Gentiles would flock to Jerusalem as the temple becomes the focal point of the new nation of God. But Mark completely reverses the direction of fulfillment. John leads the people, not toward the national, religious, and commercial center, but away from that center as he prepares for the ministry of Jesus. That ministry will bring with it a complete reversal of traditional values, ambitions, and expectations.

In a simpler but no less profound way, Matthew adapts the quotation of Zechariah 9:9 (and Isa. 62:11) to interpret the entry of Jesus into Jerusalem (Matt. 21:1-11). The Old Testament text says:

> Rejoice greatly, O daughter Zion!
>   Shout aloud, O daughter of Jerusalem!
> Lo, your king comes to you;
>   triumphant and victorious is he,

> humble and riding on a donkey,
> on a colt, the foal of a donkey.   (Zech. 9:9)

Matthew deliberately omits the phrase "triumphant and victorious is he" so that the emphasis now falls on the words "humble and mounted on a donkey, on a colt, the foal of a donkey," a beast of burden. Zechariah was looking for a mighty king who would lead the mighty men of Israel in a victorious battle, "trampling the foe in the mud of the streets" (Zech. 10:5). In direct contrast, Matthew deletes the reference to triumph and victory and emphasizes the lowliness, the humility of the King of the little people. The one who is to be the judge of all the world disclaims power, glory, triumph, and military victory, entering Jerusalem in lowliness and humility on the way to the cross. For Matthew, Jesus is the Christian Messiah, the King who is to be crucified.

We could go on at great length exploring the many hundreds of ways that the Evangelists work to present through their Gospels powerful and unmistakable messages to their churches. Each Gospel has its own story line, and they are different because each Evangelist has a different message to convey.

One more illustration may serve to show how we need to keep in mind the whole of a Gospel when interpreting any particular story. In the Gospel of Mark, it is James and John, the sons of Zebedee, who ask for the leading seats in the kingdom of God (Mark 10:35-45). But Matthew considers that this reflects unfairly on the apostles and has their *mother* make this request (Matt. 20:20-28). The story does not end there, however, for in the list of women at the foot of the cross, Matthew (and Matthew only) includes "the mother of the sons of Zebedee" (Matt. 27:56). Anyone who asks that question about power and glory must stand at the foot of the cross to receive the ultimate answer!

The Four Basic Maps

Those who read the New Testament will soon be aware that we have in our possession four different maps: Matthew, Mark, Luke, and John. The maps are different because they are prepared by different people to mark out the road of the future for different churches encountering different situations. They are preparing their people to travel through different terrain. Their destination is the same, and they are following the same leader, but details of their routes vary, for they are setting out from different starting points.

From our starting point we still seek to follow the stranger of Galilee on the road to the kingdom. In each chapter we begin with the distinctive insights of Jesus of Nazareth, and next we look at how these insights are reinterpreted in three Gospel stories. Then we explore ways in which the principles embodied in their interpretations mark out the direction for our journey into the future.

We share with the Evangelists the conviction that the image of Jesus on the road with his disciples is fundamental for understanding the life of faith. It is fundamental even for those of us who, like the early churches of the Gospels, have settled down and are not physically traveling anywhere with Jesus. Certainly we were not fishing on the sea of Galilee when he called us, and we are obviously not traveling the dusty roads of Palestine with him. Our journey is from the present to the future rather than from Galilee to Jerusalem, but the risen Christ who leads us is the Jesus who led his disciples, and he is seeking to lead us in the same basic direction. We will therefore seek to treat the Gospels with extreme seriousness while at the same time seeking, with equal seriousness, to interpret them into our contemporary situation.

Let us then head for the road and travel into the future, following the tall man with a beard and a long robe who once stood on the shore of the Sea of Galilee and called his first disciples to follow him. Sometimes the road will head uphill through terrain which may be strange for some of us. But if we are following the stranger from Nazareth, it will be an exciting trip—a journey full of hope, for us and for all humanity!

1

The Call to a Life on the Road

The Call to Discipleship

The Good News of the Kingdom

Mark 1:14-15: "Now after John was arrested, Jesus came to Galilee, proclaiming the good news of God, and saying, 'The time is fulfilled, and the kingdom [AG: kingly reign] of God has come near; repent, and believe in the good news.' "

Matthew 4:17: "From that time Jesus began to proclaim, 'Repent, for the kingdom [AG: kingly reign] of heaven has come near.' "

Luke 4:16, 18-19, 43: "[Jesus] stood up to read. . . . 'The Spirit of the Lord is upon me, because he has anointed me to bring good news to the poor. He has sent me to proclaim release to the captives and recovery of sight to the blind, to let the oppressed go free, to proclaim the year of the Lord's favor. . . . I must proclaim the good news of the kingdom of God to the other cities also; for I was sent for this purpose.' "

With these words the three Evangelists present what they

believe to be the essence of the preaching of Jesus. Though they express it in words appropriate to their differing situations and theologies, they are united in their testimony that in the parables and miracles of Jesus, in his life and ministry, in his death and resurrection, God's reign of grace has begun to break into human history.

The idea of the kingdom of God does not begin with Jesus. It has a long history behind it. From early days the people of Israel celebrated the Lord's kingly reign in their temple liturgies, particularly in the Psalms and in enthronement festivals (Pss. 47, 93, 96—99). However, as time went by, they came to the increasing realization that all was not well within Israel and that the present occupants of the throne of David fell far short of divine (and human) expectations. They began to dream of a day when God's kingly rule would be revealed in all its glory (Isa. 24:23; 33:22; Zeph. 3:15; Zech. 14:16-17).

This hope for a new future flowered during the exilic and postexilic periods, when Israel was under the domination of the Gentiles. Laboring under the oppression of foreign rule, the people looked forward in eager anticipation to the day when God's rule would break into their world, when Israel would be free and all the nations would acknowledge that Yahweh was King (Isa. 25:3; Zech. 14:9, 16). At present his royal rule might be hidden and unrecognized by the majority, but they believed that one day God would fulfill their hopes and dreams, vindicating his word and liberating his people (Zeph. 3:15; Mal. 1:14).

Then Jesus comes preaching and teaching that the time of fulfillment has drawn near. It is knocking at the door! With an authority recognized even by his opponents, Jesus affirms that, contrary to all appearances, God's kingdom is a present reality. When asked for a word of assurance, he points to the fact that his reign is already breaking into human history as, in his words and works, Satan is being defeated (Luke 11:20), the blind are receiving their sight, the lame are walking, the lepers are being cleansed, the deaf are hearing, the dead are being raised, and the good news is being preached to the poor (Matt. 11:5).

The words and actions of Jesus are controversial and run

counter to the religious and political ambitions of the authorities (Mark 2:1—3:6; 11:27-33). Jesus is convinced that through him, God's absolute future is breaking into the present age. Accordingly, he heals the sick (1:29-34, 40-45), casts out demons (1:23-28; 5:1-20), ignores the Sabbath regulations (2:23-28; 3:1-6), and speaks of the end of the temple (13:2; 14:58). He abolishes the rigid food regulations (7:15) and associates with the nobodies of society (2:14-17; Luke 7:36-50).

Jesus pronounces God's blessing on the poor and demonstrates God's presence with the persecuted (Matt. 5:1-14; 25:31-46). He declares the forgiveness of sins (Mark 2:1-12) and invites the outcasts and infidels to the messianic banquet (2:15-17; Luke 14:15-24). All without exception are invited, and all without distinction are welcome. This is to be a festival of grace and joy, a carnival celebrating the coming of God's kingly reign.

Though the kingdom has begun to break into the world, it is in many ways still veiled and hidden. It can only be described in parables and metaphors (Mark 4:1-34) and can only be understood by faith. Through these stories which Jesus relates from everyday life, listeners are gripped in their hearts and minds, and they respond—either in faith or unbelief. Drawn irresistibly into the drama of the story, they either affirm, "Yes, that is how it is with God!" or they deny that God could ever act in such a way.

Many of the religious and political leaders are unable to understand the truth of Jesus' teaching, and they are indignant at the way he behaves. Spending so much time in bad company! Surely God approves only of the upright, the moral, the religious (Mark 2:15-20)—the sort of people with whom they themselves associated. After all, people may always be judged by the company they keep, and for a wandering charismatic preacher from Galilee to associate with the riffraff of society is to invite both the wrath of God and the ready condemnation of the authorities.

The little people of society, however, instinctively recognize in the stranger from Nazareth the fulfillment of their desires and ambitions. Wherever he goes in Galilee, the poor and the outcasts, the women and the children, the sick and the demon-possessed—they all flock to greet him. When they arrive, they find that they are welcome. Not only welcome, but especially invited! The messianic banquet has been prepared for them (Luke 14:16-24). The kingdom is theirs (Matt. 5:3, 10; Mark 10:14). What a celebration! But also what a reversal of values! The first are finding out that they have now become last, whereas those who were always considered to be last are now being invited to take their places in the kingdom of God (Mark 10:31).

In the light of the coming kingdom, Jesus teaches with authority (Mark 1:21-28), preaches the good news, and invites people to a life of repentance and faith (1:14-15). In an action without parallel in the ancient world, he takes the initiative and calls disciples to follow him (1:16-20). He calls them to leave the security of their homes, families, and jobs to travel with him as he journeys the dusty roads of Palestine, preaching the good news and teaching the ways of the kingdom, healing the sick and casting out demons. They might well be from the margins of society; but he is inviting them to share his life, to be his people (3:13-19), to take part in his mission in the world (6:7-13).

After Easter, as Christianity was spreading throughout the empire, the early Christians continued to tell the stories of the way Jesus called his disciples to follow him through Palestine. Even when they lived in communities scattered throughout the Mediterranean world, they remembered these stories and reinterpreted them as the call of Christ to them. Most had never seen the Sea of Galilee and knew little about tax collecting, much less about fishing. Yet they saw in these stories definitive examples of the way Jesus works in the world. As these stories were recounted, many continued to hear Jesus calling his people to faith, bringing them together as his people, and thrusting them out to continue his mission in the world.

We will look at three different examples of the way these stories were used in the early church: the simple accounts of the call to follow Jesus (Mark), the dramatic story of why they left everything to follow Jesus (Luke), and the invitation to come and meet the Messiah (John).

The Call to Follow Jesus (Mark 1:14-20; 2:13-14)

Mark arranges the material of his Gospel into three major sections. The introduction (Mark 1:1-13) declares that Jesus of Nazareth is the Messiah, the Son of God. He is the one through whom God is about to speak and act in a decisive and definitive way.

In the first major section (Mark 1:14—8:26), Jesus reveals his authority in word and action only to be greeted by the increasing darkness of the world. How hard it is to open the eyes of the blind! In the second major section (8:27—10:52), Jesus repeatedly reveals to his disciples his true identity as the suffering Son of Man and calls on them to live in the light of this reality. After many attempts, eyes are opened as Bartimaeus follows on the way to the cross. The third major section (11:1—15:47) recounts the passion, death, and resurrection of the Son of God, through whom judgment is passed on unbelieving Israel and the promise of grace is extended to the Gentiles. When a centurion standing at the foot of the cross sees how Jesus dies, he makes his confession of faith! The conclusion (16:1-8) shows God's affirmation of the way of the cross and points the disciples back to Galilee where the story will begin again.

The first major section of the Gospel (Mark 1:14—8:26) is divided into three smaller sections (1:14—3:6; 3:7—6:6a; 6:6b—8:26). Each of these smaller sections commences with a statement summarizing one particular aspect of the ministry of Jesus: Mark 1:14-15, preaching the good news and calling for repentance and faith; 3:7-12, healing the sick from all over the countryside and beyond; 6:6b, teaching among the villages. This is immediately followed by a story about discipleship: Mark 1:16-20, the call of the first disciples; 3:13-19, the naming of the disciples; 6:7-13, the sending out of the disciples on mission. Each section concludes with a representative group opposed to Jesus: 3:6, the religious and political leaders plot to kill him; 6:1-6, his own townspeople in Nazareth reject him; 8:14-21, even his disciples harden their hearts.

According to Mark's presentation, there are only two possible ways of responding to the revelation of God in Jesus: discipleship or rejection. One either joins with those seeking to follow Jesus or joins with those who are taking their stand against him. The call of the first disciples (Mark 1:16-20) is a pictorial presentation of the meaning of repentance and faith. Here is the Christian faith lived out in response to the preaching of the good news that God's kingly reign is breaking into the world. Mark tells the story in such a way that it is good news for members of the church to which he is writing. The call of the fishermen becomes their call, and the challenge is for them to allow the response of the fishermen to become their response to the kingdom of grace in Jesus.

> Now after John was arrested, Jesus came to Galilee, proclaiming the good news of God, and saying, "The time is fulfilled, and the kingdom [AG: kingly reign] of God has come near; repent, and believe in the good news."
> As Jesus passed along the Sea of Galilee, he saw Simon and his brother Andrew casting a net into the sea—for they were fishermen. And Jesus said to them, "Follow me and I will make you fish for people." And immediately they left their nets and followed him. As he went a little farther, he saw James son of Zebedee and his brother John, who were in their boat mending the nets. Immediately he called them; and they left their father Zebedee in the boat with the hired men, and followed him. . . .
> Jesus went out again beside the sea; the whole crowd gathered around him, and he taught them. As he was walking along, he saw Levi son of Alphaeus sitting at the tax booth, and he said to him, "Follow me." And he got up and followed him.   (Mark 1:14-20; 2:13-14)

For over forty years before Mark writes, these stories were handed down by word of mouth in the early church as preachers and teachers called men and women to follow Jesus Christ. In this process of telling and retelling, all of the irrelevant details were omitted so that what now remains is of intense theological interest. Nothing is told by chance. The picture, more like a woodcut than an etching, is presented in boldest outline only: As Jesus was traveling along, he saw certain people, he called them, and they responded. Or, from Mark's perspective: Jesus sees the people, he calls them, and they respond! For Mark the good news is always to be expressed in the present tense!

Life on the Road Begins with Jesus of Nazareth

As we have seen, Mark begins each section with a statement about Jesus and his ministry (Mark 1:14-15, preaching; 3:7-12, healing; and 6:6b, teaching). Then, and only then, does he recount a story about discipleship (Mark 1:16-20, the call; 3:13-19, the community; 6:7-13, the commission). This is his way of emphasizing that discipleship begins with Jesus, not with the disciples. The divine dimension is fundamental to his understanding of the meaning of following Jesus.

Within each of the three call narratives (Mark 1:16-18, Simon and Andrew; 1:19-20, James and John; 2:14, Levi) the story begins with Jesus already on the move. Mark tells us of the arrest of John the Baptist, the messianic forerunner who lost his head because of his loyalty to God (6:14-29). Just afterward, Jesus comes into Galilee preaching the good news of the kingdom (1:14-15). He has already begun his ministry, and as he is traveling on the mission that will ultimately lead to his crucifixion outside Jerusalem, he calls the fishermen to follow him (1:16-20). When later he is embroiled in conflict with the religious authorities (2:1—3:6), Jesus returns to the lake and teaches the crowds. Again, as he is going along, involved in a ministry of conflict and controversy, he calls a tax collector to follow him (2:14).

The call itself begins when Jesus sees the person. In Mark 1:16 he sees Simon and Andrew; in 1:19 he sees James and John; in 2:14 he sees Levi; later, in 10:21 Jesus sees the rich young man, and in Luke 19:5 he sees Zacchaeus. For Mark, and the early church before him, discipleship does not begin when people see Jesus and come to him. Rather, it begins when Jesus takes the initiative, when he sees them and calls them to follow him.

Through familiarity with the Gospels, we are accustomed to the fact that Jesus takes the initiative in the call to discipleship. Yet such an action was without parallel in the ancient world. The story of Elijah and Elisha provides the nearest parallel, but there are significant differences (1 Kings 19:19-

21). In the Old Testament it was regarded as an exceptional case and was not continued.

In the first century, charismatic leaders, miracle workers, and freedom fighters all had their followers. But the closest parallel to the action of Jesus is that of the Jewish rabbis, whose disciples followed a respectful three paces behind their teachers. However, in the case of the rabbis, the initiative was always taken by the would-be disciple who came and offered himself. If the rabbi was suitably impressed, he might well accept him into his school. But if the would-be disciple's pious practices were not sufficiently orthodox, if his exegesis was not suitably skilled, or if his memorization of Scripture was in some way deficient, he was likely to be rejected. In each instance the would-be disciple had to take the initiative and offer himself—as in the story in Matthew 8:19, the scribe promises to follow Jesus wherever he goes.

In the Gospel stories about discipleship, the action is quite the reverse. Jesus takes the initiative, he sets his eye on the person, and he issues the call to follow. More than that, as we will see later, he declares that their eternal destiny, their acceptance into the kingdom of God, depends on their acceptance of his call (see Luke 9:62).

For Mark, and for the early church before him, this aspect of the story is of immense theological importance. It indicates that a person does not choose to become a disciple of Jesus (on response, see below). It is the divine Son from Nazareth who takes the initiative and issues the call. Discipleship does not depend on us. It depends upon the authoritative and all-powerful Jesus Christ. He is the author and finisher of discipleship, the alpha and the omega of the new life of faith.

The Invitation to Follow Jesus Is an Act of Grace

Because life on the road begins with Jesus and because he is the goal of the journey, the call to follow is a call of grace and love. It is a call of grace and love because the Jesus who takes the initiative and issues the call is the incarnate grace and love of God.

In these brief stories, from which every nonessential detail has been wrung, we are repeatedly told that those whom

Jesus calls are, at the time, engaged in their ordinary occupations: two are fishing (Mark 1:16), two are overhauling their nets (1:19), and one is at work in the tax office (2:14). They are not involved in religious activity; they are not attending the temple or the synagogue; they are not praying or studying the Scriptures. They are pursuing their ordinary everyday occupations and, in Mark at least, they are not even thinking about Jesus. Indeed, in this Gospel they have never seen him before. With Jesus, discipleship clearly depends on the grace of God, not on the worth, or even the potential worth, of the one who is called. Thus, contrary to much popular opinion, Levi is not called because of his ability in handling finances—otherwise the purse would not have been entrusted to Judas!

In the story of the call of Levi (Mark 2:14), we see most plainly that the call to discipleship is an act of grace. He is engaged in his profession of tax collecting, seated in the tax office, when Jesus calls him. As Hans Küng has explained, "Tax collectors were the downright sinners, miserable sinners in the proper sense of the term, practicing a proscribed trade, afflicted with permanent uncleanness as collaborators to the national cause, incapable of repentance simply because they could not remember how many they had cheated and how much they had swindled" (Küng, 271). Levi, the professional swindler and archsinner, is called from his filthy profession to become a follower of Jesus.

The ministry of Jesus is an open invitation to everyone, and all are welcome. Yet the distinctive feature of his ministry is that it is directed primarily toward those whom the orthodox, the establishment, regard as beyond the fringes of respectability. The ministry of Jesus is directed especially to those considered to be beyond the realm of salvation, according to the theology of the day: lepers who have to live outside the camp, regarded as unclean and denied fellowship with others; Gentiles who have no share in the privileges of Israel; women and children who have no status within the community; notorious sinners, despised tax collectors, drunkards, and prostitutes. The ministry of Jesus is open to all, but it is directed primarily toward the oppressed and the outcast, for it is a ministry of grace and love.

This unexpected dimension in the ministry of Jesus is indicated already in Mark's opening summary statement (1:14-15), which introduces his story of the call of the first disciples. Here is the grace and truth which bring with it a radical reversal of values. The imprisonment of John the Baptist, the wild and woolly wilderness preacher, signals the start of Jesus' mission—not the death of the great King Uzziah, as was the case with Isaiah. And Jesus' mission begins among the dispossessed people of Galilee—not among the priestly classes of the capital city of Jerusalem. It is a mission from the periphery, from beyond the borders of respectability, and it begins out in the country among the marginalized. His first disciples are fishermen and tax collectors.

The Demand Is Unconditional, the Response All-Embracing

The invitation to discipleship, since it is an invitation given by Jesus, is an invitation of grace and love. But this grace and love evokes, demands, and makes possible a radical response to the call of Jesus. The demand of Jesus is unconditional and the response is all-embracing. When Jesus issues his call of grace, there can be no delay, no half-hearted response.

When called by Elijah, Elisha made the request, "Let me kiss my father and my mother [good-bye], and then I will follow you," and the prophet granted him permission (1 Kings 19:20). When a would-be disciple says to Jesus, "I will follow you, Lord, but let me first say farewell to those at my home," that one is told, "No one who puts a hand to the plow and looks back is fit for the kingdom of God" (Luke 9:62). The one who offers to follow Jesus is warned, "The Son of Man has nowhere to lay his head" (Matt. 8:20). And when one who is called wants first to go and bury his father, Jesus says, "Let the dead bury their own dead" (8:22); "as for you, go and proclaim the kingdom of God" (Luke 9:60).

"The Son of Man has nowhere to lay his head! Let the dead bury their own dead!" Following Jesus plunges the disciple into a total lack of security and requires a break with even the strongest and most sacred of human relationships. In the present stories, the tax collector leaves his ledgers, and the fishermen abandon their boats. When later they temporarily return to their fishing business (John 21:1-4), it is clearly regarded as an act of apostasy on the part of those who had deserted their Master—hence the recommissioning of Peter in John 21:5-19.

Again, we may notice that in the three call narratives we have been considering from the Gospel of Mark, all irrelevant details are omitted. It is repeatedly said that the ones who are called leave what they are doing and follow Jesus: "Immediately they left their nets and followed him" (Mark 1:18). "They left their father Zebedee in the boat with the hired men, and followed him" (1:20). Levi "got up" from his desk in the tax booth "and followed him" (2:14). The earlier statements about their work underline the gracious nature of the call of Jesus. Now the descriptions of them leaving their jobs underline the radical nature of the response demanded by Jesus. In response to his gracious call, they leave the security of jobs and family to follow him.

There is an obvious and real danger for those who seek to harmonize the accounts of the call of the disciples in Mark and John. They miss what Mark is seeking to say to his church. There is no evidence for the often-repeated suggestion that John's account preceded Mark's, making it "completely understandable" for the disciples to entrust their futures to Jesus as soon as he called them. If Mark wants us to understand the text in that way, he would tell it in that way. Instead, he wants us to understand the stories exactly as he has told them. When Jesus encounters and calls a person, no previous knowledge is required, and the response is immediate and unconditional. Jesus sees them, he calls them, and they respond!

T. W. Manson has written: "Discipleship means the risk of being reckoned undutiful sons [and daughters], bad husbands [and wives], dangerous agitators; and [the one] who becomes a disciple accepts these risks with eyes open, and is prepared to accept all the consequences that may follow. And this is not just a matter of a single moment of decision in a burst of enthusiasm. It demands dogged endurance, the maintenance of the first enthusiasm right through to the end" (*Sayings*, 132).

Johann Baptist Metz even goes so far as to refer to discipleship as "class treason." He says, "It is possible that what love demands of us here may look like treason—a betrayal of affluence, of the family, and of our customary way of life." He then asks, "Did not Jesus himself incur the reproach of treason? Did not his love bring him to this state? Was he not crucified as a traitor to all the apparently worthwhile values?" (Metz, 14-15).

The call to discipleship is a call of grace, for it depends on Jesus, the incarnate grace and love of God. But as Dietrich Bonhoeffer rightly reminds us, "Such grace is *costly*, because it calls us to follow, and it is *grace* because it calls us to follow Jesus Christ. It is costly because it cost a person his life, and it is grace because it gives a person the only true life" (Bonhoeffer, 39). It is grace because it offers us new life, but it is costly because it runs counter to so many of our dreams, ambitions, and desires, and it carries as its consequence the charge of class treason. The universal punishment for such a crime is death, either in the palace (Mark 6:17-29) or, more frequently, outside the gate (Heb. 13:7-16).

Again, the setting of the call narratives underlines this emphasis. Mark's opening summary (Mark 1:14-15) declares that "after John was arrested," Jesus began his ministry. This is not merely a chronological notice. It is an important theological statement. The Greek word that is used in the arrest of John, that he "was handed over," is precisely the word that is used in the "handing over" of Jesus to death (9:31; 10:33; 14:21, 41). Both the beginning (6:17-29) and the ending of the ministry of Jesus are bathed in blood. The call of the fishermen (1:16-20) follows immediately after John's arrest. The call of the tax collector occurs in the midst of the first set of conflict stories (2:1—3:6), conflicts which will result in the death of Jesus. Following Jesus is demanding and costly. It involves following the crucified Messiah on his mission in the world.

Thus, for Mark, the simple stories of the call of the disciples to follow Jesus are profound interpretations. They are pictorial representations of God's kingly reign breaking into human history and of people responding to this good news in repentance and faith. These stories encapsulate the message proclaimed by Jesus as an act of grace making possible and demanding a life-changing response.

They Left Everything to Follow the Lord (Luke 5:1-11)

The Gospel of Matthew tells the story of the calling of the first disciples in basically the same location and wording as in Mark (Matt. 4:18-22). There is one significant change. Mark says that when Jesus saw James and John, *he immediately called them*, and they followed him (Mark 1:19-20). In Matthew, when Jesus saw James and John, he called them, and *they immediately followed him* (Matt. 4:21-22). Thus Matthew stresses further the obedience of the disciples (1:24; 21:6; 26:19). In the calling of the tax collector, "Levi" (Mark 2:14) is named "Matthew" (Matt. 9:9), making it apparent that he is one of the twelve (10:2-4). Perhaps Matthew is indicating that the twelve were the only ones called in this special way. Although the emphasis differs, the stories are essentially the same.

In Luke and John, the situation is different, and the stories have little in common. If we are going to hear what Luke and John are saying to their churches, we must allow the texts to speak to us *as they now stand*. Let us understand the emphases and interpret the theological directions which the Evangelists have so clearly marked out for us. Some people attempt to harmonize Luke and John, either with one another or with Mark or Matthew. This is futile and succeeds only in closing the texts off from us, changing the proclamation of the gospel into none-too-accurate reminiscences of former heroes of the faith. The Gospels make abundantly clear to us that by hearing and responding to the good news, we become disciples of Jesus, followers of the risen Lord, who continually encounters his people through his word.

Therefore, let us hear what the Spirit of the Lord is saying to the churches through Luke:

> Once while Jesus was standing by the lake of Gennesaret, and the crowd was pressing in on him to hear the word of God, he saw two boats there at the shore of the lake; the fishermen had

gone out of them and were washing their nets. He got into one of the boats, the one belonging to Simon, and asked him to put out a little way from the shore. Then he sat down and taught the crowds from the boat. When he had finished speaking, he said to Simon, "Put out into the deep water and let down your nets down for a catch." Simon answered, "Master, we have worked all night long but have caught nothing. Yet if you say so, I will let down the nets." When they had done this, they caught so many fish that their nets were beginning to break. So they signaled their partners in the other boat to come and help them. And they came and filled both boats, so that they began to sink. But when Simon Peter saw it, he fell down at Jesus' knees, saying, "Go away from me, Lord, for I am a sinful man!" For he and all who were with him were amazed at the catch of fish that they had taken; and so also were James and John, sons of Zebedee, who were partners with Simon. Then Jesus said to Simon, "Do not be afraid; from now on you will be catching people." When they had brought their boats to shore, they left everything and followed him. . . .

After this he went out and saw a tax collector named Levi, sitting at the tax booth; and he said to him, "Follow me." And he got up, left everything, and followed him.

Then Levi gave a great banquet for him in his house; and there was a large crowd of tax collectors and others sitting at the table with them. The Pharisees and their scribes were complaining to his disciples, saying, "Why do you eat and drink with tax collectors and sinners?" Jesus answered, "Those who are well have no need of a physician, but those who are sick; I have come to call not the righteous but sinners to repentance."

(Luke 5:1-11, 27-32)

When Luke begins "to set down an orderly account of the events that have been fulfilled among us" (Luke 1:1), he uses the Gospel of Mark as his basic geographical framework. But he extends the lines backward into the Old Testament and forward into the history of the church. In so doing, he divides the history of salvation into three periods.

First, there is the time of Israel centering on the Law, as the faithful remnant gather in the temple to await the coming of the Spirit-filled Liberator of his people (Luke 1—2). Then there is the time of Jesus as the centerpoint of salvation history (3—24). Finally comes the time of the church in the power of the Spirit as the gospel is spread from Jerusalem to Rome to encompass the ancient world. Christianity is changed from being a Jewish sect to a worldwide religion (Acts). Each story in Luke and Acts is thus placed within this framework of salvation history and is to be interpreted within the context of the church's mission in the world. This emphasis can be clearly seen in Luke's account of the calling of the first disciples.

Called to Participate in the Mission of Jesus

In Mark the story of the call of the first disciples (Mark 1:16-20) is recounted immediately after the opening summary statement about the preaching of Jesus in Galilee (1:14-15). In Luke the setting is somewhat different.

According to Luke, Jesus is empowered by the Spirit when he begins his ministry by teaching in the synagogues throughout Galilee (Luke 4:14-15). In his inaugural sermon at Nazareth, he declares that in him and his mission of liberation, the Old Testament promises are finding their fulfillment (4:16-30). At Capernaum he casts out a demon in the synagogue (4:31-37), heals Simon's mother-in-law (4:38-39), and in the evening heals all who were sick, and casts out many demons (4:40-41). The next day when the people of Capernaum seek him out and ask him to stay with them, he declares that, as a matter of divine necessity, he must preach the good news in other cities as well (4:42-43). After preaching in the synagogues of Judea (4:44), he returns to Galilee and meets Simon and the sons of Zebedee at the lake of Gennesaret (Sea of Galilee; 5:1-11).

In Luke's presentation, then, the mission of Jesus is well under way by the time he encounters Simon and the others at the lakeside, and the entire story is told from that perspective. This is probably the reason why Luke prefers this particular story, with its parallel in the resurrection appearance in the Fourth Gospel (John 21:1-14), rather than the Marcan account of the call of the fishermen (Mark 1:16-20). He certainly has the Marcan story before him and could use it if he chooses to do so. Mark includes the statement "I will make you fish for people" (1:17). But the parallel story illustrates more vividly the fact that the call to discipleship is a call to participate in the mission of Jesus and the church. So Luke chooses to use it instead.

The crowd is pressing in upon Jesus, eager to hear "the word of God" (Luke 5:1); this is a phrase used in Acts to describe the missionary preaching of the apostles. When Jesus sees two boats pulled up on the shore, he uses one of them as a floating pulpit. At the end of his teaching, he tells Simon to go fishing again, even though they had failed to catch anything the previous evening and could hardly have expected to do any better fishing in deep water during the daytime. When Simon obeys, a miraculous catch results, his partners come to his aid, and even then there are so many fish that the boats are in danger of sinking. They are staggered at the size of the catch, and the story reaches its climax with the declaration to Simon that from now on he will be engaged in the business of catching people.

We will look more carefully at Luke's understanding of the church's mission when we consider the theme of discipleship and mission, but already a few things are clear. The ministry of Jesus fulfills the Old Testament promises of liberation (Luke 4:16-30) and anticipates the mission of the church, teaching "the word of God" (5:1). It is therefore not surprising that much of the language used to describe the ministry of Jesus here is taken up again in Acts in connection with the mission of the early church: teaching in the synagogues (4:15-30), preaching the good news of the kingdom (4:43-44), healing the sick (4:38-40), and casting out demons (4:33-37, 41). It is a ministry accomplished "with the power of the Spirit" (4:14): "his teaching" is "with authority" (4:32), he casts out the demons "with authority and power" (4:36), he is "praised by everyone" (4:15), and "the power of the Lord was with him to heal" (5:17).

Moreover, Luke provides a sharp contrast to Mark and Matthew, in which Jesus has only just begun to preach in Galilee (Mark 1:14-15; Matt. 4:12, Capernaum). Now we learn that Jesus has exercised an extensive ministry both in Galilee (Luke 4:14-15) *and in Judea* (4:44) prior to the calling of the disciples. He has worked in Capernaum on at least two occasions (4:23, 31-41) and has preached in Nazareth (4:16-30) and in many other synagogues (4:15) and cities (4:43). Reports about Jesus have already spread through "all the surrounding country" of Galilee (4:14) and "every place in the region" of Capernaum (4:37). Soon even Pharisees and teachers of the Law would be coming to him "from every village of Galilee and Judea and from Jerusalem" (5:17)!

Certainly Simon already knows about Jesus and his mission because of the healing of his mother-in-law (Luke 4:38-39; again in contrast to Matthew and Mark, in which the healing takes place later). According to Luke, Jesus is well into his ministry by the time he meets Simon and his partners at the lake. Hence, it is unmistakable that to follow Jesus is to become involved in his ministry and in the mission of the church.

Two other features of the story are also probably to be understood in the light of the later mission of the church—the role of Simon and the size of the catch. No mention is made of Andrew in this story, even though he plays a significant role in the other accounts (especially in John 1:35-42). In fact, he is not mentioned anywhere else in Luke other than in the list of the twelve, where he is introduced after Peter and called "his brother" (Luke 6:14). Simon is the first of the great apostolic preachers (Acts 2:14-36), and the story at Gennesaret focuses on him. It is to him that the assurance is given, "Do not be afraid; from now on you will be catching people" (Luke 5:10).

The mention of the large shoal of fish (Luke 5:6) belongs to the heart of the story. John 21:11 says that they caught 153 "large fish," and they are surprised that the net is not torn. Luke emphasizes the large catch and gives it as the reason for Simon's amazement. But Simon is not the only one who is amazed; "all who were with him" (Luke 5:9) are similarly astonished! This is not surprising in view of Luke's emphasis on the worldwide success of apostolic preaching (Acts 1:8; 2:41, 47; 5:13-15; 6:1, 7; 17:6). Simon instinctively knows the meaning of Jesus' words "from now on you will be catching people," and he and his partners leave everything and follow Jesus. They don't even have to be called: Levi is "called" to follow Jesus, but Simon and his partners simply leave everything and follow him. Thus discipleship clearly involves mission in the Lucan story.

Participation in the Mission of Jesus Is an Act of Grace

One of the greatest surprises in the early church must have been the fact that it was Peter, of all people, who became the first of the great apostolic preachers (Acts 2:14-36). Only a short while earlier, despite his outspoken profession of allegiance (Luke 22:31-34), he had denied Jesus three times in the courtyard of the high priest (22:54-62). Yet this broken and defeated leader became the successful spokesman for the church on the day of Pentecost.

This mystery of divine grace, revealed so clearly in Peter's life, is reflected in Luke's account of Simon's encounter with Jesus at the lake of Gennesaret. Simon falls on his knees before Jesus and begs him to leave him (Luke 5:8). He recognizes that he is unworthy of such a divine visitation, even as later he will recognize the scandal of his denial (22:62). When he confesses, "I am a sinful man," he is perhaps reflecting only a sense of general unworthiness and fear that all people would experience in the presence of the divine (Isaiah 6:5). But when this story was told and retold in the early church, those who listened would have recognized the appropriateness of the term "sinner" for Peter, the one who had denied Jesus in the hour of his deepest need.

Yet because the call to discipleship is an act of grace issued by the gracious Lord of the church, Jesus refuses to leave Peter, either on the lake of Gennesaret or in the city of Jerusalem. Certainly Peter is a sinner, a fact which Jesus does not dispute, but discipleship is of grace, not of works. Jesus declares him forgiven, which is the meaning of "do not be afraid," and commissions him to a new life in the kingdom of God with the promise that "from now on you will be catching people." Jesus will not leave the sinner. Instead, he calls Simon Peter to participate in his mission, showing that a new life is opening up for him as he leaves his old life of catching fish and joins with Jesus in catching people for the kingdom.

Also true to this form, Paul, the persecutor of the church, becomes the second great preacher in Acts!

Simon is not called to participate in the ministry of Jesus or in the mission of the church because of his moral character, intellectual capacities, or ability to withstand the pressures that will come to him in the life of discipleship. His call, like every other call to participate in the mission of Jesus, comes to him on the basis of grace. It depends on the one who calls him and, though he might fail many times, that one will never forsake him. This is not only the experience of Simon. James and John experience the same grace (as does Paul), and it has been the testimony of the leaders of the people of God throughout the ages.

A Spontaneous Response of Radical Obedience

In Luke, Simon's call takes place after a disappointing night on the lake—absolutely nothing to show for their efforts! Tired and disappointed, they haul their boats out of the water and begin washing their nets—light work after a good night, but frustrating and irksome when it was all in vain. But surprisingly, when the carpenter of Nazareth tells them to try again, Simon merely hints at the unusualness of the suggestion: as an experienced fisherman he knows that they are unlikely to catch anything in the deep water during the daytime, especially after such a hopeless night.

Nonetheless, Simon obeys. A word from the Master is sufficient, even though Simon realizes that the command runs counter to all that he has learned, even though previous experience assures him that it is totally unrealistic. But it is not only Simon who displays an unusual obedience. At the conclusion of the story (taken over from Mark's account), we are told that "when they had brought their boats to shore, they left everything and followed him" (Luke 5:11).

The statement that "they left *everything*" and followed Jesus (Luke 5:11) has proved more difficult for twentieth-century commentators than the command of Jesus to fish in deep water during the daytime. One writes: "Jesus would not have let them catch the fish to be cast into the sea again or wasted. Undoubtedly the Lord allowed them to divide and sell the fishes and to provide for their dependents before commencing to follow him continuously" (Geldenhuys, 182). Another writes: "Luke does not lay particular stress on the thought of giving up all to follow Jesus (Mark 1:18, 20): the accent is on verse 10 with its call to mission" (Marshall, 206). Yet another says: "Probably the verse should not be pressed to mean a complete and immediate abandonment of their trade" (Ellis, 103). How difficult it is for us when the Scripture runs counter to all that we have learned, when all previous practice assures us that it is totally unrealistic!

The call to discipleship is a call to share in the mission of Jesus. It is a call of grace, but, as Luke continually emphasizes, it requires single-minded obedience. When he retells the story of the call of Levi, he says that "he got up, left everything, and followed him" (Luke 5:28, adding to Mark's story that he "left everything"!). Similarly, in Luke's version of the story of the rich young ruler, Jesus says, "There is still one thing lacking. Sell all that you own and distribute the money to the poor, and you will have treasure in heaven; then come, follow me" (18:22, with "all/everything" again added to Mark's account).

When Jesus is teaching the disciples on the need for an absolute concern for the kingdom of God, the same saying is given: "Sell your possessions, and give alms" to the poor (Luke 12:33). Finally, this is applied to everyone after the twin parables of the tower builder and the king contemplating a campaign. Jesus says, "So therefore, none of you can become my disciple if you do not give up all your possessions" (14:33). In the opening description of life in the early church, Luke stresses that the Christians "would sell their possessions and goods and distribute the proceeds to all, as any had need" (Acts 2:45). Whatever else may be said, it is clear that Luke wishes to stress the need for a single-minded obedience in following Jesus in his mission in the world.

As in Luke's account of the sharing in the early church (Acts 2:44-45; 4:32), Jesus does not command Simon and his partners to give up everything and follow him (Luke 5:11). It is a spontaneous response of trustful obedience. The same is true in the case of Levi (5:27-28), but the converted tax collector goes even further: he holds a great feast for Jesus in his house, celebrating his liberation (5:29-32). The response is spontaneous, radical, and joyful!

Thus Luke has a different version of the commissioning of Simon from that found in Mark and Matthew. He carries through some of the same insights, but he has his own emphases as well. More than any other Gospel, he integrates discipleship into the ministry of Jesus and the mission of the church. He stresses again the gracious nature of the divine visitation in Jesus. He underlines in a most emphatic way that Simon and his partners respond to Jesus with a spontaneous and radical act of single-minded obedience. They go with Jesus, trusting him for the present and for the future.

Come and Meet the Messiah (John 1:35-51)

The Gospel of John has been aptly described as "a book in which a child can wade and an elephant can swim." It is frequently recommended as the Gospel for young Christians, and yet it continues to tantalize even the most experienced theologians. It appears easy to understand, and yet its interpretation presents some of the most difficult problems of New Testament research.

Like the other Gospels, John has been written so that "you may come to believe that Jesus is the Messiah [the Christ], the Son of God, and that through believing you may have life in his name" (John 20:31). It is a document of faith: written from the perspective of faith, it confirms and strengthens an already-existing faith, while at the same time it seeks a response of faith from those who hear the message for the first time.

Like the others, the Fourth Gospel is a writing in which sayings and stories have been arranged and interpreted in such a way as to present the significance of Jesus for a specific situation that has developed within the life of the early churches. It stands apart from the others, however, in the thoroughgoing way the writer's theology dominates his presentation. The Jesus whom he describes speaks a different language, performs different miracles, visits different places, meets different people, and even approaches his death with a different attitude.

The Gospel of John is not a collection of historical reminiscences of an aging apostle. It is a vigorous and robust attempt to present the good news to its readers in a meaningful way and with customary terms, telling them who Jesus is and how they might respond to this divine revelation. The total presentation is written from the standpoint of faith in the risen Lord. The Evangelist seeks to provide a systematic and thorough expression of the meaning of faith in Jesus Christ.

The Fourth Gospel was written late in the first century to churches which were already excluded from the synagogue (John 16:2) and were struggling to survive in a syncretistic world of competing religious claims (4:20-42). The Evangelist seeks to strengthen their faith in Jesus as the messianic Son of God and universal Savior of the world. As Eduard Schweizer expresses it, "More than any other New Testament writer, John expects all salvation from Jesus Christ; in everything he says, he seeks only to emphasize this one point, that everything is to be found in Jesus" (Schweizer, *Jesus*, 168).

John differs from the other Gospels because it was written for Christian communities living in quite a different historical situation from the churches of the other Gospels. It was written by someone (or, more likely, a circle of people) with a unique understanding of the person of Jesus Christ and of the message he proclaims. If we are to hear what the Spirit is saying to the churches, we must listen carefully to what John is saying, renouncing any attempt to harmonize the Gospels.

The next day John again was standing with two of his disciples, and as he watched Jesus walk by, he exclaimed, "Look, here is the Lamb of God!" The two disciples heard him say this, and they followed Jesus. When Jesus turned and saw them following, he said to them, "What are you looking for?" They said to him, "Rabbi" (which translated means Teacher), "where are you staying?" He said to them, "Come and see." They came and saw where he was staying, and they remained with him that day. It was about four o'clock in the afternoon. One of the two who heard John speak and followed him was Andrew, Simon Peter's brother. He first found his brother Simon and said to him, "We have found the Messiah" (which is translated Anointed [AG: Christ]). He brought Simon to Jesus, who looked at him and said, "You are Simon son of John. You are to be called Cephas" (which is translated Peter [AG: Rocky]).

The next day Jesus decided to go to Galilee. He found Philip and said to him, "Follow me." Now Philip was from Bethsaida, the city of Andrew and Peter. Philip found Nathanael and said to him, "We have found him about whom Moses in the law and also the prophets wrote, Jesus son of Joseph from Nazareth." Nathanael said to him, "Can any good thing come out of Nazareth?" Philip said to him, "Come and see." When Jesus saw Nathanael coming toward him, he said of him, "Here is truly an Israelite in whom there is no deceit!" Nathanael asked him, "Where did you get to know me?" Jesus answered, "I saw you under the fig tree before Philip called you." Nathanael replied, "Rabbi, you are the Son of God! You are the King of Israel!" Jesus answered, "Do you believe because I told you that I saw you under the fig tree? You will see greater things than these." And he said to him, "Very truly, I tell you, you will see heaven·opened and the angels of God ascending and descending upon the Son of Man." (John 1:35-51)

It is striking that John's account of the call of the disciples occupies such a large amount of space within the first chapter of his Gospel. Probably nowhere else in the New Testament do we find such a concentration of exalted Christology. This simply serves to underline again the way Christology and discipleship belong together. How one thinks about Jesus determines how one thinks about discipleship; and one's style of living influences the way one thinks about Jesus. John's distinctive Christology, his description of the nature of Christ, provides the key to his particular understanding of the life of discipleship.

Mark begins his Gospel with an account of the ministry of John the Baptist (Mark 1:1-8), Luke with parallel accounts of the birth of John and Jesus (Luke 1—2), and Matthew with a genealogy reaching back to David and Abraham (Matt. 1:1-17). John reaches back further still, right to the beginning of creation, and declares that at creation Jesus as the Word was with God already and belonged to the same reality of being as God himself. The Word, Jesus, finally becomes a human being and makes his dwelling among humanity (John 1:1-18).

In this majestic introduction to his Gospel, John incorporates an early Christian hymn of praise (1:1-5, 10-12, 14, 16). John adds verses about John the Baptist (1:6-9, 15) to link Jesus firmly into history and to prepare for John's ministry as "testimony/witness" to Jesus (1:19-34). When John bears witness that Jesus is the Lamb of God (1:29) and the Son of God (1:34), two of his disciples leave to become followers of Jesus (1:35-42).

As with the other Gospels, the location of the call to discipleship stories gives the clue to their meaning. In Mark the story is placed immediately after the initial preaching of Jesus as an illustration of the inbreaking of the kingdom and the meaning of repentance and faith (Mark 1:14-20). In Luke the ministry of Jesus is well under way and the call of Simon is a commissioning for apostolic ministry (Luke 5:1-11). But here in John, the ministry of Jesus has yet to begin. The opening chapter is the prelude to the ministry and concentrates on introducing the person of Jesus Christ. It is this christological context which determines the contours of John's presentation.

The Disciples Bear Witness to Jesus the Messiah

In the first three Gospels, as we have seen, Jesus and Jesus alone takes the initiative and calls people to follow him (Mark 1:16-20; Matt. 4:18-22; Luke 5:1-11). In the Gospel of John, the disciples take initiative, "testify/bear witness," and bring people to meet Jesus.

In John's story, John the Baptist bears witness to Jesus (John 1:29-34), and two of his disciples leave him and follow Jesus (1:35-42). One of the two is Andrew, who finds his brother Simon, witnesses to him, and brings him to Jesus (1:40-42). Simon finds Philip (1:43-44)—although the Greek of 1:43 is ambiguous. Jesus, Simon, or Andrew (who "first" finds Simon, 1:41; Brown, 1:85) may be the one who finds Philip, though in the context it is more likely Simon or

Andrew. Then Jesus issues the call, "Follow me." Next Philip finds Nathanael, bears witness to him, and brings him to Jesus (1:45-51).

The chain of witnesses begins with John the Baptist and continues through Andrew and Simon to Philip and Nathanael. To Nathanael is given the promise that he (and by implication all who have commenced to follow Jesus) "will see heaven opened and the angels of God ascending and descending upon the Son of Man" (John 1:51). Even Simon Peter, whose importance for the later church is indicated through the new name that he is given (Matt. 16:18), is not encountered by Jesus directly. He is brought to Jesus by Andrew, who had previously heard the witness of the Baptist. This Evangelist is writing long after the resurrection of Christ, and in his account Jesus is no longer understood primarily as walking among his people as he did in Galilee. He is the exalted Son in heaven, and it is through his witnesses, the church, that he continues to call people to faith in him.

In this process of reinterpretation in the Fourth Gospel, John the Baptist has become the first Christian evangelist, the model for all others. As he repeatedly stresses, his whole purpose is to bear witness so that people might come to faith in Jesus (John 1:7-8, 19-23, 29-34; 3:26-28; 5:33-34). He is not known by any exalted title (1:19-23); he is but a voice testifying to the one whom they do not know (1:26-27). He tells them what he has seen (1:32-34) and bears witness that Jesus is the Son of God (1:34), the Lamb of God who takes away the sin of the world (1:29, 36), the one on whom the Spirit descends and remains (1:32). All of his words point to Jesus, and his final testimony is: "He must increase, but I must decrease" (3:30). With these words, John disappears from view. Here at the outset, John acknowledges that he is not even worthy to unfasten the straps of Jesus' sandals (1:27). Jesus occupies the center stage throughout the entire Gospel.

In a similar way, Andrew has become the first Christian disciple, the model for all others. The first thing he does after being with Jesus is to find his brother Simon; to testify, "We have found the Messiah"; and to bring Simon to a face-to-face encounter with Jesus (John 1:40-42). Later, when the

Greeks want to see Jesus, they come to Philip. Philip then goes to Andrew, and together they tell Jesus (12:20-22).

The language which John is using is that of the law court where the witness appears and openly affirms what he has seen and heard. John affirms that he saw the Spirit descending as a dove from heaven and remaining with Jesus (John 1:32). First the two disciples of John "see" where Jesus lives and "remain" with him; then Andrew can say, "We have found the Messiah" (1:41). Simon is changed (1:42), Philip is called (1:43), and Nathanael has experienced the divine insight of Jesus (1:48); only then are they able to make their affirmations.

Notice, too, that apart from John the Baptist (who naturally stands alone), the others bear witness corporately. Andrew says, "We have found the Messiah" (John 1:41), and Philip declares, "We have found him about whom Moses in the law and also the prophets wrote" (1:45). This possibly also reflects the language of the courtroom, where every word has to be established by the mouth of two or three witnesses. It certainly indicates that the church bears witness through the disciples, the church which has already made its liturgical response to the revelation of the Word: "From his fullness we have all received, grace upon grace" (1:16). As witnesses to the reality of Jesus, the disciples take their place in the story of revelation alongside the Old Testament (5:39), John the Baptist (5:33-34), the works of Jesus (5:36), and even the Father (5:37) and the Spirit (14:26).

John the Baptist testifies that Jesus is "the Son of God" and "the Lamb of God" (John 1:29, 34, 36); Andrew tells Simon, "We have found the Messiah" (1:41); Philip says to Nathanael, "We have found him about whom Moses in the law and also the prophets wrote" (1:45). When Nathanael meets Jesus he makes his confession, "Rabbi, you are the Son of God! You are the King of Israel!" (1:49). In fact, almost all of the titles of Christ that occur in the Fourth Gospel are to be found in this opening chapter. What an amazing array it is!

Jesus is the Logos, the Word (1:1, 14), God (1:1, 18), the life and light (1:4-5, 9), the only begotten (1:14, 18), the Son (1:18), the Lamb of God (1:29, 36), the Son of God (1:34, 49), the Chosen of God (1:34, some manuscripts), the Messiah (1:41), the King of Israel (1:49), and the Son of Man (1:51). By implication, through the Baptist's emphatic denial, he is also designated the Christ, Elijah, and the coming eschatological Prophet (1:20-21). There is nothing like this anywhere else in the New Testament. In a world of many gods and saviors, this is John's way of indicating right at the start that all of the God-inspired hopes and expectations of humanity have found their fulfillment in Jesus Christ, the one to whom the disciples (the church) bear witness.

People Come to Faith Through an Encounter with Jesus

The disciple-evangelists (the church) make their testimony to the things which they have experienced in their encounter with Jesus. But those who hear their testimony do not become disciples on the basis of a secondhand experience. They are brought to Jesus, and through an encounter with him, they come to faith.

The disciples of John go off after Jesus when they hear their teacher's testimony to the Lamb of God. But it is not until they "come" and "see" and "remain" with Jesus that Andrew can say, "We have found the Messiah" (John 1:35-41). Possibly John's account is only meant to indicate that the disciples lodged with Jesus on Friday evening and Saturday until the Sabbath was over and they were able to travel again (2:1). There is some support, however, for the idea that the tenth hour (four o'clock in the afternoon, by Jewish reckoning; 1:39) was meant to indicate "the hour of fulfillment." Thus the verb "remain" likely has theological overtones of "abiding," as elsewhere in this Gospel. If so, this is John's equivalent to Mark's statement that the disciples were called "to be with" Jesus, to be part of his community (Mark 3:14).

While we infer that Andrew is part of Jesus' community, John clearly makes this point with respect to Simon. Through Simon's encounter with Jesus, he receives a new name (John 1:42). He becomes a new person. In the Gospel of Mark, Simon receives his new name later, when the twelve disciples become the nucleus of the new community of faith (Mark 3:13-19). To John, however, it is important to indicate that this change takes place here through the first encounter with Jesus. In John's presentation, this is when Simon becomes a new person.

When Philip hears the call "Follow me," he is able to testify to Nathanael, "We have found him about whom Moses in the law and also the prophets wrote" (John 1:44-45). When Nathanael expresses doubt that anything good could come from the tiny and despised town of Nazareth, Philip does not bother to argue with him. He simply says, "Come and see." The encounter with Jesus renders all proofs and arguments irrelevant. Nathanael makes his confession and receives the promise of sharing the future glory of the Son of Man (1:46-51).

The disciples testify to their experience of Jesus in their own ways and using different words and titles. There is no one orthodox confession which must be used by everyone, and there is no title which does not find its fulfillment in Jesus. Through a meeting with Jesus, the barriers are finally removed, and they are able to make their own confessions of faith. The witness of others prepares the way for faith, but faith itself comes through an encounter with the one who is both the source of faith and the object of faith, Jesus Christ. In John's account, the experience of the disciples is finally designated "faith" when they see the revelation of the glory of Jesus in his first sign at Cana and come to believe in him (John 2:11).

Meeting the Messiah Marks the Beginning of a New Life

In each of the Gospels, discipleship involves a break with the old way of living and the beginning of a new life of following Jesus. Once again, John stands somewhat apart from the others. The Fourth Gospel no longer expresses this change of lifestyle in terms of leaving boats, families, and professions to follow Jesus. In John, the disciples leave behind other prophets, teachers, lords, and saviors to give wholehearted allegiance to Jesus. He, and only he, is the way, the truth, and the life (John 14:6); this is the meaning of the emphatic "I am" formulas. Through their encounters with Jesus, the disciples recognize that he is "the Son of God" (1:34), "the Lamb of

God" (1:29, 36), "the Messiah" (1:41), "the King of Israel" (1:49), "the Son of Man" (1:51). Jesus is the one on whom the Spirit descends and remains (1:32), the one who takes away the sin of the world (1:29), the center of their lives.

In these beginning discipleship stories, John expresses the new life in terms which indicate a new understanding of the person of Jesus. But as John makes clear elsewhere, such a new understanding of the person of Jesus leads to a new ethic through this new allegiance to Jesus. For John, this ethic is the ethic of love, the commandment which Jesus gives to his disciples (John 13:34; 15:12, 17). This love is grounded in the self-giving love of God in Jesus (3:16 and many other places) and shows itself in sacrificial service. Through sacrificial love, life is to be found. Those who wish to serve must follow Jesus, the servant of all, and those who wish to follow must become the servants of all (13:1-20). To be with Jesus is to render him absolute allegiance and to become a servant of humanity with him.

The Lifestyle of the Kingdom

We have seen in the Gospel of Mark that the simple stories of the call of the first disciples (Mark 1:16-20) are profound pictorial representations of God's kingly reign breaking into human history and of people responding to this good news in repentance and faith. They encapsulate the good news proclaimed by Jesus as an act of grace making possible and demanding a life-changing response. Jesus takes the initiative and calls people from their everyday occupations; they in turn leave behind their jobs and families and follow him.

Luke has a different account of the commissioning of Simon (Luke 5:1-11) from that found in Mark and Matthew. He carries through some of Mark's insights but has his own distinctive understanding as well, especially on the ministry of Jesus and the mission of the church. He stresses again, in his own way, the gracious nature of the divine visitation in Jesus. In a most emphatic way, he underlines that Simon and his partners respond to Jesus with a spontaneous and radical act of single-minded obedience. They go with Jesus, trusting him for the present and for the future.

The stories of the call to discipleship in the Fourth Gospel (John 1:35-51) are dramatically different from anything found in the earlier accounts. The incidents take place before the commencement of Jesus' ministry, as part of the Evangelist's opening presentation of Christ's exalted status, in a compact Christology. Everything is subordinated to this emphasis. The disciples bear witness to Jesus, using a wide range of christological titles. Then, through an encounter with Jesus, the disciples come to faith, leaving behind other prophets, lords, and saviors to give wholehearted allegiance to Jesus.

The stories of the call of the first disciples are very different because they are written in response to different situations in the early churches and by different people who had different Christian theologies. Indeed, it is surprising that they have so much in common. Each story is dominated by the person of Jesus. In Mark, Jesus takes the initiative, sees the people, and calls them to follow him. In Luke, Jesus is the Lord of the church and the world, already well into his ministry of teaching, healing, and preaching. He shows the disciples where fish are to be found in most unpropitious circumstances, forgives their sins, and promises them an amazing future in the worldwide mission of the church. In John, Jesus is the one in whom all of the hopes and dreams and expectations of humanity find their fulfillment. There never has been and never will be anyone to match this Jesus.

More than any of the others, Luke emphasizes that the call to discipleship is a call to participate in the ministry of Jesus and in the mission of the church. The location, form, and features of his story all serve to underline this emphasis. But he is not alone in this. As we will see later, Mark has arranged his opening three stories on discipleship so that there is a deliberate progression toward mission. The first disciples are promised, "I will make you fish for people" (Mark 1:17). The twelve are called "to be with him, and to be sent out to proclaim the message, and to have authority to cast out demons" (3:14-15). And they are finally sent out to continue his mission in the world (6:7-13).

The fourth Evangelist has so reinterpreted his stories that

John the Baptist has become the first Christian evangelist, the model for all others, and Andrew has become the first Christian disciple, the model for all others. The Baptist's total concern is to bear witness to Jesus, and as soon as Andrew becomes a Christian, he brings his brother to Jesus.

Again, it is Luke who emphasizes more strongly than the others the radical nature of the response of the early disciples. In his account, they spontaneously leave everything and go off after Jesus. But this feature is present already in Mark, where the disciples leave their jobs and families to follow him. It is there also in John, where the disciples leave other prophets, teachers, lords, and saviors to follow Jesus.

The significance of a number of these aspects of the stories will become clearer as we examine them more closely and realize the extent to which our lives are to be determined by the Jesus whom we are seeking to follow. At the outset, though, before anything else, we must recall that life on the road is an act of grace—before we come to consider the cost of following Jesus and of being involved in his mission in the world, before we look at the question of renouncing dependence on material possessions and of becoming involved in the community of the new people of God, and before we talk about rejecting traditional patterns of power and oppression and of learning to live a life of prayer and dependence upon God. By God's grace we have been called to follow Jesus. By grace we are able to continue in our life with him. And it will be solely on the basis of God's grace that life will be brought to its conclusion with Jesus.

When called, the first disciples are not involved in religious activities. They are not worshiping in the temple or synagogue, nor are they praying or reading the Scriptures. They are not doing anything especially meritorious; they are just going about their business. And what a business it is—fishing and tax collecting! There is nothing particularly great which marks them out as important people who simply must be included in a successful missionary enterprise. Quite the contrary! These are not choice jobs!

The fact that Jesus comes from a despised town like Nazareth, works with his hands, and ministers primarily among marginalized people is the "pre-Easter scandal" of Christianity. In Western churches we have long grown accustomed to the idea of a crucified Messiah; this scandal is a stumbling block for us. We find it so difficult to accept that Christianity is based on grace, and therefore that our background, upbringing, education, and social standing do not grant us special privileges with God. Because the church is based on grace, the Christian life and the community of faith are open to everyone. And because this involves the justice of God, the poor and the outcasts have a special place.

We are Christians not because of who we are or what we do, but because of who Jesus is and what he does! If only we could believe this, the life and lifestyle of Western Christianity would be radically transformed and churches would again become centers of grace and justice for all. Jesus would again be walking among us, converting our society to the kingdom of God—a kingdom of peace, justice, and freedom for all. With this promise in view, let us go on to consider more fully the life of discipleship as we follow the wandering preacher from Nazareth, the crucified and risen Lord of all.

Questions for Discussion

1. How can a call to discipleship be recognized as authentic? How can we know that Jesus is the one calling us?

2. What is new in the call of Jesus compared with the Jewish tradition? How may the call to discipleship differ from the teaching of traditional Christianity?

3. The call to discipleship is also a call to community. Who are to participate in this community?

4. Is not the idea of costly grace a contradiction in terms? If it is grace, how can it be costly? If it is costly, how can we call it grace?

5. Do you really think the disciples would have left everything to follow Jesus? Why? Why not?

6. What did you leave behind when Jesus called you?

7. How can an encounter with Jesus convince someone like Nathanael when arguments have failed to impress?

8. How can anyone call discipleship "class treason"?

2

The Cost of Living on the Road

The Cost of Discipleship

Following Jesus in Palestine

The central feature of the preaching and teaching of Jesus is that in his words and works the kingly reign of God has drawn near. The reign of grace, the time of joy for the downtrodden, the sinners and the outcasts, the era of good news for the poor has begun to break into human history. The time of overflowing love and unsurpassable freedom, of universal reconciliation and everlasting peace has drawn near. It is at the very door, even in their midst. The time for the fulfillment of God's promises in the salvation of his people has arrived.

According to the Gospels, Jesus is convinced that through him God's future is already breaking into the present. Thus Jesus heals the sick and casts out demons, ignores the Sabbath regulations and speaks of the end of the temple. He abolishes the rigid food laws and associates with the nobodies of society, pronounces God's blessing on the poor and demonstrates his presence with the persecuted. He declares the forgiveness of sins and invites the outcasts and notorious sinners to the messianic banquet. The time of God's joyful celebration has arrived, and all of his people are invited to join in the festivities. All, without exception, are invited, and all, without distinction, are welcome. This is to be a festival of peace and love.

In the light of the inbreaking of the kingdom, Jesus teaches with divine authority, preaches the good news, and invites sinners to repentance and faith. In an act without parallel in the ancient world, he takes the initiative and calls disciples to follow him. He invites them to leave the security of homes, families, and jobs to be with him in a special way as he travels the length and breadth of Palestine telling the good news.

The invitation to go with Jesus is a call of grace, for the hearers have done nothing to deserve the divine invitation. But it is a call of costly grace, for they have to leave everything to follow him. Time and again, Jesus warns of the cost involved. When a scribe brashly offers to follow Jesus wherever he goes, he is told in no uncertain terms: "Foxes have holes, and the birds of the air have nests; but the Son of Man has nowhere to lay his head" (Matt. 8:20). A disciple wants to wait until he has discharged his family responsibilities, and Jesus commands: "Follow me, and let the dead bury their own dead" (8:22). The disciples and the crowd are told: "If any want to become my followers, let them deny themselves and take up their cross and follow me" (Mark 8:34).

As Günther Bornkamm has observed: "Discipleship means decision; Jesus' decision as regards certain individuals, but then it means no less their own decision to follow him. It consists, in actual fact, in the determination to abandon everything and, in the first instance quite literally, to follow Jesus from place to place, and to accept the fate of the wanderer with all its privations" (*Jesus*, 146).

Jesus does not hide his scars to win disciples. In Luke, he teaches the people: "Whoever comes to me and does not hate [Matt. 10:37: love less] father and mother, wife and children, brothers and sisters, yes, and even life itself, cannot be my disciple" (Luke 14:26). In the double parable of the man planning to build a tower and of a king contemplating a military campaign, Jesus warns against rash decisions. Those who desire to follow him ought first to sit down and count the cost (14:28-33). "No one who puts a hand to the plow and looks back is fit for the kingdom of God," says Jesus (9:62).

Undoubtedly, many of the sayings about the cost of living on the road with Jesus are originally addressed to those who are to follow him while he is traveling through Palestine as a wandering charismatic preacher and miracle worker. Not all of his supporters are called to leave house and home to follow him. Some who want to go with him are, in fact, sent home to share the good news with their family and friends (Mark 5:18-20).

After the resurrection of Jesus, however, as the early church sought to depict the kind of response God required to the good news of grace and love in Jesus Christ, they saw in the stories of Jesus and his disciples supreme illustrations of the life of faith. This is why Mark places the call of the fishermen (Mark 1:16-20) immediately after the opening summary of the preaching of Jesus (1:14-15). The call of the disciples is, for Mark, an example of God's kingly rule of grace breaking into the world, and their following of Jesus is, for him, an illustration of the meaning of repentance and faith.

In the same way, the warnings of Jesus about the cost of following him are reinterpreted as warnings to the church in every age. They are seen as examples of the way discipleship covers every area of life and involves a radical obedience to Jesus and a renunciation of the ways of the world. The Gospel of Mark specifically says that Jesus summoned "the crowd" with his disciples before giving his teaching about taking up the cross and following him (8:34). In other words, this saying has, for Mark, a universal application which is not to be restricted to the original followers of Jesus.

After Easter, as with the call narratives, the warnings and the illustrations of faith were reinterpreted and adapted in the light of the differing contemporary situations encountered by each Evangelist. We will look at three examples: the cross as the only way to glory (Mark), the experience of the stormy sea (Matthew), and the warning to count the cost (Luke).

The Cross Is the Only Way to Glory (Mark 8:27—9:8)

Throughout the first part of Mark's Gospel, Jesus reveals his authority in word and action only to be greeted by the increasing blindness of the world. The religious and political leaders (Mark 3:6), his own townspeople at Nazareth (6:1-6), and even his own disciples (8:14-21) take their stand against him or fail to grasp his mission. In words reminiscent of the fearful pronouncement of Isaiah's prophecy, Jesus has to ask his disciples: "Do you still not perceive or understand? Are your hearts hardened? Do you have eyes, and fail to see? Do you have ears, and fail to hear?" (8:17-18). How hard it is to open the eyes of the blind (8:22-26)!

With the report of the incident at Caesarea Philippi (Mark 8:27—9:1), there is a distinct change in Mark's presentation. Up to this point, Jesus has revealed himself only in a veiled way, and those who perceived his true identity were not allowed to reveal it to others (3:11-12). Now he speaks openly to his disciples. Three times he tells them that the Son of Man will be put to death (8:31; 9:31; 10:32-34). On the first occasion (8:31-33), Peter is incensed and rebukes Jesus for speaking in such terms. Jesus is not so easily turned aside, and he goes on to teach the disciples, and the crowd, that those who follow him must do so by way of the cross (8:34-38).

Jesus tells of his impending death a second time (Mark 9:31-32), but they still do not understand and spend their time discussing who is the greatest. Jesus takes a child, places the little one in their midst, and teaches them at length concerning the true nature of discipleship (9:35-50). A third time he foretells his death (10:32-34), but immediately James and John ask for positions of honor and glory in the kingdom of God. They still do not understand, so Jesus teaches them about discipleship as sacrificial service (10:38-40). The story of the transfiguration (9:2-8), presented as a divine affirmation of the way of the cross, underlines the importance of the opening teaching on the cost of discipleship (8:27-9:1).

Jesus went on with his disciples to the villages of Caesarea Philippi; and on the way he asked his disciples, "Who do people say that I am?" And they answered him, "John the Baptist, and others, Elijah; and still others, one of the prophets." He asked them, "But who do you say that I am?" Peter answered him, "You are the Messiah." And he sternly ordered them not to tell anyone about him.

Then he began to teach them that the Son of Man must undergo great suffering, and be rejected by the elders, the chief priests, and the scribes, and be killed, and after three days rise again. He said all this quite openly. And Peter took him aside and began to rebuke him. But turning and looking at his disciples, he rebuked Peter and said, "Get behind me, Satan! For you are setting your mind not on divine things but on human things."

He called the crowd with his disciples, and said to them, "If any want to become my followers, let them deny themselves and take up their cross and follow me. For those who want to save their life will lose it, and those who lose their life for my sake, and for the sake of the gospel, will save it. For what will it profit them to gain the whole world and forfeit their life? Indeed, what can they give in return for their life? Those who are ashamed of me and of my words in this adulterous and sinful generation, of them the Son of Man will also be ashamed when he comes in the glory of his Father with the holy angels." And he said to them, "Truly I tell you, there are some standing here who will not taste death until they see that the kingdom of God has come with power."

Six days later, Jesus took with him Peter and James and John, and led them up a high mountain apart, by themselves. And he was transfigured before them, and his clothes became dazzling white, such as no one on earth could bleach them. And there appeared to them Elijah with Moses, who were talking with Jesus. Then Peter said to Jesus, "Rabbi, it is good for us to be here; let us make three dwellings, one for you, one for Moses, and one for Elijah." He did not know what to say, for they were terrified. Then a cloud overshadowed them, and from the cloud there came a voice, "This is my Son, the Beloved; listen to him!" Suddenly when they looked around, they say no one with them any more, but only Jesus.   (Mark 8:27—9:8)

At Caesarea Philippi, on the border between Israelite territory and the Gentile lands, Jesus begins the fateful journey which will reach its climax with his death outside Jerusalem. At the beginning of this journey, as he is "on the way" to his death, Jesus takes the initiative and for the first time speaks plainly about his identity and about the cost of following him. As Jesus sets out for the center of political, economic, and religious power, he begins to explain to his disciples exactly who he is and how they should follow him. He is the suffering Son of Man (Mark 8:27-33). Those who follow him must do so by way of the cross (8:34—9:1), for the cross is the only way to glory (9:2-8).

Jesus Is the Suffering Son of Man

Throughout this Gospel, Mark emphasizes that discipleship begins with Jesus. In an event unprecedented in the ancient world, Jesus, unlike the rabbis and other leaders, takes the initiative and calls people to follow him (Mark 1:16-20). He calls the twelve out from the larger group of his followers so that they might enter into a special relationship with him (3:13-19). A little later he calls them together and sends them out on mission (6:7-13). And now, again in contrast to the rabbis who normally gave their teaching in response to the questioning of their disciples, Jesus takes the initiative. He questions them about his identity as they are about to be led into a new revelation of the meaning of following him.

It is important to notice that before Jesus speaks about discipleship, he speaks about himself. This is the primary issue, for the way we think about discipleship is largely determined by the way we think about Jesus. According to the disciples, the people generally have been associating Jesus with the great prophetic heroes of the Israelite faith. This is not sufficient, and Jesus presses them further. Peter acts as their spokesman and confesses that they see in Jesus the messianic Son of David who would restore the fortunes of Israel, defeat the Gentiles, and establish his kingdom in Jerusalem.

Jesus neither accepts nor rejects Peter's orthodox confession of faith, but within the context of Mark's Gospel it is clearly inadequate. Matthew, on the other hand, is able to affirm Peter's confession because he has redefined and Christianized the concept of messiahship. But according to Mark, in many ways such an understanding has not even risen to the heights of the demons who have already recognized in Jesus the Son of God (Mark 3:11; 5:7). When they reach Jerusalem, they will find out just how their traditional expectations are being turned upside down in Jesus of Nazareth.

Jesus ignores Peter's confession and goes on to speak of himself as the Son of Man. This is perhaps a humble self-designation in the tradition of the prophets, or perhaps a title for the exalted figure of Jewish apocalyptic expectations, but more likely and specifically the messianic figure representing the suffering people of God, who are to receive the kingdom, as in Daniel 7. Jesus predicts that he will be rejected by the religious hierarchy in Jerusalem, suffer many things, and be put to death. He speaks this plainly, openly, and confidently, for the days of parables and veiled sayings have ended. The time of open revelation has begun, but it is open revelation of the humble one who is to be rejected, suffer, and die—and rise again.

Peter is not able to accept such a despicable fulfillment of his religious hopes and ambitions (Mark 8:32). That Jesus should suffer many things would hardly have troubled him, for Israel knew of many righteous leaders who had suffered for their faith. But that he should be rejected by the religious leaders in Jerusalem and be put to death is a scandal to him. Jerusalem is to be the center of the messianic kingdom, not the place of rejection and death. It is not that Peter misunderstands what Jesus said. He understands perfectly. He understands that the words of Jesus speak of a way of lowliness and humiliation rather than a way of worldly power and glory. He understands what Jesus said, but he rejects it and takes the unparalleled step of rebuking Jesus for suggesting such a thing. Peter's way is the way of worldly power and glory.

Jesus, for his part, radically disassociates himself from Peter's hopes and their projected fulfillment. He designates them as demonic, issuing from Satan himself (Mark 8:33). They are totally opposed to the way of God in Jesus.

In the face of the darkness of the world in which the religious leaders will destroy God's messenger outside the center of power, the plain words of revelation have been spoken. The way of God is the way of rejection, suffering, and death. Those who cannot accept this way stand with the powers of darkness. This applies as much to the disciples as to anyone else, perhaps even more so. Discipleship confers responsibility, not positions of privilege.

Discipleship Is the Way of the Cross

The disciples, who up till now have been following Jesus, must decide whether they wish to follow the way of God or turn aside into the ways of humanity. They must choose between the way of traditional security, power, and glory suggested by Peter and the way of humiliation, rejection, and death offered by Jesus. It is not only the disciples, however, who must make this decision. As Mark emphasizes, before Jesus begins to teach, he calls the crowd as well as the disciples (Mark 8:34). The crowd has not been sighted in Mark since the feeding of the four thousand (8:1-10), and now they must hear this teaching. What Jesus has to say is not reserved for Christian leaders, and its validity is not restricted to his own time. This is the choice which is laid before the people of God in all generations, the choice between the way of power and glory and the way of the cross.

The decision, for all its importance, is not forced upon anyone (Mark 8:34). Like all decisions which arise through an encounter with Jesus, it is a personal decision and it is a free decision. When Jesus approaches the disciples for the first time and calls them to follow him, they are free to continue fishing or mending nets or collecting taxes (1:16-20; 2:14). The rich young man continues to make his money and care for his large estates (10:17-21). The choice is open to him, and he makes it. Jesus offers a free choice, but the options are strictly limited. The first disciples can not continue fishing, mending nets, collecting taxes, and still follow Jesus. The rich young man can not continue making money and still follow Jesus. It is one thing or the other. There is no middle way. The choice has to be made between the way of God and the ways of humanity. We must make the same· choice. The options are the way of power and glory or the way of the cross.

The way of God (Mark 8:34) begins when the disciples forsake their selfish pretensions and desires for earthly security, power, and glory for the sake of Jesus. It does not end there, however, for the disciple must also take up the cross and follow Jesus. As Dietrich Bonhoeffer says, "The cross is laid on every Christian. . . . When Christ calls a man he bids him come and die" (*Bonhoeffer*, 79).

This saying about taking up the cross and following Jesus (Mark 8:34) has lost its horror and dread. The cross has become a divine ornament, an ecclesiastical trinket; the saying about carrying the cross has been reduced to the level of enduring our little daily troubles. In the first century, the cross was the Roman gallows. Crucifixion was the dreaded method of public execution reserved for criminals and insurrectionists, and the condemned person was forced to carry the crossbeam to the place of execution.

To take up the cross is to set off on the terrible path of a person condemned to death, carrying on your shoulder the heavy beam to which you will be nailed and on which you will die. Martin Hengel writes, "For the men of the ancient world, Greeks, Romans, barbarians and Jews, the cross was not just a matter of indifference, just any kind of death. It was an utterly offensive affair, 'obscene' in the original sense of the word, . . . a 'barbaric' form of execution of utmost cruelty" (*Crucifixion*, 22-23).

But if the saying about taking up the cross (Mark 8:34) has been robbed of its horror and dread, it has also been robbed of its glory. One can never travel the way of the cross alone. The call is to take up the cross and *follow Jesus*. The one who first made that fearful journey to Golgotha makes the journey again and again before his followers. One of the profound paradoxes of Christianity is to be found in the fact that the one who was not able to carry his own cross (15:21) is the one who enables us to carry ours. When we carry the cross, we shall never walk alone, for we are following Jesus. But if we follow Jesus, we must carry the cross.

The picture of Simon of Cyrene carrying the cross behind Jesus (Mark 15:21) has become one of the most poignant pictures of discipleship in the Christian tradition. At Caesarea Philippi, Jesus laid the options before his disciples. There it is emphasized that we are not forced to carry the cross. It is a free choice. We have to decide whether or not we will carry the cross. The story of Simon, however, is told from a different perspective. Simon was forced to carry the cross and was therefore not even given any credit for making the decision. It was forced upon him. He had no choice. Discipleship, therefore, is not to be understood as a "work meriting salvation." In our obedient following, we do no more than is expected.

The scene of Simon of Cyrene carrying the cross behind Jesus (Mark 15:21) also expresses most clearly the literal meaning of discipleship. Discipleship, in the New Testament, is not a subjective experience; it is not a frame of mind, a way of thinking. Discipleship takes place when we carry the timber behind Jesus. It is ultimately a down-to-earth experience, and it changes one's entire life. We are not only told that the man's name was "Simon," we are also told that he was "the father of Alexander and Rufus." It seems almost certain that he became a Christian and that his family was known to the Marcan church. The life of Simon and his family was never the same again, not after he had carried the timber behind Jesus.

The sacrifice of which Jesus speaks is not self-mortification for the purification of our souls. It is self-denying discipleship for the sake of Jesus and the gospel (Mark 8:35, with Mark himself adding "and . . . the gospel"). Made possible by Jesus, this self-denying discipleship has as its goal the glorification of Jesus and his church. The church has often lost its glory because it has pointed people to Peter's way rather than to Jesus' way. It has sought to offer Jesus and the way of power and glory at the same time. But it is through weakness that strength is to be found (8:35). It is through the renunciation of power and glory that power and glory will come to the church. Those who follow Jesus must do so by way of the cross (8:34). But many are ashamed of the crucified Messiah and his message about suffering and rejection (8:31) and the cross as the way of discipleship (8:34). In return, they will find that they will be rejected on the day of glory (8:38).

Divine Affirmation of the Way of the Cross

The revelation of the resurrection triumph and final glory of Jesus in the transfiguration is a story rich in theological symbolism but not without its difficulties in interpretation. It follows on closely from the previous section on death before rising (Mark 8:27-33) and discipleship (8:34—9:1). Mark has bound these stories together by the specific mention that the incident took place "six days later" (9:2, the only place outside the passion narrative where Mark uses such precise chronology). As another tie, he immediately leads from the transfiguration to the talk on the way down the mountain, discussion about the meaning of the resurrection and the suffering of the messianic forerunner (9:9-13).

The revelation of the divine glory (Mark 9:2-8) follows closely upon the prediction of the crucifixion of the Son of Man (8:31) and the call to the disciples to walk the way of the cross (8:34). There is no other way to participate in the glory than to travel the road which leads to Jerusalem. The way which leads to Jerusalem, however, also leads on to glory. The crucifixion and the resurrection belong together—for Jesus and for his disciples. A number of scholars have suggested that the transfiguration is a misplaced resurrection story. While this theory has many difficulties, it does underline Mark's emphasis that the cross and resurrection belong together. Whatever else it may be, in this Gospel the transfiguration is certainly understood as an anticipation of the resurrection.

Jesus takes Peter, James, and John up the mountain to experience the revelation of the divine glory (Mark 9:2), and the whole account is directed toward them, the inner circle of the new people of God. These are the very ones who are having such difficulty in recognizing the way of God in Jesus' prediction of his death and in his teaching on the way of discipleship. The three chosen to receive the divine revelation are Peter, who disagrees with Jesus' teaching (8:32-33); and

James and John, who misunderstand and ask for leading positions in the kingdom (10:35-37)!

The great heroes of the faith around which so many Jewish hopes had gathered, Elijah and Moses (Mark 9:4), appear to the disciples and talk with Jesus. They reinforce the decisive nature of Jesus' coming as the final revelation of God. It is in Jesus and his teaching, in his death and in his call to follow in the way, that their hopes are being fulfilled.

Traditionally, Elijah and Moses have been interpreted as representing the Law and the Prophets, the totality of Old Testament revelation. This is the understanding in Matthew, where the order of names is "Moses and Elijah" (Matt. 17:3) and may well have been the same in the story as it came down to Mark. However, by changing the sequence to the unusual "Elijah and Moses" (Mark 9:4), Mark points to a more profound interpretation: "Elijah and Moses" are the two suffering righteous ones of the Israelite tradition.

Jesus has just spoken of his own suffering and death (8:31) and called the disciples to take up the cross and follow him (8:34). They are talking about this on the mountain. The discussion during the descent (9:9-13) confirms the role of Elijah as the forerunner of the suffering Son of Man. In Mark, John the Baptist is the "suffering Elijah" who is to come first to restore all things (9:12) and loses his life as he fulfills his ministry (6:14-29) of preparing the way of the Lord (1:2-3). This is what the people do not understand when, at the cross, they wait to see if Elijah will come and take Jesus down (15:35-36)—Elijah has come *first* to prepare the way for this event! He cannot come and take Jesus down.

Final support for this understanding of the dramatic role ascribed to Elijah and Moses as the suffering righteous ones of Israel is to be found in an old story in the book of Revelation, dating back at least to the time when the Gospel of Mark was written. This story tells of two faithful martyrs and witnesses (Rev. 11:1-8), "the two olive trees and the two lampstands that stand before the Lord of the earth" (11:4). The two faithful witnesses and martyrs are clearly identified as Elijah and Moses. They are said to have "authority to shut the sky, so that no rain may fall" (as Elijah did in 1 Kings 17:1).

They also have "authority over the waters to turn them into blood, and to strike the earth with every kind of plague" (as Moses did in Exod. 7:14-19).

When these two faithful martyrs and witnesses appear on the mount of transfiguration with Jesus, they affirm again the relationship between discipleship and death. The two who were put to death in the city "where also their Lord was crucified" (Rev. 11:8) appear and talk with Jesus in anticipation of his death outside the city. But more than that, the story in Revelation goes on to say that after a short while "the breath of life from God entered them, and they stood on their feet" (11:11). Discipleship, death, and resurrection belong together, both in the Revelation story and in Mark's account.

When Peter witnesses the divine glory, he does not know what to say, for "they were terrified" (Mark 9:6; as in Rev. 11:11, "those who saw them were terrified"). But that does not inhibit Peter. His attitude is still the same as at Caesarea Philippi (Mark 8:32), and he suggests that they erect three temporary shelters so that they can remain on the mountain, enjoy the festival, and prolong the glory. Earlier he had been rebuked (8:33), but this time his advice is simply ignored—he is still on the side of man, not of God. The one who does not listen to the story of the cross does not understand the resurrection either.

As at the baptism of Jesus (Mark 1:9-11), so also here the heavenly voice affirms Jesus' divine sonship (9:7). This time, however, the affirmation is directed to the disciples ("listen to him!") rather than to Jesus. They are the ones who must learn that Jesus is the Son of God. They must also hear the command, "Listen to him!" Listen to him? But Jesus has not spoken to them. He has remained silent throughout the entire story! But God has already spoken in Jesus, and the revelation has been made plain (8:31). If they wish to follow him, they must do so by way of the cross (8:34). There is nothing more to be said. To those who will not hear the words of Jesus about death and discipleship, nothing more can be said. Nothing more will be said! They will be left in the silence, the awful silence of a God who has nothing more to say.

When we do not like what Jesus has said, we frequently

wait for another word from him, a different word, an easier word. The divine voice assures us that no other word will come. The divine Son has spoken. He has pointed the way to God in the suffering Son of Man and in the call to take up the cross and follow him. It only remains for us to decide whether we will accept the way of God or turn aside into the ways of humanity.

The heavenly vision passes quickly, and the story ends abruptly. All that remains is the harsh reality of life on earth. The disciples are left with Jesus and with him alone (Mark 9:8). On the way down the mountain, they are commanded to tell no one about what has happened until after his resurrection (9:9). Only the church which has experienced the cross and resurrection can understand and enter into his glory. The disciples do not understand what the resurrection means, and they still cannot fit the idea of rejection and death into their theological framework (9:10-11). They still have to come to an understanding that the two belong together: crucifixion and resurrection, suffering and glory. You cannot have the one without the other. The way to glory is the way of the cross; the way of the cross is the way to glory.

The Experience of a Stormy Sea (Matthew 8:18-27)

Matthew was writing toward the end of the first century in an urban community of relatively secure middle-class Christians. He used materials drawn from a number of different sources and fashioned his Gospel to meet the needs of a rather conservative, charismatic Jewish-Christian church. Matthew presents Jesus as the messianic Son of God, the Christian Messiah, and calls the members of his community to a single-minded devotion to God through Jesus Christ. The church has settled down and is in no sense a moving congregation. Yet Matthew takes up the stories about Jesus and his disciples and, like Mark before him, reinterprets them so that they now convey to his church the essential meaning of discipleship for their situation. They are still called to follow Jesus, even though they are no longer traveling anywhere with him. The stories of Jesus and his disciples, rightly reinterpreted, mark out the way they should live.

Matthew has taken over the basic framework from Mark, but he has incorporated a good deal of additional material from other sources. He extended the story backward through the birth stories and genealogy to David and Abraham, and forward through the great commission to the worldwide mission of the church. His Gospel is, in fact, a fresh and expanded edition of Mark, modified and rewritten in response to a new situation which had arisen in the early church.

The Sermon on the Mount (Matt. 5—7), Matthew's sermon on the sermons of Jesus, presents the words of the Messiah. It is immediately followed by his collection of miracle stories (Matt. 8—9) depicting the works of the Messiah. In contrast to Mark and Luke, who have miracle stories spread throughout the ministry of Jesus, Matthew has collected them primarily in this one section of his Gospel (Matt. 8—9; see the answer given to the messengers from John the Baptist in 11:2-5). He has carefully arranged his material around four themes: Christology (8:1-17), discipleship (8:18-34), community relationships (9:1-17), and faith (9:18-31). In the midst of these stories of Jesus, the Christian community, and the meaning of faith, Matthew tells of the experience of the disciples on the stormy sea:

> Now when Jesus saw great crowds around him, he gave orders to go over to the other side. A scribe then approached and said, "Teacher, I will follow you wherever you go." And Jesus said to him, "Foxes have holes, and birds of the air have nests; but the Son of Man has nowhere to lay his head." Another of his disciples said to him, "Lord, first let me go and bury my father." But Jesus said to him, "Follow me, and let the dead bury their own dead."
>
> And when he got into the boat, his disciples followed him. A windstorm arose on the sea, so great that the boat was being swamped by the waves; but he was asleep. And they went and woke him up, saying, "Lord, save us! We are perishing!" And he said to them, "Why are you afraid, you of little faith?" Then he got up and rebuked the winds and the sea; and there was a dead calm. They were amazed, saying, "What sort of man is this, that even the winds and the sea obey him?"
>
> (Matt. 8:18-27)

This story is an excellent example of the way Matthew has written his Gospel. He begins to recount the stilling of the storm from Mark (Matt. 8:18) and then inserts two discipleship sayings (8:19-22) which occur in quite a different context in Luke (Luke 9:57-61). Finally he tells the rest of the story about the storm on the lake (Matt. 8:23-27). Matthew recasts the story of the storm in such a way that it not only tells what happened once upon a time on the sea of Galilee, but, more importantly, what happens to disciples time and again as they follow Jesus. Matthew has transformed the original miracle story into a sermon on discipleship. He describes Jesus leading his disciples into the church and rescuing them from trial and tribulation when they are in danger of sinking. To follow Jesus is a costly and risky business, but he may be trusted to care for his people in times of difficulty and danger.

Hardship, Loneliness, and Separation

Jesus prepares to go to the other side of the sea to escape the crowds who have been attracted by his teaching (Matt. 7:28; 8:1) and his miracles (8:18). Just then a "scribe" comes to Jesus seeking acceptance into his wandering school of discipleship (Matt. 8:19).

For Matthew it is important that this first person is a "scribe" (Matt. 8:19), whereas in Luke he is described simply as "someone" (Luke 9:57). Together with the Pharisees, the scribes have become the major opponents of Jesus and his followers in Matthew (hence the long list of woes against them in Matt. 23). Some of them accuse Jesus of blasphemy (9:3), and others seek a sign (12:38). They charge the disciples with breaking the traditions of the elders (15:1), and they are indignant when, in the temple, he reveals himself as the merciful Son of David (21:15). They condemn him to death (26:59, 66) and mock him as he hangs upon the cross (27:41).

However, as Matthew is quick to point out, not all the scribes oppose Jesus and his church. Some are still open to the gospel (Matt. 13:52; 23:34; and the references to "some of the scribes" in 9:3; 12:38). This particular scribe acknowledges Jesus' authority and, following the usual rabbinic practice (cf. Mark 1:16-20), presents himself as one who wishes to be included among his students. He declares his willingness to follow Jesus anywhere. Such is his enthusiasm for the new rabbi and his teaching.

Jesus displays no interest whatsoever in the scribe's background or training. The matters of greatest importance to the rabbis do not even rate a question. Rather, he warns the scribe of the intense hardship and continuing loneliness that are involved in following him. For Jesus, discipleship is not so much a matter of training as it is a matter of living. He knows the dangers involved in living as one of his disciples, and he warns the scribe who is so keen to follow him. Even the animals and birds have protection and places to rest, but Jesus and those who travel with him have to live with rejection and homeless insecurity (Matt. 8:20).

We are not told whether the scribe follows Jesus or not. Almost certainly he does not, for in Matthew's Gospel, disciples and followers of Jesus address him as "Lord" (Matt. 8:21), never as "Teacher." Matthew does not bother to record this, however, for he is seeking to focus attention on the hardship and loneliness involved in following Jesus. The question of whether the scribe follows or turns aside is deliberately left open so that the readers of the Gospel may make their own decision. For Matthew the important question is not whether this particular scribe followed Jesus. The important question was whether his *church*, aware of the hardship and loneliness involved, will follow Jesus.

Next, one of the disciples, one who has already decided to follow Jesus, requests time off so that he may fulfill his family responsibilities in burying his father (Matt. 8:21). He acknowledges the authority of Jesus and addresses him as "Lord" (contrast 8:19), for he is one of his followers.

The proper burial of the dead was a matter of great importance in ancient Israel. This can be seen from the numerous Old Testament references and from the many thousands of ancient Jewish graves which have been excavated in recent times. Burial usually took place on the day of death and was followed by six days of mourning. Lack of a proper burial was considered a tragedy, and to provide a burial for another was considered an act of great piety (see Mark 15:42-46 for the account of Joseph of Arimathea providing for the burial of Jesus).

The burial of one's father was a matter of supreme importance (Tobit 4:3; 6:15), and only the high priest and the Nazirite were excluded from the responsibility (Lev. 21:11; Num. 6:6-7). Even a priest, who ordinarily must avoid the defiling contact with the dead, was permitted to bury his father (Lev. 21:1-2). The rabbis considered that the responsibility for family burials took precedence over such important acts of daily piety as saying the Shema (Deut. 6:4-5) and the Eighteen Benedictions. In his exhaustive study of these sayings, the German historian Martin Hengel adds: "Refusal of burial had always been considered among the Greeks and Jews as an unheard-of act of impiety and as the severest of punishments for criminals. . . . Burial of the dead was for the ancients always both a human and a religious duty" (*Charismatic Leader*, 10).

.The demand of Jesus to leave the spiritually dead to bury their own dead involves a total disregard for one of the most revered customs of the day. The only action in Scripture which can be considered in any way parallel to the demand of Jesus at this point is in the command of God to two of his prophets. As a sign of his judgment on Israel, God forbade Ezekiel to carry out the mourning ritual on the occasion of his wife's death (Ezek. 24:15-24). For the same reason, he demanded that Jeremiah abstain from marriage and from participation in banquets and celebrations, and that he not visit a house of mourning or take part in the lamentations for the dead (Jer. 16:1-9).

Thus, in the Old Testament the demand to keep from burial rites was made only on an isolated prophet and was not intended to have wider application. But such is the radical nature of the teaching of Jesus! The work of the kingdom requires a total commitment. The mission of Jesus must take priority even over our most sacred customs.

Again, we are not told whether this disciple continues to follow Jesus; is able to transcend traditions and customs, rules and regulations; and can continue giving absolute allegiance to Jesus. Matthew probably wants us to understand that he does persevere in following Jesus for the title "Lord" is used only by the disciples and people of faith in his Gospel. Still, he avoids discussing the question so that his church might more readily focus on the issue of their own obedience. The important question is not whether this particular disciple continues to follow Jesus, but whether Matthew's church will rise to the challenge and continue faithfully to follow their Lord. The scene therefore shifts immediately to Jesus and those who are following him into the boat.

The Storm of a Persecuted Community

In the story as we read it in the Gospel of Mark, Matthew's source at this point, Jesus is already in the boat and the disciples take him across to the other side of the lake. Other boats are with him (Mark 4:36). Matthew has rewritten this section so that Jesus now leads the way and the disciples "follow" him into the boat (Matt. 8:23). He uses the very same word as in the command to the disciple who wants to go and bury his father. Thus with his picture of the disciples following Jesus into the boat, Matthew is talking about the experiences of discipleship.

The boat is once again intended as a symbol for the church (see Matt. 14:22-33). Jesus issues the command to follow and leads his disciples into the church. In obedience they follow him. Almost immediately, however, a mighty storm is unleashed on the church. According to Mark's description, the waves are beating on the boat, and it is already "filling" with water (Mark 4:37, AG). Here the situation is even worse, for the boat is in grave danger of sinking (Matt. 8:24).

This now is no ordinary tempest. With an eye on the significance of the story for his church situation, Matthew has converted Mark's gale into an apocalyptic storm. He uses a rare word which can refer to a storm at sea, but which is more frequently used for cosmic disturbances. It is the word used in the book of Revelation to describe the fearful catastrophes which were expected to come upon the world before the end of the age (Rev. 6:12; 8:5; 11:13, 19; 16:8). Persecution of the church is an essential ingredient in traditional pictures of apocalyptic catastrophe, and Matthew's is a persecuted church (Matt. 5:10-12; 10:16-33; 22:6; 23:29-39). His readers would immediately have understood what he was talking about, for he was describing the reality of their situation.

Jesus sleeps on (Matt. 8:24; note that the "cushion" of Mark 4:38 is deleted since in this story the Son of Man has nowhere to lay his head; Matt. 8:20). He is not troubled by outward circumstances and is confident of the outcome. Jesus is confident that he can control the situation no matter what happens, for he is the Lord of the lake. The powers of chaos which threaten the church are ultimately under his control. The disciples, however, are frightened. They wake him and appeal for help, using the same words as Peter after his abortive attempt at walking on water (Matt. 14:30), "Lord, save us! We are perishing!" (8:25).

In Mark's account, Jesus speaks first to the wind and the sea (Mark 4:39) in the description of the stilling of the storm. Matthew has altered the sequence so that Jesus speaks to his troubled flock before he calms the storm. He rebukes the disciples for having "little faith," again in contrast to Mark, where they are described as having "no faith" (Mark 4:40). There is a world of difference between having "no faith" and having "little faith," for faith, even the size of a mustard seed, can remove mountains (Matt. 17:20).

Still, Matthew's church is shown up for what it is, a community willing to follow Jesus and yet failing and doubting when trouble strikes. Frequently they are described as a community of little faith (Matt. 6:30; 8:26; 14:31; 16:8), unwilling to allow God to provide for their needs (6:30; 16:8) or rescue them in times of trouble (8:26; 14:31). They are not a community without faith, but it is such little faith that the Evangelist repeatedly calls them to a single-minded devotion to Jesus and the kingdom. The persecuted community must learn to trust its Lord even in the most trying conditions.

Revelation of the Lord of the Lake

After chastising them for their little faith, Jesus nonetheless stands up and rebukes the storm. It disappears as quickly as it appears (Matt. 8:26). He is the Lord of the lake as well as Lord of the disciples (8:21-22) and of the church (8:25). He is in control of the chaos and of the cosmic upheavals and may be trusted even in times of persecution. The storm subsides, the disciples have been rescued, and the people marvel (8:27). The disciples and those who hear the story throughout the ages are amazed at the Lord's power to save. This is the reason he may be trusted in any situation arising in the life of the community. The disciples may trust him, for he is always in control. Such is the power and dependability of Jesus Christ, Lord of the lake and Lord of the church.

Strong Words on Counting the Cost (Luke 14:25-35)

In practical terms, Luke lays even more stress on the radical cost of discipleship than do the other Evangelists. Already in his account of the call of the first disciples, as we have seen, he emphasizes that "they left everything" to follow Jesus (Luke 5:11, with "everything" added to the account of Mark 1:20). When Luke retells the story of the call of Levi, he says that "he got up, left everything, and followed him" (Luke 5:28, adding to Mark 2:14 the words "left everything"). Similarly, in Luke's version of the story of the rich young ruler, Jesus says, "There is still one thing lacking. Sell all that you own and distribute the money to the poor, and you will have treasure in heaven; then come, follow me" (Luke 18:22, with "all" again added to Mark 10:21).

When, in Luke, Jesus is teaching the disciples on the need for an absolute concern for the kingdom of God, the same saying is given to all of them: "Sell your possessions, and give alms" (Luke 12:33). Finally, this teaching is applied to everyone when, after the twin parables of the tower builder and the king contemplating a campaign, Jesus says, "So, therefore, none of you can become my disciple if you do not give up all your possessions" (14:33). Luke stresses the same in his opening summary of life in the early church, a description designed to commend that form of corporate discipleship to his readers. Christians "would sell their possessions and goods and distribute the proceeds to all, as any had need" (Acts 2:45).

But it is not only with respect to material possessions that Luke emphasizes the cost involved in following Jesus. The warning words about the hardship, loneliness, and separation involved in following Jesus (Luke 9:57-62) are strategically placed at the commencement of the long journey to Jerusalem. During this journey to the heart of Israel, Jesus spends much of his time teaching about the way of discipleship. The initial warnings set the scene for the teaching that follows. Twice during the journey, Luke records the saying about carrying the cross (9:23; 14:27). The first time, when the saying is taken over from Mark (8:34), he emphasizes the need for daily obedience (9:23, with "daily" added to Mark's saying). The second, when he formulates the saying himself, he uses it as the conclusion to the teaching about the need to renounce traditional family ties (14:27).

Similarly, in his teaching on the need to renounce traditional patterns of family life for the sake of Jesus, Luke goes beyond the parallel in Matthew to include not only father and mother, son and daughter (Matt. 10:37-38), but also wife and brothers and sisters (Luke 14:25-26). The saying about divisions within households is intensified. In Luke it includes not only son against father, mother against daughter, daughter-in-law against mother-in-law (Matt. 10:35), but also the reverse: father against son, mother against daughter, mother-in-law against daughter-in-law (Luke 12:53).

The present passage (Luke 14:25-34), which Luke has built up from material taken from many different sources, provides his clearest teaching on the need to count the cost of discipleship. He has placed it at this point in his Gospel to prevent a possible misunderstanding of the story of grace depicted in the parable of the great banquet (14:15-24). Facing the danger of the misinterpretation of Jesus' invitation as cheap grace, Luke immediately warns of the cost of following Jesus:

> Now large crowds were traveling with [Jesus]; and he turned and said to them, "Whoever comes to me and does not hate father and mother, wife and children, brothers and sisters, yes, and even life itself, cannot be my disciple. Whoever does not

carry the cross and follow me cannot be my disciple. For which of you, intending to build a tower, does not first sit down and estimate the cost, to see whether he has enough to complete it? Otherwise, when he has laid a foundation and is not able to finish, all who see it will begin to ridicule him, saying, 'This fellow began to build and was not able to finish.' Or what king, going out to wage war against another king, will not sit down first and consider whether he is able with ten thousand to oppose the one who comes against him with twenty thousand? If he cannot, then, while the other is still far away, he sends a delegation and asks for the terms of peace. So therefore, none of you can become my disciple if you do not give up all your possessions.

"Salt is good; but if salt has lost its taste, how can its saltiness be restored? It is fit neither for the soil nor for the manure pile; they throw it away. Let anyone with ears to hear listen!"

(Luke 14:25-35)

For some time now Jesus has been on his way to Jerusalem, the place of crucifixion and exaltation (Luke 9:51-56). As he travels, he is instructing the disciples and the crowds on the significance of the kingdom (14:14-36; 13:18-21) and the meaning of discipleship (9:57-62; 11:1-13) and engaging in confrontation with the Jewish leaders (12:1-3; 14:1-6). Large crowds are now going with Jesus, encouraged no doubt by the offer of grace and salvation to the poor, the crippled, the lame, and the blind (14:13, 21) and by the declaration that it is God's intention to have as many as possible share in the banquet of salvation (14:23). Those who receive this free invitation, however, must count the cost of acceptance, for Jesus is not a dispenser of cheap grace.

Renunciation of Traditional Family Relationships

The saying about family relationships (Luke 14:26-27), probably the most uncompromising statement about the claims of the kingdom to be found anywhere in the New Testament, occurs in a much starker form in Luke than in Matthew's parallel (Matt. 10:37-38). To begin with, Matthew's list mentions "father and mother," "son and daughter," but Luke has expanded it to include "wife" and "brothers and sisters" as well.

The mention of "wife" is particularly significant, for they appear only in Luke ("brothers and sisters" also occurs in the related saying in Mark 10:29-30). Moreover, the third excuse offered by people declining the invitation to the messianic banquet (the call to salvation in the kingdom of God) was "I have just been married, and therefore I cannot come" (Luke 14:20)! Later, in response to Peter's declaration that they have left their homes to follow him, Jesus replies, "Truly I tell you, there is no one who has left house or wife or brothers or parents or children, for the sake of the kingdom of God, who will not get back very much more in this age, and in the age to come eternal life" (18:29, again adding the reference to "wife").

Within Luke's church, apparently, as among many Western churches today, the early period of marriage represented a time of particular testing for Christians. The relationship which Luke has established with the following sayings on possessions (Luke 14:29-33) suggests that the danger was related to materialism and the quest for security.

The major difference between Matthew and Luke with respect to this saying, however, is not its scope but its intensity. Whereas Matthew requires followers of Jesus to love their parents and children less than they love Jesus, Luke requires that they "hate" their own family. They both go back to the same saying of Jesus, but they have been interpreted differently by Matthew and Luke.

In the Old Testament are many passages where "love" and "hate" stand alongside one another in such a way that "hate" obviously is not meant to be interpreted literally but is to be taken to mean "love less." Jacob, for instance, loves Rachel, but Leah is hated, unloved, or loved less (Gen. 29:31-33). There are laws about rights of inheritance for a man who has two wives, one loved, and the other hated, disliked, or loved less (Deut. 21:15-17). The original version of a well-known proverb clearly illustrates this usage: "Those who spare the rod hate their children, but those who love them are diligent to discipline them" (Prov. 13:24). This is certainly the way Matthew interpreted the saying (Matt. 10:37-38).

Luke, though, has translated the word literally, interpreting "hate" against the background of the Old Testament wisdom literature. There the word means "to leave aside, renounce, abandon" (as in Prov. 8:13: "the fear of the Lord is hatred of evil," renouncing evil). Perhaps this is why Luke has inserted "yes, even life itself" (Luke 14:26; see also John 12:25) and has concluded the section with a repetition of the saying, "Whoever does not carry the cross and follow me cannot be my disciple" (Luke 14:27). The renunciation of self must have its parallel in the renunciation of family ties. What Luke is saying, albeit in a dramatic way, is that those who would become disciples of Jesus must be committed exclusively to him. They cannot give their allegiance to anyone else or anything else.

In the time of Jesus this saying, like so many of the other hard sayings of Jesus, was meant to be interpreted literally, even if spoken somewhat hyperbolically. Those who traveled the length and breadth of Palestine with him had, by force of circumstance, to leave their families behind. In the situation of the later church, when the Christians were no longer following Jesus around Palestine, the Evangelists reinterpreted the saying in the light of their own situation. Matthew took the saying to mean "love less" (following one Old Testament tradition); Luke translated it literally (in accord with another Old Testament tradition and through the saying on cross-bearing) and reinterpreted it to mean denial or renunciation. It therefore was not understood so much as a call to abandon family ties, but as a call to live within them in such a way that absolute priority is accorded to the service of the kingly reign of God.

Renunciation of Traditional Forms of Security

The twin parables of tower-building and of contemplating a battle (Luke 14:28-32) are found only in the Gospel of Luke. They warn against rash emotional professions of discipleship, and they are followed once again by a warning about the dangers of material possessions.

The person building a tower, probably a farm building of considerable size, calculates the cost so he will not become an object of ridicule (Luke 14:28-29). The king contemplating a battle takes counsel to make sure that he does not underestimate the enemy's strength, prematurely declare war, and end up seeking terms of surrender (14:31-32). The apocryphal Gospel of Thomas, found in Egypt, has a rather gruesome parallel: "The kingdom of the Father is like a man who wished to kill a powerful man. He drew his sword and stuck it into the wall, in order to know whether his hand would carry through; then he slew the powerful man" (G. Thomas 98). If you choose a dangerous and difficult job, first make sure you can carry it through!

Luke's special emphasis is to be seen in the conclusion which he draws from the two parables: "So therefore, none of you can become my disciple if you do not give up all your possessions" (Luke 14:33). He applies to the community in general a stringent saying which originally applied only to one particular person in the ministry of Jesus (Mark 10:17-31). Just as a person should not begin an undertaking without having the resources to complete it, so the disciples must continually be ready to give up everything they have to follow Jesus.

It is of more than passing interest that the two people spoken about in the comparisons used by Jesus are people of substance and power. There is a somewhat wealthy farmer, not overly wealthy, otherwise the worry about having enough money to complete the tower would have hardly been a real concern. And there is a ruler with a small army, flexing his muscles but not really strong enough to go to war. These are appropriate images in a Gospel addressed to a community that has long been poor, but which now has a number of its members on the way up the social scale, with some apparently reaching the stage of the nouveau riche! The warning is clear! Discipleship is costly and one should not embark upon it without first carefully considering the issues involved. Particular attention needs to be paid to matters relating to money and family.

The reason for one of the changes we observed in Luke's presentation of the call of Simon is now apparent. In sharp contrast to Mark's account, where Peter is called at the beginning of Jesus' ministry (Mark 1:16-18), Luke shows that Jesus' ministry is well under way (Luke 4:14-44) by the time he encounters Simon (5:1-11). Indeed, he has already healed Simon's mother-in-law (4:38-39). In Luke's account, therefore, Simon already knows Jesus and has seen his ministry in action. Thus he is well aware of what is involved in following Jesus. When he decides to leave everything and follow him, it is not a rash decision. It is one that is well considered, deliberate, and radical. It is, in fact, a model decision in Luke's understanding of discipleship (14:28-33)!

Be Warned: It Is for Life

The parable of the salt which has lost its saltiness occurs in all three synoptic Gospels, but each time it has a different application. Mark applies it to the need for unity within the Christian community (Mark 9:50), Matthew relates it to the missionary responsibility of the community (Matt. 5:13), and Luke uses it to illustrate the need for a continuing life of discipleship (Luke 14:34-35).

According to Luke, disciples who give up their life of renunciation and return to traditional family relationships and traditional forms of security are as useless as salt which has lost its taste. In Palestine, salt was not artificially prepared but was simply dug from evaporated pools near the Dead Sea. It contained many impurities, so if rain drenched it on the way to market, the salt dissolved and what remained was useless. It was thrown away. Be warned, says Luke. Discipleship is a life-and-death issue; the stakes are high, and those who do not make it to the end will be thrown out.

Luke's teaching is so harsh at this point that it would be difficult for us to accept it as authentically Christian were it not for the fact that it is placed among parables of grace. It follows the parable of the great banquet (Luke 14:15-24). And it precedes those of the lost sheep (15:1-7), the lost coin (15:8-10) and the lost son (15:11-32), all of which stress the all-embracing grace and love of God.

Wandering bands of Christian prophets who followed an austere lifestyle presented a serious threat to church authorities throughout the first century of Christian history. Even the apostle Paul had to defend himself against their attacks on him (2 Cor. 10—11) when he sought to support himself by tentmaking rather than, as they saw it, by trusting the Lord to supply all his needs. The church struck back by laying down stringent rules governing their behavior. These are recorded in a well-known passage in the Didache, an important work of early second-century church fathers: "About apostles and prophets, follow the rule of the Gospel, which is this: 'Let every apostle who comes to you be welcomed as the Lord. But he shall not stay more than one day, and if it is necessary, the next day also. But if he stays three days, he is a false prophet. And when an apostle leaves, let him take nothing except bread to last him until he finds his next lodging. But if he asks for money, he is a false prophet' " (Did. 11:3-6).

While the Didache seeks to denigrate the wandering preachers and to control their excesses, it overlooks the problem of its own people. They were settling down to live a comfortable life, even though this involved ignoring many aspects of the teaching of Jesus. Luke is concerned about these very people who have begun to build bigger barns. For him, the radical detachment of the preachers' lifestyle points to the essence of Christian discipleship: a willingness to hang loose from traditional forms of security and to say farewell to anyone or anything which might prevent them from following Jesus. This is the spirit Luke would like to see at work among his communities. He later describes the lifestyle of the early church (Acts 2:42-47; 4:32-35) as an indication of how this spirit might work itself out in daily living.

The Conflict of Values in the Kingdom

The church continued to tell the stories about Jesus and his disciples, reinterpreting them in the light of the cross and resurrection. The Evangelists carried on this process as they included the stories in their Gospels, reinterpreting them in the light of the new situations which had emerged in the churches to which they were writing.

Mark writes in the context of a highly successful church which has tended to overemphasize the power and glory of Christ. He seeks to redress the balance and to restore the cross to its rightful place at the heart of Christian reflection and action. At the beginning of a lengthy section devoted to the meaning of discipleship, he stresses that Jesus is the crucified Son of Man and that the disciples must take up the cross and follow him, for the cross is the only way to glory (Mark 8:27—9:8). As he indicates in the chapters which follow, this principle of cross-bearing discipleship relates to all areas of life. Personal relationships, power, and material possessions alike are all to be subjected to this fundamental concept of Christian living. Mark stresses time and again that the disciples (the church) fail to understand and want to continue on the way of power and glory.

Matthew writes a decade or so later in an urban situation of relatively secure, conservative middle-class Jewish Christians. He seeks to present Jesus as the Christian Messiah and to call the members of his community to a single-minded devotion to Christ. Matthew warns them that to follow Jesus is a costly and risky business, but he assures them that this Lord may be trusted to care for his people in times of difficulty and danger (Matt. 8:18-27).

Bringing together the radical sayings of Jesus and the story of the stilling of the storm, Matthew paints a brilliant picture of the life of a disciple. Hardship, loneliness, and separation are the marks of discipleship, for to follow Jesus is to embark on a life of insecurity and danger. Following Jesus into the church leads not to peace and tranquillity, but to trial and tribulation. In many situations the opposition will be so great that there is a real danger of going under altogether. However, Jesus may be trusted to rescue his people in their times of deepest distress.

Luke is a contemporary of Matthew, but he is writing for a predominantly Gentile church which had long been poor but was beginning to include some on the way up through the social scale to the nouveau riche. He issues a stern warning: that kind of living is completely incompatible with the gospel! Their model should instead be the wandering prophets who are willing to hang loose from traditional forms of security and to say farewell to anyone or anything which might prevent them from following Jesus (Luke 14:25-35). He warns them of the need to renounce traditional family relationships and traditional forms of security. And he warns them that this is not to be a temporary renunciation, but a permanent attitude and lifestyle. The Christian life is one of grace, but costly grace. A radical response is required.

Within the Western church, this teaching is very difficult to accept, whether it be in the radical form espoused by Luke or in the more moderate approach of Matthew. It runs counter to our culture, our expectations, and all of the apparently worthwhile values which we have been taught from earliest times. The need for a start in life so that we might get a good job, be able to buy a good house, and provide for our families both for the present and the future—these are all part of a value system which is the lifeblood of our society. It is not simply that, like the early follower of Jesus in Matthew's story, we need to have time off to go and bury our father. Instead, we need time off to go and provide for our children and, when we have finished that, it is almost time for them to go and bury their parents!

The Christian church has been one of the prime agents in spreading this gospel of "responsible living." In the process, the good news of Jesus has been reduced to the level of a motivational force designed to ensure the success of every venture we undertake, whether it be in the business world, on the sporting field, or in the realm of international diplomacy. Jesus is supposed to be the guarantor of this success.

Half an hour with the television preachers on any Sunday morning is enough to indicate how complete is the cultural containment of Christianity within right-wing religion. Some are perhaps extreme, albeit eminently successful, representatives of contemporary Christianity. But even within the mainstream, especially within white Protestantism, the aims and ideals of Christian living have often been tailored to the needs of individualism and consumerism. It often seems that only a few prophetic figures and small groups on the fringes of churches are doing serious work on living out the costly discipleship that is depicted for us in the Gospels. And their impact seems so small when compared with the controllers of the mass media.

Western Christians have not deliberately turned their

backs on the good news of Jesus. There is a great reservoir of goodwill and good intention. Yet the life of Jesus and his disciples seems so totally foreign to the presuppositions of our contemporary society that we are almost unable to see any way forward—short of a fundamental conversion. Here is the rub: radical conversion is a risky business. It is a call to live life according to a different set of values, and with no guarantee of success.

It is one thing to follow Jesus into the eye of the storm. But how are we to know that it will work out all right in the end? Matthew tries to tell us that it is a matter of trust and faith, even a little faith! This is what is at stake in Western Christianity; we are on trial for our faith. Not the fiery trial of persecution, but the warm and comfortable experience of conformity and acceptance. The corporations can deliver the goods, but can the Christian faith provide an alternative? Their corporate dividends are guaranteed, but if we follow Jesus into the eye of the storm, will we even be able to survive? In Matthew's terms, it is a question of trust in the Lord of the lake!

As Mark portrays it, so many of us have gone for the Peter option (the way of Jesus *and* the way of power and glory) in preference to the Jesus option (the way of Jesus *instead of* the way of power and glory). Of course, Luke is right; this is particularly a problem for those of us who have begun to climb the social scale and are in a position to make quite a spectacle with our displays of wealth. Those who are on the bottom of the heap don't face this problem. But what of those of us who are in a position of making a name for ourselves?

Jesus does not simply leave us in our dilemma. He comes time and again and calls us to follow him, offering us the opportunity of a fresh start in the life of discipleship. The options don't vary, but the choices continue.

Questions for Discussion

1. Where do you see a conflict between the values of the kingdom and the values of our society?

2. Is it wrong to look for security?

3. Have you experienced the call to live according to a different set of values? What difference has it made to your life?

4. Isn't responsible living just being responsible as adults? Should we take risks?

5. Does family life make following Jesus easier or harder for you?

6. Is Jesus calling us to disregard any contemporary social customs?

7. How much money do you think you need? For what?

8. In what way might following Jesus still be a costly and risky business?

3

You Will Have to Travel Light

Discipleship and Possessions

The Life of Repentance and Faith

The central feature of the teaching of Jesus is that in his words and works, the kingly reign of God is beginning to break into human history. The kingdom of God for the Old Testament was but a vision of the future. It would be the reign of grace, the time of joy for the downtrodden, the sinners, and the outcasts. It was to be the era of good news for the poor and of table fellowship for the little people of society. Now this very kingdom begins to dawn in the life and teaching, the parables and miracles, the death and resurrection of Jesus of Nazareth.

On the basis of what Jesus believes to be the decisive and definitive intervention of God in human history, he calls for a radical reorientation of life. According to his preaching, nothing less than repentance and faith will suffice (Mark 1:15).

Repentance, in the teaching of Jesus, is not just a change

of mind. It is not just feeling sorry for your sin. It is changing your way of living. "God's definitive revelation demands final and unconditional decision on man's part. It demands a radical conversion, a transformation of nature, a definitive turning from evil, a resolute turning to God in total obedience. . . . It affects the whole person, first and basically the center of personal life, then logically his conduct at all times and in all situations; his thoughts, words and acts" (Behm, 1002).

Faith, in biblical terms, is not to be confused with mental assent to a doctrine or creed, with faithfulness to a dying cause, or with irrational credulity. It is a life of trustful obedience, the surrender of the total personality to God. Faith is life lived as a radical reorientation to God. It is the attitude of genuine obedience made possible by God's gracious action in Christ. Thus believers stand in marked contrast to those who think they are masters of their own affairs.

The life of repentance and faith is set forth in the Gospels as the life of obedience—life on the road following Jesus. It is the unconditional response to the unconditional demand, both made possible by the supreme act of costly grace in Jesus Christ.

The radically reoriented life of trustful obedience "is more than generalizations—it has to do with specific acts of self-sacrifice in concrete situations" (Padilla, 128). John the Baptist, for instance, has a fitting word for each person who becomes convicted by his message. In each case, his ethical demand touches the point at which the person is enslaved to the powers of the old age, thus remaining closed to God's new action in the world. To the people in general, he says, "Whoever has two coats must share with anyone who has none; and whoever has food must do likewise." To the tax collectors, "Collect no more than the amount prescribed for you." To the soldiers on active service, "Do not extort money from anyone by threats or false accusation, and be satisfied with your wages" (Luke 3:10-14).

The same principle can be seen in the teaching of Jesus. To the rich young man who asks, "What must I do to inherit eternal life?" he says, "You lack one thing; go, sell what you

own, and give the money to the poor, and you will have treasures in heaven; then come, follow me" (Mark 10:17-22). In
his presence Zacchaeus perceives the truth and declares,
"Look, half of my possessions, Lord, I will give to the poor;
and if I have defrauded anyone of anything, I will pay back
four times as much." To this Jesus responds, "Today salvation has come to this house, because he too is a son of Abraham. For the Son of Man came to seek out and to save the
lost" (Luke 19:1-10).

The crisis created by the inbreaking of the kingly reign of
God cannot be resolved by resorting to our traditional way of
living (Luke 3:8), and salvation cannot be found in traditional
confessions of faith (Matt. 7:21-23). The only way of averting
the crisis is to be found in the life on the road following Jesus
(Mark 10:21). An adequate response can be made to the
grace and the love of God in Jesus Christ only through a
change in our way of living (1:15) and through a life of continuing obedience to the moral demands of the kingly reign
of God (Matt. 7:24-27).

The Gospels are full of proof that this life of obedient
faith is not an easy thing. Those who wish to respond to the
grace and love of God must count the cost of their allegiance.
Jesus reminds one of the scribes who wishes to follow him,
"Foxes have holes, and birds of the air have nests; but the
Son of Man has nowhere to lay his head" (Matt. 8:20). He
warns the disciple who wants to go off and first bury his father, "Follow me, and let the dead bury their own dead"
(8:22). The one who wishes to go and say good-bye to those
at home is told in no uncertain terms that "no one who puts a
hand to the plow and looks back is fit for the kingdom of
God" (Luke 9:62).

To follow Jesus on his preaching missions throughout
Palestine, the first disciples have to leave behind their families and friends (Mark 1:20), their professions and profits
(1:16-20; 2:14), for they are in Capernaum one day and Cana
the next. Following the wandering prophet of Galilee, they
are able to take with them only what they can carry, and
sometimes not even that much (6:7-13).

As they travel on the road with Jesus, the disciples hear

Jesus tell the rich young man that if he wishes to find life, he must reorder his priorities (Mark 10:17-22). They see the liberating power of the gospel totally transform the attitude of the moneygrubbing tax collector of Jericho (Luke 19:1-9). The disciples hear Jesus commend the poor widow who gives all her money to God (Mark 12:41-44). They witness his emphatic approval of the woman who squanders her money in an act of single-minded devotion as she anoints his body in anticipation of his death (14:3-9).

Jesus teaches his followers that they can not serve God and money at the same time (Matt. 6:24). He encourages them to learn from the birds of the air and the flowers of the field that God can be trusted to care for them (6:25-34). Jesus pronounces God's blessing on the poor and declares that their place in the kingly reign of God is secure. At the same time, he denounces the rich whom, he says, have already received any reward that belongs to them (Luke 6:20-24).

In the countries of the overdeveloped Western world, it is frequently our bondage to material possessions that prevents us from wholeheartedly following Jesus on the road. In the realm of dollars and cents, we need to experience the liberating power of the gospel.

To help us in our reflection on these important issues, we will again look at three texts: the encounter of Jesus with the rich young man (Mark), his teaching about seeking first the kingdom of God (Matthew), and the blessing he pronounces on the poor (Luke).

Keep an Eye on the Camels (Mark 10:17-31)

To understand Jesus' encounter with the rich young man and its significance in relation to our own material possessions, we first need to understand the context into which Mark deliberately places this story. The Evangelist has carefully arranged his material. Three times Jesus tells of his impending death (Mark 8:31; 9:31; 10:32-33), but on each occasion his followers misunderstand his teaching (8:32-33, Peter; 9:32-34, the disciples; 10:35-40, James and John, the sons of Zebedee). Jesus therefore has to take them aside and repeatedly teach them concerning the real nature of discipleship (8:34—9:1; 9:35—10:31; 10:41-45).

On the first occasion when Jesus teaches about discipleship in this part of the Gospel, he speaks in terms of principle, calling on the crowd and the disciples to take up the cross and follow him. The cross is the only way to glory (Mark 8:34—9:1). On the last occasion, Jesus again speaks in general terms, this time of sacrificial service in the world with the Son of Man as the model and motivating force of all genuine discipleship (10:41-45). In the intervening central section (9:35—10:31), Jesus teaches his followers about personal and communal relationships (9:35-50), the use and abuse of power (10:1-16), and material possessions (10:17-31). Discipleship must cover every aspect of life.

Mark has arranged the material carefully so that his readers will not miss the import of his message on these three selected crucial issues facing his church: personal relationships, abuse of power, and material possessions. Each section begins with a fresh geographical notice: "They went on from there and passed through Galilee . . . to Capernaum" (9:30, 33); "He left that place and went to the region of Judea and beyond the Jordan" (10:1); "As he was setting out on a journey"(10:17). The sections include a discipleship saying introduced by the solemn formula, "Truly I tell you" (9:41; 10:15, 29).

Since the teaching is directed primarily to the church, on a number of occasions "the disciples" or "the twelve" are the only ones present (Mark 9:31, 35; 10:23). Sometimes the crowd is in attendance at the beginning of the story (10:1). Only after Jesus is "in the house" does he answer the disciples' questions (10:10; see also 9:28-29). A parallel progression is to be found in the story of the rich young man (10:17-31). The discussion begins in public on the open road (10:17-22). But after the young man leaves, it focuses on the disciples (10:23-27) and finally on Peter, their spokesman (10:28-31). The arrangement of the story shows us, once again, that Mark's primary interest is not so much in the teaching which Jesus gives to one particular person in one particular situation during his ministry. Instead, Mark wants readers to catch the significance of the teaching which Jesus repeatedly gives to his church through the experiences of the disciples (10:23-27) and of Peter (10:28-31).

> As [Jesus] was setting out on a journey, a man ran up and knelt before him, and asked him, "Good Teacher, what must I do to inherit eternal life?" Jesus said to him, "Why do you call me good? No one is good but God alone. You know the command-ments: 'You shall not murder; You shall not commit adultery; You shall not steal; You shall not bear false witness; You shall not defraud; Honor your father and mother.' " He said to him, "Teacher, I have kept all these since my youth." Jesus, looking at him, loved him and said, "You lack one thing; go, sell what you own, and give the money to the poor, and you will have treasure in heaven; then come, follow me." When he heard this, he was shocked and went away grieving, for he had many possessions [AG: large estates].
>
> Then Jesus looked around and said to his disciples, "How hard it will be for those who have wealth to enter the kingdom of God!" And the disciples were perplexed at these words. But Jesus said to them again, "Children, how hard it is to enter the kingdom of God! It is easier for a camel to go through the eye of a needle than for someone who is rich to enter the kingdom of God." They were greatly astounded and said to one another, "Then who can be saved?" Jesus looked at them and said, "For mortals it is impossible, but not for God; for God all things are possible."
>
> Peter began to say to him, "Look, we have left everything and followed you." Jesus said, "Truly I tell you, there is no one who has left house or brothers or sisters or mother or father or children or fields [AG: farmlets], for my sake and for the sake of the good news, who will not receive a hundredfold now in this age—houses, brothers and sisters, mothers and children, and fields with persecutions—and in the age to come eternal life. But many who are first will be last, and the last will be first."   (Mark 10:17-31)

The story of the rich young ruler begins in the public are-na, where all may see and hear, but the focus of attention shifts to the disciples and finally concentrates on Peter. In Luke, the magistrate or ruler is present throughout the whole incident. But in Mark, only after the rich person has left does

Jesus give instructions to his disciples about the danger of wealth (Mark 10:23-27). Then, through speaking to Peter, Jesus promises overflowing rewards to all who renounce families and possessions for the sake of the gospel (10:28-31). The story originally recounted the individual experience of one particular rich person who declines the invitation to follow Jesus (10:17-22). Mark has transformed it into an address to the church on the danger of material possessions (10:23-31). He inserted it into the Gospel narrative to be the climax of his instruction on the meaning of discipleship as it relates to contemporary issues.

Mark explains that it is because the rich person has large estates that he does not follow Jesus (Mark 10:22). He then gives the twofold reference to the renunciation of fields or farmlets (10:29-30), reflecting the rural situation of his church. Since Luke is writing for a city congregation, it is only natural that he should have omitted the references to farmlets (Luke 18:29) and to the dialogue beginning out on the open road (Mark 10:17).

Those who give up farms and families will receive "a hundredfold" (Mark 10:30; but "very much more" in Luke 18:30 and some manuscripts of Matt. 19:29). This statement indicates that Mark sees a close relationship between our present story and the situation described in the interpretation of the sower (Mark 4:13-20). That parable highlights that Mark's rural church was facing a crisis situation as "the cares of the world, and the lure of wealth, and the desire for other things" had already begun "to come in and choke the word" (4:19). This crisis of faith provides the context for interpreting the story of the rich man seeking eternal life.

Sell What You Have and Give to the Poor

Mark's arrangement of the discipleship material (Mark 8:27—10:52) is held together by the journey of Jesus to Jerusalem, the city of rejection, suffering, and death. Starting in the north near Caesarea Philippi, on the border between Gentile lands and Jewish territory (8:27), Jesus moves on to Capernaum (9:33) and crosses over into the territory of Judea and beyond the Jordan (10:1). At each place he seeks to teach his disciples on the true meaning of discipleship. As he embarks on the next stage of his fateful journey and is on the way again (10:17), a man comes and falls at his feet in worship, asking how he might inherit eternal life. This is life's ultimate question. It should be asked only by a person on his knees before the one who will shortly suffer and die outside Jerusalem, for it is in his death that the meaning of life will be revealed. In following Jesus on the way to Jerusalem, the inquirer will find eternal life (10:52).

Mark finally tells us that the man is very rich as the initial story draws to its conclusion and he rejects Jesus' invitation to follow him (Mark 10:22). But at the beginning of the story, he seems deliberately to avoid identifying the person in any way. Matthew (19:22) says he is "young" and Luke (18:18) calls him "a ruler," hence, the traditional designation of him as "the rich young ruler." Mark, however, deliberately starts by giving him no name, no rank, and no title. He tells us nothing about his family background or professional status and describes him simply as "a man" (Mark 10:17). Mark does this so we might more readily identify with him in his quest for life. The Evangelist begins by encouraging us to write our own name into the story line and to follow through the narrative in our own experience and in the experience of our churches.

The man broaches the question regarding life's meaning with obvious reverence; nowhere else in contemporary Jewish or Greek writings do we find students using such a respectful form of address as "Good Teacher" (Mark 10:17). Even Nicodemus, who approaches Jesus with obvious deference, addresses him only with the traditional title "Teacher" (John 3:2). This person, then, is shown to be earnestly sincere in his quest for life. Jesus, however, refuses such rich titles and points to the source of all goodness, to God himself. God is the ultimate reference point in the question of life. Although life is to be found in following Jesus, it must never be forgotten that God is the one who makes such following possible (10:27). God is the origin and power of all Christian discipleship. God is the source of all goodness.

To the surprise of the questioner, and of the church retelling the story through the ages, Jesus simply endorses the traditional teaching of the priests: "You know the commandments: 'You shall not murder; You shall not commit adultery; You shall not steal; You shall not bear false witness; You shall not defraud; Honor your father and mother' " (Mark 10:19). In the tradition of many of the prophets, however, Jesus concentrates on the second half of the Ten Commandments, referring only to those commandments which deal with our relationships to other people. The statement "no one is good but God alone" may be a veiled allusion to the earlier commandments governing our relationship to God. Yet there can be no missing the emphasis that Jesus makes: the way to God, the way to eternal life, of necessity, leads through our neighbor. Do not murder, commit adultery, steal, give false evidence, defraud; honor your father and mother (10:19).

So what's new? the inquirer asks. Ever since he was a youth, he has been observing the commandments in a life of day-to-day obedience under God (Mark 10:20). As his own experience has shown him, he already knows that the answer to the meaning of life is not to be found in keeping commandments. He thinks he sees something better in the ministry of Jesus and feels that through his teaching his life might realize its full potential. He is hoping that in Jesus he might find the way to life.

Jesus is instinctively drawn to such a respectable, clean-living, and earnest young man (10:21). His declaration of daily obedience is neither hypocritical nor insincere. Jesus recognizes how diligent he has been in his religious observances and how serious he is in his quest for life. He knows, however, that for the quest to be fulfilled, the young man must become one of his followers. Before he will be able to do that, he will have to sell his possessions and give the proceeds to the poor.

The choice involved in following Jesus is an either-or decision. Some have to choose between following Jesus and fishing (Mark 1:16-17), mending nets (1:19-20), collecting taxes (2:14), burying the dead (Matt. 8:21-22), or saying good-bye to those at home (Luke 9:61-62). For some, repentance involves sharing the second shirt; for others, it means exacting no more than the assessment or even making do with their pay (3:10-14).

Just as Jesus expects the tax collector to stop cheating (Luke 19:8) and the conceited person to turn away from pride (Matt. 6:1-18), so he also expects the rich man to turn away from his materialism. If he wishes to find the meaning of life, he will have to learn that his life must be governed by an obedience to Jesus which comes before all other relationships and responsibilities.

Repentance and following Jesus have to do with the concrete realities of life. The encounter with Jesus touches the point at which we are enslaved to the powers of the present age and are thereby unable to respond to the incarnate grace of God. For this young man, his large estates stand in the way of hearing the call of Jesus (Mark 10:22).

The term here translated large estates can have the more general meaning of "great wealth" or "many possessions" (RSV, NRSV, and most translations). But in the other two places where it occurs in the New Testament, it designates landholdings (Acts 2:45; 5:1). In view of the rural setting of Mark's church and the unusual later mention of fields or farmlets (Mark 10:29-30), this is probably its meaning here as well. He cannot manage his estates and follow Jesus at the same time, for it is a case of Capernaum today and Cana tomorrow! This rich man will have to change his lifestyle if he wants to follow Jesus.

The experience of the young man with his large estates stands in stark contrast to that of Zacchaeus, the notorious tax collector of Jericho. In the presence of Jesus, he perceives the truth and declares, "Look, half of my possessions, Lord, I will give to the poor; and if I have defrauded anyone of anything, I will pay him back four times as much" (Luke 19:1-10). Zacchaeus, according to contemporary religious standards, is the epitome of a sinner. The rich man of our story, according to those same contemporary religious standards, is a model of righteousness. Yet Zacchaeus gives away his possessions and rejoices in salvation, while the rich man holds onto his estates and goes away in sorrow.

The American psychoanalyst Erich Fromm rightly comments, "In the New Testament, joy is the fruit of giving up having, while sadness is the mood of the one who hangs onto possessions" (Fromm, 118). As the German theologian Johann Baptist Metz expresses it, "The meaning of loving cuts across having" (Metz, 2).

In the Gospels this is the only time we are specifically told of a person declining the call of Jesus. Let the Western church mark and understand well that he does so because of his material possessions! Yet Mark records the fact simply and unemotionally. The young man, who has such great potential, disappears from the stage, and we hear nothing more about him. Not even his name is recorded.

It Is Easier for Camels Than for Cadillacs

In the Gospel of Luke, the rich ruler is present throughout the story, but in Mark's account the young man disappears immediately. The scene switches to Jesus and his disciples, and the discussion quickly changes from what happened once upon a time to what happens time and time again in the history of the church. As always, it is here that Mark's interest is primarily to be seen. He continues to write as an evangelist rather than as an antiquarian.

The disciples are naturally staggered at Jesus' teaching on how hard it is for the rich to enter the kingdom of God, but their leader is not deterred by their continued lack of understanding. He goes on to declare that it would be easier for a camel to pass through the eye of a needle than for a rich person to enter the kingdom of God (Mark 10:25). This typically oriental metaphor is effective. How absurd the scene of a camel, the largest animal in Palestine, trying to get through the smallest hole imaginable! So, says Jesus, is the picture of the rich trying to get into the kingdom of God!

Throughout the ages, the church has found it difficult to accept the teaching of Jesus at this point and has looked for other explanations. Though spelled differently, the Greek word for "camel" was in later times pronounced the same as the word for "ship's cable" or "rope," and some early writers adopted this suggestion. While it makes the saying marginally more acceptable, it destroys the imagery and neglects the parallel analogy of straining gnats and swallowing camels (Matt. 23:24). There the contrast is between the smallest insect and the largest animal. Other explanations also ignore the parallels with the later rabbis who, probably in dependence upon this saying of Jesus, spoke of the absurdity of an elephant trying to get through the eye of a needle. The Koran, too, has the threat: "They shall not enter Paradise until a camel goes through the eye of a needle."

The suggestion of a ninth-century commentator has become popular worldwide: There was a small gate in the wall of Jerusalem called the Eye of the Needle, so it is said. When the main gate was closed at sunset, the camel of a traveler arriving after dark could just barely get through this smaller gate by humbly bowing its head and crawling through on its knees! However, there is no evidence to suggest that there was such a gate in the Jerusalem wall; it is probably a figment of an early commentator's fertile imagination. This pious spiritualization has become widely accepted because it allows the rich to keep their possessions and still enter the kingdom of God, so long as they are humble like the camel! This is not a reinterpretation; it is a blatant renunciation of the teaching of Jesus. For him, it was simply easier for a camel (one hump or two!) to get through the eye of a needle than for a rich person to enter the kingdom of God.

According to Mark's graphic portrayal, the disciples' astonishment is almost beyond belief (Mark 10:26)! They rightly see that what Jesus has been talking about has implications for everyone and would make salvation a human impossibility. Jesus agrees. He looks straight at them and declares that the life of discipleship, with the sacrifices and suffering involved, is possible only by the grace of God. It is beyond the capacities of people and becomes a possibility only as the grace of God permeates the reality of their being, as they accept what God has made possible. Through the grace of God, dependence upon material possessions can be abolished as the followers of Jesus are liberated to the joyful obedience of following him.

The disciples ought to have realized this truth already, for it was enshrined in their own experience: the call to follow Jesus had come to them as the enabling word of grace. In response to this grace, they had left behind their families and their professions to follow Jesus (Mark 1:16-20). Such a response, though, is not to be interpreted as a human achievement. It is possible only because of the power and the presence of God in Jesus. The call of Jesus energizes and enables the response of believing obedience.

The Great Reversal

People may make their sacrifices, and indeed they must—though Peter exaggerates: he has not yet completely broken his ties with home, he still goes back to his fishing, and he has certainly not given up his old ways of thinking about the Messiah. But God's gift is immeasurably greater than anything a person can give in the service of God and the gospel (Mark 10:28-30). Throughout the Gospels, sayings of renunciation focus primarily on families and jobs. So it is only natural that in a rural situation, Mark emphasizes the renunciation of fields—farms or farmlets (as in 5:14; 6:36, 56). The giving up of such country property, for the sake of Jesus and of the gospel, gains greater poignancy through the way Mark has edited his material in order to secure a direct relationship between these promises and the story of the rich person who failed to follow Jesus because of his large estates (10:22).

According to Matthew and Luke, the promise is that those who have left home and family for the sake of Jesus will simply "very much more" (Matt. 19:29, some manuscripts; Luke 18:30). Mark, though, has an eye on the interpretation of the parable of the sower (Mark 4:8, 20). It is important that the word of discipleship which falls upon such good soil should be seen to bear fruit in an appropriate "hundredfold" superabundance, the blessing of God (as in Gen. 26:12). The seed that is sown is "the word," the preached word of the gospel of Jesus Christ (Mark 4:14-20). For the sake of Jesus and of the gospel, disciples have abandoned families and fields (10:29). Through "the good news," Jesus is present in the midst of his community. Thus, sacrifices made for the sake of the gospel are always to be understood as sacrifices made for the sake of Jesus.

God's gift, however, includes persecutions, for as we have already seen, the grace which issues in discipleship is costly grace. Those who follow Jesus enter into his pain as well as his joy, his sorrow as well as his glory, his crucifixion as well as his resurrection. Jesus is on the way to Jerusalem (Mark 10:17), and he calls his disciples to follow him to the cross, for as Mark has already indicated, the cross is the way to glory (8:27—9:1).

Following Jesus is a gift from God. It exceeds all human expectations in such a way that "the first will be last, and the last will be first" (Mark 10:31). This wisdom saying about reversal of roles and values in the kingdom is not intimately linked to the preceding discussion on possessions and probably circulated at one time as an isolated word of Jesus. Mark, however, has deliberately placed it here as the climax to his entire discussion on the priorities of discipleship (9:35—10:31).

The powerful will find themselves marginalized as, in a totally unexpected way, the powerless, the women, and the children become paradigms for acceptance into the kingdom of God (Mark 10:13-16). Those who consider themselves the greatest will be the least, and those regarded as little people will be examples for everyone (9:33-37). The rich, with their large estates, will find themselves "grieving" (10:17-22), while those who have abandoned everything for the sake of Jesus and the gospel will have family and fields in abundance (10:29-30).

At one stage this reversal of roles may well have been understood as taking place solely in the future kingdom, but Mark sees it as being fulfilled in the realities of the life of the early church. There members spontaneously and joyously shared their property and possessions (presumably in a way similar to that described in Acts 2:44-45; 4:34-35).

The rich person comes to Jesus seeking eternal life, but he goes away sad, missing out on life, because he is unwilling to part with his large estates so that he might follow Jesus (Mark 10:17-22). Disciples who abandon everything for the sake of Jesus and the gospel are promised that they will be richly rewarded in this life, and in the age to come they will gain the eternal life that the rich young man was so earnestly seeking (10:30).

Watch Out for the Fork in the Road (Matthew 6:19-34)

Matthew is particularly interested in questions of finance and discusses them within the context of his own middle-class community. His starting point is the teaching of Jesus about seeking first the kingdom of God, and he reinterprets the economic implications of each Gospel story to bring out their significance to his own situation. We can observe this most clearly when we see his teaching on money alongside that of the other Evangelists. Matthew mentions some form of money forty times, Mark only eight times, and Luke ten times. On each occasion paralleled by the other Gospels, Matthew has the largest figure.

For example, in the sending out of the missionaries, Mark says they should take with them no copper money (Mark 6:8, Greek: *chalkos*); Luke says no silver money (Luke 9:3, Greek: *argurion*); and Matthew says no gold, silver, or copper money (Matt. 10:9, Greek: *chruson, arguron, chalkos*). This is the only mention of gold coins in the Gospels, and Matthew has eight of the thirteen references to silver coins; Mark has one, Luke four. Clearly Matthew's church was becoming more prosperous and accustomed to a wider range of financial dealings than were the churches of Mark and Luke.

Writing for a more middle-class urban community, Matthew has omitted Mark's story of the poor widow who gives everything to God (Mark 12:41-44), feeling that it was not a relevant model discipleship story for his church. He has made significant modifications to the stories of the rich young man (Matt. 19:16-30) and of the anointing at Bethany (26:6-13) for the same reason. In this Gospel, the model disciple is no longer the poor widow who gives everything she has, but Joseph of Arimathea, a "rich man," "also a disciple of Jesus," who buries Jesus in his own tomb (Mark 15:42-47; Matt. 27:57-61). Note that in Mark, Joseph is neither "rich" nor a "disciple." But for Matthew, it is important to present

Joseph in this way. His church had a greater need for the challenge of a rich man who used his possessions for Jesus than for the example of a poor widow.

Matthew shares with Luke the answer which Jesus gives to John the Baptist (Matt. 11:2-6; Luke 7:18-23). But Matthew has placed it in a different context so the messengers can tell John what they had heard (the Sermon on the Mount) and what they had seen (the miracles that follow the Sermon). He has shaped his account of the miracles of Jesus in accord with Jesus' answer: the blind see (Matt. 9:27-31), the lame walk (9:2-8), the leper is cleansed (8:1-4), the deaf hear (*kōphos* is translated "deaf" in 11:5 and "mute" in 9:32-33), and the dead are raised (9:18-19, 23-25).

Within this context, the tax collectors and sinners are the poor to whom the gospel is preached (Matt. 11:5). They may be quite well off financially, but they come and are "sitting with" Jesus in the fellowship of the kingdom (9:10). They are the "poor in spirit," those who look to Jesus for salvation, to whom the opening beatitude of the Sermon on the Mount is addressed (5:3).

In the story of the rich young man, Matthew (19:16-26) has made many alterations to Mark's account. To the list of commandments, he has added his favorite, "You shall love your neighbor as yourself" (19:19). In Matthew, to do this is to fulfill the Law and the Prophets (7:12; 22:40). When the man asks what he still lacks, Jesus replies, "If you wish to be perfect, go, sell your possessions, and give the money to the poor, and you will have treasure in heaven; then come, follow me" (19:21). To be perfect, in Matthew's understanding, is to fulfill in a radical way the Law as it has been renewed and radicalized in Jesus Christ (5:48). The rich young man must stop seeking to serve both God and mammon/wealth (6:24) and turn away from his trust in material possessions which obviously are a stumbling block to his discipleship (19:22).

The parable of the sheep and the goats (Matt. 25:31-46) indicates the importance which Matthew ascribes to acts of compassion. The Jewish trilogy of almsgiving, prayer, and fasting (6:1-18) are included in Matthew's understanding of justice, provided the almsgiving is extended even to one's enemies (5:43-48). The most important thing for Matthew, however, is the need to seek first the kingdom of God and his justice through acts of reconciliation, forgiveness, and love (5:21-48).

In his more solidly middle-class church, Matthew's primary concern in this regard is that some are seeking their security in God and material possessions, while others are self-righteously finding status in their acts of charity.

[Jesus said,] "Do not store up for yourselves treasures on earth, where moth and rust consume and where thieves break in and steal; but store up for yourselves treasures in heaven, where neither moth nor rust consumes and where thieves do not break in and steal. For where your treasure is, there your heart will be also.

"The eye is the lamp of the body. So, if your eye is healthy, your whole body will be full of light; but if your eye is unhealthy, your whole body will be full of darkness. If then the light in you is darkness, how great is the darkness!

"No one can serve two masters; for a slave will either hate the one and love the other, or be devoted to the one and despise the other. You cannot serve God and wealth.

"Therefore I tell you, do not worry about your life, what you will eat or what you will drink, or about your body, what you will wear. Is not life more than food, and the body more than clothing? Look at the birds of the air; they neither sow nor reap nor gather into barns, and yet your heavenly Father feeds them. Are you not of more value than they? And can any of you by worrying add a single hour to your span of life? And why do you worry about clothing? Consider the lilies of the field, how they grow; they neither toil nor spin, yet I tell you, even Solomon in all his glory was not clothed like one of these. But if God so clothes the grass of the field, which is alive today and tomorrow is thrown into the oven, will he not much more clothe you—you of little faith? Therefore do not worry, saying, 'What will we eat?' or 'What will we drink?' or 'What will we wear?' For it is the Gentiles who strive for all these things; and indeed your heavenly Father knows that you need all these things. But strive first for the kingdom of God and his righteousness, and all these things will be given to you as well.

"So do not worry about tomorrow, for tomorrow will bring worries of its own. Today's trouble is enough for today."

(Matt. 6:19-34)

The Sermon on the Mount is the first of five major discourses which constitute one of the most striking features of Matthew's presentation of the ministry and message of Jesus Christ. A formula, "When Jesus had finished . . . ," follows each of the five discourses: the Sermon on the Mount (Matt. 5—7), the missionary sermon (10), parables of the kingdom (13:1-54), the messianic community (18), and parables of the end (23—25). On each of these occasions, the Evangelist has taken over parables and sayings from a variety of sources. He edits and rearranges them to build them into the structure of the Gospel in such a way as to proclaim to his readers the contemporary significance of Jesus the Christ. Thus he teaches them how they ought to respond in lives of daily obedience.

The Sermon on the Mount is therefore one of Matthew's sermons on the sermons of Jesus. Delivered on a mountain to the disciples (Matt. 5:1), it is intended as God's revelation to his people through his new lawgiver, the Christian Messiah, the bringer of the kingdom. This Sermon is placed immediately after the proclamation of the gospel (4:17) and the call of the first disciples (4:18-22). Hence, it is presented as teaching primarily to those who have heard the call of grace in Jesus and have begun to follow him. Yet Jesus also addresses all of Israel; the "crowds" (5:1; 7:28) can hear and have the opportunity to respond (Gardner, 92-93).

The Sermon on the Mount sets out the life of discipleship in relation to the world (Matt. 5:13-16), the Law (5:17-48), religious devotion (6:1-18), material possessions (6:19-34), and other people (7:1-12). The introduction to the Sermon sets forth the terms and conditions of entry into the kingdom of heaven (5:3-12). The concluding sayings warn about the dangers of half-hearted discipleship (7:13-23) and stress the need of responding to the teaching of Jesus in a life of daily obedience (7:24-27). As in the Gospel of Mark, Jesus' teaching on material possessions is placed within the context of teaching on discipleship covering all areas of life. For both Matthew and Mark, teaching on material possessions is an integral part of teaching on discipleship; and discipleship, they are telling us, must include material possessions.

Only Heavenly Treasure Is Secure

The accumulation and hoarding of material possessions is due to the desire for security, the desire to be rid of anxiety about the future. Jesus does not argue against this natural desire for security, but he disputes the popular notion that security is to be found in material possessions (Matt. 6:19-21). Far from removing anxiety, material possessions are frequently a source of anxiety, for they are liable to loss and decay—moth, rust, and thieves (inflation, devaluation, and economic uncertainty) can soon see to that. No matter how sure and certain our valuable possessions, estates, houses, ornaments, and money may seem, they are really quite fragile. Moths can eat holes in precious clothes, rust can ruin fine ornaments, thieves can carry off the most priceless of treasures.

The only source of lasting and ultimate security is to be found in God and in God alone. Marauding moths and treacherous thieves have no effect on heavenly treasures. Investments with God cannot be squandered or devalued. Good works (Matt. 5:16), justice which extends even as far as loving enemies (5:21-48), forgiveness of those who have caused offense (6:14-15), doing for others what you desire they should do for you (7:12)—these are the permanent investments which will last long after the moths, rust, and thieves have done their work.

All persons set their hearts on what they count as ultimately important (Matt. 6:21). This allegiance determines the direction of their life. If the heart clings to earthly treasures, if the will is consumed by the love of material possessions, then one is as susceptible to destruction as the earthly possessions themselves. But if the life is governed by the real values of justice and forgiveness, then it has the prospect of living forever, secure in God. This, for Matthew, is the meaning of the parable of the eye as the lamp of the body (5:22-23) with its horrific warning, "If then the light within you is darkness, how great is the darkness!" If the foundation on which the building is constructed proves unsafe, it is sure to fall. The larger the building, the greater the crash. If the insights by which a life is lived turn out to be false—what a disaster! If you have set your heart on material possessions as providing the meaning of life, how terribly dark it will be. Life and security are to be found in God and his justice and mercy.

You Cannot Serve God and Mammon

The claims of God and mammon/wealth are mutually incompatible; their demands on people are irreconcilable. The service of God calls for self-dedication and self-sacrifice; the service of mammon calls for self-assertion and self-interest. The disciple of Jesus is called to a life of devotion to God, which requires hanging loose from all material possessions. The parallel text in Luke (16:13) says, "No slave can serve two masters." But here in Matthew (6:24), "No one can serve two masters" is made universal, both in scope and in significance. Thus it can be more easily applied to the situation of his readers—few of whom were probably servants. The apocryphal Gospel of Thomas follows Luke, but extends the metaphor, "It is impossible for a man to mount two horses and to stretch two bows, and it is impossible for a servant to serve two masters; otherwise he will honor the one and offend the other" (G. Thomas 47a).

"Mammon" denotes "material possessions," but it always carries with it the idea of "trust." The Wisdom of Ben Sirach (a Jewish wisdom writing from court circles about 200 B.C.E.) provides an interesting background to the idea here:

> One who loves gold will not be justified;
> one who pursues money will be led astray by it.
> Many have come to ruin because of gold,
> and their destruction has met them face to face.
> It is a stumbling block to those who are avid for it,
> and every fool will be taken captive by it.
> Blessed is the rich person who is found blameless,
> and who does not go after gold.   (Sirach 31:5-8)

In some circles within Judaism, "mammon" seems to have already acquired overtones of "dishonesty" (see Luke 16:9). In the pseudepigraphical book of Enoch, the rich who trust in dishonest wealth are repeatedly denounced: "Woe unto you who gain silver and gold by unjust means; you will then say, 'We have grown rich and accumulated goods, we have acquired everything that we have desired' " (1 Enoch 97:8; also 94:6, 8; 96:5, 8; 98:8-11).

Thus mammon is not simply material possessions; it is materialism, blind faith in material possessions to supply the ultimate meaning of life. It is the attitude directly opposed to faith in God. Mammon is highly seductive and enslaves those who have been lured into thinking they are being liberated. It easily leads to dishonesty and oppression.

"The life of discipleship can only be maintained so long as nothing is allowed to come between Christ and ourselves—neither the law, nor personal piety, nor even the world. The disciple looks only to his master, never to Christ *and* the law, Christ *and* religion, Christ *and* the world" (Bonhoeffer, 154). Again, we are reminded that the call to follow Jesus involves an either-or decision. The legalist who wants Christ and the law, the pietist who wants Christ and religion, the materialist who wants Christ and the world—these all refuse to face the radical nature of the call to follow Jesus. The demands of God and of materialism are irreconcilable.

Seek First God's Kingdom and His Justice

The disciple who lives entirely for God (Matt. 6:24) will no longer be driven by concern about his earthly life. His primary concern will be directed toward God's kingly reign and the justice and righteousness which it reveals and which it demands (6:25-33). The either-or decision involved in following Jesus is depicted here as the decision between worldly wisdom and effort and childlike faith; between those who ruin their lives by worrying and working for food and clothing, and those who are prepared to take God seriously as the Creator and sustainer of life. Those with faith and trust in God join forces with him in his kingdom and his justice.

The key word for the understanding of this passage is

usually translated "take anxious thought" or "worry" (Matt. 6:27). But it also means "put forth an effort" with a view to securing the future, and this is almost certainly involved here. We are not to expend all our effort in gaining material possessions, not even food and clothing. The primary focus of our attention, the chief concern of life, is the kingly rule of God and his justice. We therefore will wish to devote our time to securing God's justice in the world. In the face of this primary concern, all other concerns wither away and are lost. In this redirection of life, liberation in Christ is to be found.

Matthew encourages his readers to look at the birds (Matt. 6:26) and to learn a lesson from the lilies (6:28-29). In Luke's version, the reference is to "the ravens" (Luke 12:24), and this is probably the original form of the saying which Matthew (6:26) has generalized to "the birds of the air." In the Old Testament ravens were considered unclean (Lev. 11:15; Deut. 14:14), and in the ancient world they were often regarded as careless because they frequently fail to return to their nests. If God feeds even the unclean and careless birds, whose incessant pecking is a sign of his abundant provision, will he not care for his children?

And what about "the colorful, beautiful flowers that dot the Palestinian countryside in the spring; e.g., the scarlet anemone, the Easter daisy, the autumn crocus, ranunculi, even poppy" (Fitzmyer, 979)? Here today and gone tomorrow! Yet even the proverbial wealth and colorful clothing of Solomon (1 Kings 10:1-25; 2 Chron. 9:1-28) is nothing compared with what God has provided for them. " 'Consider,' says Jesus, 'Brother Raven: does he plough, sow, and reap, and gather his harvest into his barn? And yet God gives him in abundance all he needs. Consider, too, you men of little faith, Sister Anemone: does she spin or weave? And yet the royal purple pales before the splendor of her attire! You are God's children. The father knows what you need. He will not let you starve' " (Jeremias, *Parables,* 215).

According to this passage, discipleship involves not only a simple trust in God as Creator and Sustainer, but also an active involvement with the Creator in his work of liberation in the world. "Justice" or "righteousness" (Matt. 6:33) is a key theological concept for Matthew (also 3:15; 5:6, 10, 20; 6:1; 21:32). It describes the ways of God manifested in the lives of people in terms of reconciliation (5:23-24), forgiveness (6:14-15), loving one's enemy (5:43-48), and doing for others what you desire that they should do for you (7:12). To seek first the kingdom of God and his justice is, for Matthew, to submit oneself to the lordship of God in Christ and to live in accordance with his will, as set forth in the Sermon on the Mount. Yet we always remember that this is possible only as a response to the call of God in Jesus, with both the call and the response the result of the grace of God in our lives.

To the disciples who have heard the gospel and begun to follow Jesus in a life on the road, Jesus proclaims the Sermon on the Mount as the new law for the new community. The crowds who overhear the Sermon might seize the opportunity to respond and join in this journey of faith and obedience. At the heart of the Sermon, Jesus addresses the question of material possessions. He does not deny physical needs, but he seeks to set things in an order of priority, with the kingdom and its justice at the head of the list. It is acceptable to have possessions as long as they do not possess us, as long as we continue to live in accord with God's will as set forth in the Sermon on the Mount. The poor in spirit (Matt. 5:3), those who hunger and thirst for righteousness/justice (5:6), and those who are persecuted for the sake of justice/righteousness (5:10)—such are assured of God's blessing.

The Less You Have to Carry, the Better (Luke 6:20-26)

Both Matthew and Mark give extended teaching on material possessions within the context of discipleship. Luke takes up the same theme, but looks at it from the perspective of the blessing that Jesus pronounced on the poor at the beginning of the Sermon on the Plain (Luke 6:20). In fact, this perspective so dominates Luke's portrayal of the ministry of Jesus that he has been called the Evangelist of the poor. Using materials drawn from many sources, Luke divides the history of salvation into three periods: the time of Israel (Luke 1—2), the time of Jesus (Luke 3—24), and the time of the church

(Acts). Within each of these periods, Luke not only stresses that discipleship involves material possessions. He goes on to draw the demarking line between judgment for those who have things in excess, and salvation for those who do not have even the basic necessities.

Luke introduces this theme already in the birth stories. Mary, a representative of the devout and poor holy ones within Israel, sings her song of blessing to God her Savior and declares:

> He has brought down the powerful from their thrones,
>   and lifted up the lowly;
> he has filled the hungry with good things,
>   and sent the rich away empty.   (Luke 1:52-53)

John the Baptist has ready answers when he is confronted by people who want to know how they ought to respond to his message of coming judgment and anticipated salvation: "Whoever has two coats must share with anyone who has none; and whoever has food must do likewise." He tells tax collectors, "Collect no more than the amount prescribed for you." The Baptist encourages soldiers on active service: "Do not extort money from anyone by threats or false accusation, and be satisfied with your wages" (Luke 3:10-14).

When, according to Luke, Jesus opens his ministry in the synagogue at Nazareth and delivers his manifesto of salvation history, he does so by declaring that the words of the ancient prophet have come to fulfillment in him:

> "The Spirit of the Lord is upon me,
>   because he has anointed me
>   to bring good news to the poor.
> He has sent me to proclaim release to the captives
>   and recovery of sight to the blind,
>   to let the oppressed go free,
> to proclaim the year of the Lord's favor."   (Luke 4:18-19)

In his teaching on hospitality, Jesus commands his host to "invite the poor, the crippled, the lame, and the blind" (Luke 14:13). Then in the following parable of the great feast, the host commands his servant to go out and bring back "the poor, the crippled, the blind, and the lame" (14:21), because all the invited guests have declined the invitation. In the parable of the rich man and Lazarus, the poor man is carried to Abraham's bosom while the rich man falls into Hades (16:19-31) and is cut off forever from the presence of God.

As we have seen, Luke has a different account of the calling of the first disciples, and at the end of it he stresses that "they left *everything*" to follow Jesus (Luke 5:11). When he takes over Mark's account of the call of Levi, he again stresses that "he got up, left *everything*, and followed him" (5:28, adding to Mark's story the words "left everything"!). Similarly, in Luke's version of the story of the rich young ruler, Jesus says, "There is still one thing lacking. Sell *all that* you own and distribute the money to the poor, and you will have treasure in heaven; then come, follow me" (18:22, with all again added to Mark).

In Luke, Jesus addresses the opening words of the Sermon on the Plain to the disciples who have "left everything" to follow him: "Blessed are you who are poor. . . . Woe to you who are rich" (Luke 6:20-26). In his opening description of life in the early church, Luke stresses that the Christians "would sell their possessions and goods and distribute the proceeds to all, as any had need" (Acts 2:45). For Luke, then, abandonment of material possessions is integral to the life of discipleship, as taught by Jesus, demonstrated by the disciples, and lived out in the early church. Thus in this setting, Luke has Jesus pronounce his blessings upon the poor and his woes upon those who are rich:

> Then [Jesus] looked up at his disciples and said:
>   "Blessed are you who are poor,
>   for yours is the kingdom of God.
>   "Blessed are you who are hungry now,
>   for you will be filled.
>   "Blessed are you who weep now,
>   for you will laugh.
>   "Blessed are you when people hate you, and when they exclude you, revile you, and defame you on account of the Son of Man. Rejoice in that day and leap for joy, for surely your

reward is great in heaven; for that is what their ancestors did to the prophets.

"But woe to you who are rich,
   for you have received your consolation.
"Woe to you who are full now,
   for you will be hungry.
"Woe to you who are laughing now,
   for you will mourn and weep.
"Woe to you when all speak well of you, for that is what their ancestors did to the false prophets."   (Luke 6:20-26)

The Sermon on the Plain (Luke 6:20-49) is the first major collection of teaching material that Luke has inserted into his Gospel. Almost all of it is included, along with a great deal more, in Matthew's Sermon on the Mount (Matt. 5:1—7:27). It is probable that these sayings and parables have been taken from an early collection of teaching material, usually called *Q*, which Matthew and Luke both used in writing their Gospels. Most of the material is also to be found in Matthew, but this fact does not mean that Luke has simply copied his earlier source. On the contrary, as with all of the material he uses, Luke has reshaped these sayings and parables so they express more clearly his understanding of the gospel and address more specifically the questions faced by the church to which he is writing.

In Matthew the Sermon is directed to the disciples and the crowds, but in Luke it is spoken only to the disciples (Luke 6:20). Thus it is obvious that in Luke, Jesus is directing his attention to the church. In a programmatic way, Luke has inserted four woes (6:24-26) as the negative counterpart to the four blessings (6:20-23) at the beginning of the Sermon. In this, and in other ways, Luke has radicalized the Sermon, especially on the question of material possessions.

Blessed Are You Who Are Poor

An extended list of nine blessings, in a somewhat spiritualized form, is to be found at the beginning of Matthew's Sermon on the Mount (Matt. 5:3-12). The Gospel of Thomas includes a number of blessings as well. This is a fourth-century version of a collection of sayings and parables of Jesus that probably goes back to a second-century original. It has Jesus say, "Blessed are the poor, for yours is the kingdom of heaven" (G. Thomas 54). "Blessed are you when you are hated and persecuted, and no place will be found where you have not been persecuted" (68). "Blessed are those who have been persecuted in their hearts; these are they who have known the Father in truth" (69a). "Blessed are they that are hungry, that the belly of him who desires may be satisfied" (69b). Blessings, then, are a well-known part of the gospel tradition, and it is always the poor who lead the way, who are the first to receive the promise of divine blessing.

The word translated "blessed" or "happy" refers to the distinctively religious joy which comes to people who know that they will share in God's salvation. This overwhelming joy or happiness is independent of earthly circumstances. It comes because the people on whom it is pronounced are assured that they will participate with God in his kingly reign when it finally bursts forth in all its fullness into human history. As the second and third beatitudes (Luke 6:21) stress, however, this anticipation of future joy and happiness is not simply reserved for the future. Happiness is already breaking into the present (note the twice repeated "now"!) and relegates all secular goods and values to a completely subordinate position in relation to the kingdom of God.

How can we describe this joy? It is as when someone finds a "treasure hidden in a field" and covers it again. "Then in his joy he goes and sells all that he has and buys that field" (Matt. 13:44). Nothing else matters. He is so happy, he willingly sells everything and does not consider it a sacrifice. This joy is like a merchant looking for fine pearls. When he finds "one pearl of great value, he goes and sells everything he has, and buys the pearl" (13:45-46, adapted). That is the joy of God's kingly rule, a joy which comes to all who will finally share in it.

According to the Beatitudes, the first ones to be promised this joy of ultimate salvation, the joy of the kingdom, are the poor (Luke 6:20; Matt. 5:3; G. Thomas 54). Generally in the Old Testament, "poverty" is considered evil. Divine partiality on behalf of the poor is not only recognized but is understood as an ethical model for the leaders of the community. In the Psalms the poor are often the oppressed righteous:

> O Lord, . . . an impious people reviles your name.
> Do not deliver the soul of your dove to the wild animals;
>   do not forget the life of your poor forever. . . .
> Let the poor and needy praise your name.   (Ps. 74:18-21)

In the period immediately prior to the New Testament, it was primarily the poor who remained faithful to the Law; the wealthy upper classes in Jerusalem tended to accommodate themselves to their Greek and Roman overlords. Hence, in the first century "rich" tended to mean "worldly and irreligious" while "poor" tended to mean "God-fearing and saintly." We see this illustrated clearly in the first-century B.C.E. pseudepigraphical Psalms of Solomon, where "the poor" and "the saints" are used to describe the same people:

> The saints shall give thanks in the assembly
>   and God shall have mercy on the poor
>   in the day of gladness of Israel.   (Ps. of Sol. 10:7)

Matthew seizes on the underlying thought of this first beatitude and, to prevent misunderstanding, expands it to "Blessed are the poor in spirit" (Matt. 5:3). For him, the blessing is pronounced upon the poor whose sole help is in God. This is in contrast, not only to those who are rich materially, but also and especially to those who consider that they are rich in religious knowledge and religious achievement. Therefore, *The New English Bible* translates Matthew's first beatitude as: "Blest are those who know their need of God." We should always remember, however, that when the New Testament speaks of "the poor" in an extended sense, as in Matthew, the term always still has economic associations. Likewise, when the economic aspects appear to dominate, as in Luke, it is predominantly the poverty of those who have responded to the call to follow Jesus (see Luke 5:11, 28).

It is not by chance, theologically, that the story of Jesus blessing the little people (Mark 10:13-16) is followed immediately by the story of the rich young ruler (10:17-31). In the first, Jesus declares, "Let the little children come to me; do not stop them; for it is to such as these that the kingdom of God belongs" (10:14). In the second, Jesus tells the rich man, "Go, sell what you own, and give the money to the poor, and you will have treasure in heaven; then come, follow me" (10:21). The promise of participation in the kingly rule of God is made to those who are prepared to accept it as a gift. It is the result of the grace of God, free and undeserved. Those who trust in themselves, their own abilities, and their own possessions exclude themselves. To Luke, the promise of the kingdom comes first to "the poor"; "the rich " are the prime example of those who exclude themselves."

Woe to You Who Are Rich

The economic associations of "poverty" and "riches" in the Gospel of Luke are underlined in the brief series of woes which are found only here in the New Testament (Luke 6:24-26). Those who are satisfied in this present life will find themselves in the reverse position in the future life, even as the poor and dispossessed of this life will find their roles reversed as they experience the riches of God's kingly reign.

In the Old Testament there is a development in the understanding of "the rich" similar to that which we have already seen with respect to "the poor." The Prophets denounce the ruthless rich with the same enthusiasm they show in defending the powerless poor (Amos 2:6-8; 4:1-3; Revelation Isa. 5:8-12; Jer. 5:26-31; Ezek. 22:23-31; and many places). Typical of their denunciations is Jeremiah's tirade:

> Like a cage full of birds,
>   their houses are full of treachery;
> Therefore they have become great and rich,
>   they have grown fat and sleek.
> They know no limits in deeds of wickedness;
>   they do not judge with justice
> the cause of the orphan, to make it prosper,
>   and they do not defend the rights of the needy. (Jer. 5:27-28)

While "the poor" is becoming a term synonymous with "the saints" or "the righteous," "the rich" is used as a syn-

onym for "the wicked." This is clear also in one of the best-
known of all Old Testament texts:

> They made his grave with the wicked
>> and his tomb with the rich.   (Isa. 53:9)

Like Deuteronomic theology, the later Wisdom tradition
is more positive than the Prophets in its attitude toward
wealth. It even regards it as a blessing from God: "The blessing of the Lord makes rich, and he adds no sorrow with it"
(Prov. 10:22; also Sirach 11:14-22). The positive consequences of wealth are security (Prov. 10:15), friends (14:20),
honor (Sir. 10:30), peace (Sir. 44:6), and a happy life
(1 Chron. 29:28; Sir. 44:1-8). The danger is that people will
begin to trust in riches rather than in God (Sir. 11:19) and
may even stoop to deceit in order to gain greater wealth:
"One who loves gold will not be justified; one who pursues
money will be led astray by it" (31:5-8). Surprisingly, the
Wisdom tradition's positive attitude toward wealth is not tak-
en up in the New Testament. The letter of James, which
stands nearest in form to Wisdom literature, is most stridently antiwealth (James 1:10-11; 2:5-6; 5:1).

Luke shows a dramatic interest in "the rich and wealthy"
(Luke 6:24; 12:16; 14:12; 16:1, 9, 21-22; 18:23, 25; 19:2; 21:1).
His many references to the rich contrast with only three in
Matthew, two in Mark, and none in John. Zacchaeus, the
wealthy tax collector from Jericho, is the only rich person
portrayed in a positive light in Luke. He is affirmed simply
because, in the presence of Jesus, he spontaneously gives
half of his property to the poor and volunteers to repay fourfold any money that he has fraudulently obtained (19:1-10).

Mary's song sets the tone for the entire Gospel:

> He has brought down the powerful from their thrones,
>> and lifted up the lowly;
> he has filled the hungry with good things,
>> and sent the rich away empty.   (Luke 1:52-53)

The story of the rich fool gives in parabolic form the
warning to the rich, to those who go on piling up riches for

themselves and yet are not rich in God's sight. The rich fool is able to build bigger barns and considers himself naturally lucky and self-sufficient. Then God warns him that he is facing the ultimate catastrophe, in which material possessions are of no value whatsoever (Luke 12:13-21). Another parable, also found only in Luke, warns of the judgment that awaits the rich who live careless and luxurious lives, unconcerned about the plight of the poor (16:19-31). Luke's parable about the people who refuse the invitation to the great supper (14:15-24) is also found in Matthew (22:1-10) and the Gospel of Thomas (64). But Luke alone introduces it with a declaration against the rich:

> [Jesus said,] "When you give a luncheon or a dinner, do not invite your friends or your brothers or your relatives or rich neighbors, in case they may invite you in return, and you would be repaid. But when you give a banquet, invite the poor, the crippled, the lame, and the blind. And you will be blessed, because they cannot repay you, for you will be repaid at the resurrection of the righteous." (Luke 14:12-14)

To be rich in material possessions and poor before God is to lay yourself open to the judgment of God. The completion of that judgment is still in the future, but it is so certain that the "woe" can already be pronounced; the weeping and gnashing of teeth have already begun!

Discipleship Is Decisive

In the time of Jesus, as we have seen, it was the poor who had remained faithful to Yahweh, the Lord, while the wealthy had compromised their faith through alliances with their powerful overlords. In this situation, Jesus had no fear of being misunderstood when he simply said, "Blessed are you who are poor. . . . Woe to you who are rich." The poor of his time were economically disadvantaged but religiously faithful; the wealthy were economically advantaged but religiously unfaithful. The dimensions of economics and faithfulness were bound together in that historical situation.

In the Gospel of Luke, the Sermon on the Plain (Luke

6:20-49) is delivered to the disciples, to those who have left everything to follow Jesus (5:11, 28, with "everything" added by Luke). To them, Jesus says, "Blessed are you who are poor" (6:20b), using the second person instead of Matthew's third person, "Blessed are the poor in spirit" (Matt. 5:3). The blessing is thus pronounced on the disciples, who are poor because of their decision to follow Jesus.

The corresponding "Woe to you who are rich" (Luke 6:24) is, despite the reluctance of many commentators, also addressed to members of the church, to those who have refused to leave everything to follow Jesus. Luke's account of the rich young ruler (18:18-30) reflects this situation. When, as in Mark, the young ruler claims that he has kept all the commandments, Jesus says: "There is still one thing lacking. Sell all that you own and distribute the money to the poor, and you will have treasure in heaven; then come, follow me" (18:23, with "all" added by Luke).

In Mark, the rich man immediately departs and the teaching is given to the disciples for the church. In Luke, however, Jesus looks at the rich man and says: "How hard it is for those who have wealth to enter the kingdom of God! Indeed, it is easier for a camel to go through the eye of a needle than for someone who is rich to enter the kingdom of God" (Luke 18:24-25). In the setting of Mark, the few rich people have already left the church (4:19). But in the setting of Luke, the rich are still present, and it is to them that he directs his challenge (Luke 19:24-26) and his warning (6:24-26).

Heroism in an Age of Consumerism

Life on the road is possible only by the grace of God. With the sacrifices and suffering involved, it is beyond the capacities of people. This journey becomes a possibility only as God's grace permeates our innermost being and we accept what God has made possible through Jesus Christ. By the grace of God, the seductive power of materialism may be broken as people are liberated to the joyful obedience of following Jesus along the road. This liberated lifestyle is costly, however, for it has to be lived out in daily obedience. The early Christians were acutely aware of the dangers which material possessions posed to the life of faith.

All of the Evangelists include many sayings, stories, and parables exhorting their readers to abandon their slavery to material possessions and to trust in God. Indeed, no other ethical question has captured their attention as dramatically as has the danger of materialism. Of course, they do not speak with one voice, and we should not have expected that they would do so. As the socioeconomic environment of their churches varied, so they interpreted the danger to faith differently and presented life on the road in their own distinctive ways.

Mark wrote for a poor rural community in which the few people who had had some money and possessions had already left the church. The worries of this world and the quest for material possessions had led them astray. The model disciples in this Gospel are the poor widow who gives everything she owns to God (Mark 12:41-44) and the extravagant woman who squanders almost a year's wages in a selfless act of devotion to Jesus (14:3-9). This is the kind of commitment that Mark was looking for, and he was apparently able to find it among some of the women of his community.

Certainly, Mark knew of rich farmers in his neighborhood who were seriously searching for the meaning of life, but their large estates stood in the way. He tells the story of one farmer (Mark 10:17-22) as the climax of his teaching that discipleship must cover every aspect of life (9:33—10:31). Thus he indicates that while wealth was keeping many people out of the kingdom (10:23-27), those who were prepared to give up everything for the sake of the gospel would be richly rewarded in this world and the next (10:28-31).

Matthew, on the other hand, was writing for a more middle-class urban community. He was concerned that his people were falling into the trap of seeking to find their security in both God and material possessions, rather than in God alone. For Matthew, the model disciple was not a poor widow who would give everything to God (Mark 12:41-44), but rather a rich man prepared to use his possessions in the service of Jesus (Matt. 27:57-61).

At the heart of the Sermon on the Mount, Matthew seeks to teach his church that investments with God cannot fail: justice is to extend to loving one's enemies (5:21-48), and forgiveness to those who have caused offense (6:14-15). His hearers are to do for others as they desire others to do for them (7:12). He warns them that materialism is diametrically opposed to faith in God; it enslaves those who think they are being liberated and often leads to dishonesty and oppression (6:24). Matthew does not deny that his people have physical needs, but he asks them to trust God and to set things in proper perspective with God's kingdom. God's justice and righteousness are to take priority in all things (6:25-34).

Luke, finally, was writing to a quite different church: a city church which had long been poor but which more recently had witnessed the emergence of a richer group within its membership. He took a firm stand and drew the demarking line of salvation and judgment between those who have a great deal more than they need, and those who do not have even the basic necessities of life.

Luke provides a number of different models of economic discipleship: Simon the fisherman and Levi the tax collector leave everything to follow Jesus (Luke 5:11, 28). Zacchaeus, the moneygrubber of Jericho, in the presence of Jesus gives away half his property and offers to repay fourfold everyone that he has defrauded (19:1-10). The early church spontaneously shares their possessions so that no one is in need (Acts 2:42-47; 4:32-35). As far as Luke is concerned, God is unequivocally on the side of the poor, and to them he promises the kingdom (Luke 6:20-22). God steadfastly warns the rich who refuse to leave everything to follow Jesus: they will be excluded from the presence of God (6:24-26).

Perhaps no gospel lesson is more appropriate for the churches of the Western world than this. "Success" has become a dominant theme, and it is widely believed that it is right and proper for a Christian to prosper and become rich. Instead, the good news of liberation from serving wealth must be preached and believed again. We see book covers showing authors with their flashy cars, and they proclaim that God has blessed them. They are a crass commentary on the contemporary Australian cargo cult (trying to obtain goods through magic) and show a corruption in popular Western Christianity. Mammon is a reality in our society, a seductive force. The media daily declare that even the most extravagant of luxuries are essential for a happy life and that an ever-rising standard of living is ours by right. An advertisement at Melbourne airport recently offered "The Ultimate Gift, . . . the gift of being pampered"! To a society that wants to be pampered, the gospel message warning of the dangers of materialism seems absurd. That which is central to our life on the road is in danger of being pushed to the periphery. Brother Roger of Taizé is clearly correct when he says, "To follow Christ in our consumer society becomes something heroic."

It is not that our churches are wanting to turn their backs on God. Quite the contrary; they are crying out for God. But they are converting the either-or of the gospel into the both-and of success. They want God *and* material possessions; or more precisely, they want the God who is willing and able to bless them with an abundance of material possessions! This is not the God of Jesus and the New Testament. While many of our churches are looking for the God of wealth, "the nub, the nucleus, of the biblical message . . . is in the relationship between God and the poor. Jesus Christ is precisely God become poor" (Gutiérrez, *Poor*, 13).

We have been called to a life on the road with Jesus, with "God become poor," and on this journey we have to travel light. We are not strong enough to follow Jesus and carry a mountain of material possessions with us. Those possessions will slow us down and make the journey such a struggle that, if we are not careful, we will ultimately settle down and give up life on the road.

Ed Loring, who works among the poor through the Open Door Community in Atlanta, recently said in one of his sermons, "To become a follower of Christ is to take a leap of faith into the arms of the poor." This is precisely the case, not simply because of isolated biblical texts, but because of the fundamental insight that God exists among the poor and calls us to live in fellowship and solidarity with him, through Jesus, the poor man from Nazareth.

The 1980 meetings of the Commission on World Mission and Evangelism and of the Consultation on World Evangelization placed the theme of "Good News to the Poor" at the top of the church's agenda. However, the continuing strength of success theology and the emergence of the "new right" are rapidly reversing the important biblical insights of these conferences and dulling the prophetic message of the gospel. We need to confront the wealthy entrepreneurs who have so stridently opposed every effort to reform our taxation system in the direction of justice. We must say with Archbishop Romero, martyr of El Salvador, "Whatever political issue we take up, we must see it from the perspective of the poor." The Christian test for any legislation is not "How will this affect us?" but rather "How will this affect the poor?"

We are on the road with Jesus, and we now view life from his perspective. Material possessions look different from here, and their hold upon our lives is broken as Jesus liberates us from things and grants us the security of the community of God.

Questions for Discussion

1. In the consumer society, people often seek security in material possessions. Why is the search for security so important today?

2. Brother Roger says that following Christ in our consumer society demands something heroic. Who are your heroes? In what ways are you heroic in following Christ in our consumer society?

3. Since Jesus promised persecution, should we be worried if we are not being persecuted?

4. Is it wrong to be rich? And successful?

5. How can one say that the poor are blessed? Why is God so interested in the plight of the poor?

6. Have you experienced the joy of giving up possessions? How?

7. Why is justice so important for the kingdom of God?

8. What is the perspective of the poor? How might this perspective influence our political decisions?

4

Friends for the Journey

Discipleship and Community

Traveling Together with Jesus

The central feature of the teaching of Jesus is, as we have seen, that in his words and works the kingly reign of God has drawn near. The reign of grace; the era of good news for the poor; the time of joy for the downtrodden, the sinners, and the outcasts—all this has begun to break into human history. The gospel preached and lived out by Jesus is good news of grace and love, costly grace and sacrificial love. The required response is a radical reorientation of life, a life lived out in believing obedience. In the Gospels, this life of repentance and faith is set forth as the life of discipleship.

The radical reorientation of life in discipleship means, among other things, that people are no longer to be enslaved by material possessions. As followers of Jesus, they must resolutely refuse to attempt the impossibility of seeking to serve God and money at the same time. Yet the followers of Jesus

are fully aware of the dominating power of material possessions and know that single-minded obedience to God is possible only by the grace of God. Obedience is beyond their ca-
pabilities; it reaches into the realm of their existence only as
God's grace permeates their innermost being, enabling them
to accept what God has made possible through Jesus Christ.

Through the grace of God, slavery to material possessions may be broken. Through the grace of God, people may
be liberated to the joyful obedience of following Jesus. But
the grace of God is costly, and the life of discipleship is no
easy thing. It reflects all the tensions and trials of human existence. Although it is accomplished by grace, it has to be lived
out in the concrete realities of life in the world where the attraction of material possessions is always a real threat to the
life of faith.

The disciples' detachment from material possessions
stands in stark contrast to their concern for brothers and sisters (Matt. 5:23-24), neighbors (Mark 12:31), and even enemies and persecutors (Matt. 5:43-48). They know that even if
they are in the middle of a sacrificial act in the temple and remember that a sister or brother has something against them,
they must leave their gifts there before the altar and first go
and make peace with that sister or brother. Only then should
they come back and complete their sacrifice, for only then
will it be acceptable to God (5:23-24).

The disciples have been taught that they must love God
with all their heart and soul and mind and strength, and that
they must love their neighbors as themselves (Mark 12:28-
34). This loving concern for others cannot be restricted to pious activities and religious observances. It is to be seen in forgiveness (Matt. 6:1-18), in doing for others what they expect
others to do for them (7:12), in caring for the hungry, the
thirsty, and the naked (25:31-46).

The followers of Jesus know that when they stand before
God at the judgment, all that will remain will be the goodness of goodness. By the grace of God they will be forgiven
according to their willingness to forgive others (Matt. 6:14-
15), since the willingness to forgive others is the outstretched
hand by which they are able to grasp the forgiveness of God.

Because of their openness toward God, because of their radical loneliness before God, they are in the process of being liberated from themselves and from selfish desires and ambitions. These selfish goals have held them captive for so long and have continually threatened to engulf them and to bury them in their own rubble. In this process of liberation toward God, they are being liberated toward their sisters and brothers, who are also seeking to do the will of God.

As the New Testament always makes abundantly clear, to be a follower of Jesus Christ is to be a member of the people of God, the messianic community of the disciples of Jesus. In the Gospels, there is no such thing as a solitary Christian, an isolated disciple. To respond to the call of Jesus is to embark on a journey with others. There is no shortage of friends for the journey when you travel with Jesus. Yet these friends might not always be people you would naturally choose as traveling companions. Lepers and outcasts, poor and powerless are there in abundance; they make for a challenging and adventurous journey.

We again will restrict ourselves to three passages: the reality of the community of the new people of God (Mark), the need for continual reconciliation within this community (Matthew), and the possibilities for sharing among God's people (Acts).

Finding a New Family (Mark 3:13-35)

In Mark's Gospel, the reality of the community of the new people of God is clearly established. In response to the revelation of God in Jesus Christ, you either join those who are seeking to follow Jesus, or you join forces with those who are taking their stand against him. You either join with Jesus and his people, or you align yourself with those who will nail him to the cross.

Mark puts forward these two options from the beginning. In his opening chapters, Jesus reveals his authority in both word and deed only to be greeted by increasing opposition and the progressive darkening of the world. The way Mark divides his Gospel into sections calls attention to the reality of the community of the new people of God, and the choice that each one is called to make. The first half of the Gospel is made up of three smaller sections (Mark 1:14—3:6; 3:7—6:6a; 6:6b—8:21). Each section commences with a statement summarizing one particular aspect of the ministry of Jesus: preaching the good news and calling for repentance (1:14-15), healing the sick and demon possessed (3:7-12), and teaching among the villages (6:6b).

On each occasion this opening summary statement is immediately followed by a story about discipleship which highlights the community aspect of Mark's teaching: the call of the first disciples (Mark 1:16-20), the community of the disciples (3:13-19) and the mission of the disciples (6:7-13). And each section concludes with a representative group opposed to Jesus. This draws attention to the need to choose between Jesus and his enemies. The religious and political leaders plot to kill Jesus (3:6); his own townspeople at Nazareth reject him, and he is consequently not able to perform many miracles there (6:1-6a); and even his own disciples harden their hearts (8:14-21).

Mark's message is clear: there is a choice to be made. Some respond to the call of Jesus, and these he brings into the community of the new people of God (Mark 3:13-35) and then sends them out on mission in the world (6:7-13).

> [Jesus] went up the mountain and called to him those whom he wanted, and they came to him. And he appointed twelve, whom he also named apostles, to be with him, and to be sent out to proclaim the message, and to have authority to cast out demons. So he appointed the twelve: Simon (to whom he gave the name Peter); James son of Zebedee and John the brother of James (to whom he gave the name Boanerges, that is, Sons of Thunder); and Andrew, and Philip, and Bartholomew, and Matthew, and Thomas, and James son of Alphaeus, and Thaddaeus, and Simon the Cananaean, and Judas Iscariot, who betrayed him.
>
> Then he went home; and the crowd came together again, so that they could not even eat. When his family heard it, they went out to restrain him, for people were saying, "He has gone out of his mind." And the scribes who came down from Jerusalem said, "He has Beelzebul, and by the ruler of the

demons he casts out demons." And he called them to him, and spoke to them in parables, "How can Satan cast out Satan? If a kingdom is divided against itself, that kingdom cannot stand. And if a house is divided against itself, that house will not be able to stand. And if Satan has risen up against himself and is divided, he cannot stand, but his end has come. But no one can enter a strong man's house and plunder his property without first tying up the strong man; then indeed the house can be plundered.

"Truly I tell you, people will be forgiven for their sins and whatever blasphemies they utter; but whoever blasphemes against the Holy Spirit can never have forgiveness, but is guilty of an eternal sin"—for they had said, "He has an unclean spirit."

Then his mother and his brothers came; and standing outside, they sent to him and called him. A crowd was sitting around him; and they said to him, "Your mother and your brothers and sisters are outside, asking for you." And he replied, "Who are my mother and my brothers?" And looking at those who sat around him, he said, "Here are my mother and my brothers! Whoever does the will of God is my brother and sister and mother."   (Mark 3:13-35)

This is not the first time the Gospel of Mark features the disciples or even the community of the disciples. When Jesus calls the fishermen (Mark 1:16-20), we are told that they go off after him. It is clear that Simon and Andrew are soon joined by James and John to form the initial group of followers. When Levi is called (2:13-17), we meet the group called "the disciples" for the first time as Jesus and his followers enjoy a celebratory feast with the liberated tax collector and a house full of his friends. Mark has, however, placed the call of the twelve at this particular point in his story of Jesus as an exposition of the healing ministry of Jesus (3:7-12), which creates a new people of God (3:13-19).

Mark is using a number of earlier stories and has carefully woven them together into a powerful portrayal of the essentials of the messianic community. He has taken over a traditional list of twelve disciples (Mark 3:13-14a, 16b-19) and has added the statement that they were called "to be with him, and to be sent out to proclaim the message, and to have authority to cast out demons" (3:14b-15). The repetition of "the twelve" is a sign that Mark has inserted the intervening material. As a result, it is clear that Mark wants us to understand that this story occupies a central position between the call of the disciples who are told they will become fishers of people (1:17), and their later appointment to the mission of preaching the good news and casting out demons (6:7-13).

He has followed the story about the twelve (Mark 3:13-19) with a composite narrative. This he created by placing the account of the conflict with the scribes (3:22-30) between the two halves of the story about his family trying to take him in hand (3:20-21, 31-35). The section reaches its climax with the declaration of Jesus, "Whoever does the will of God is my brother and sister and mother" (3:35). We will gain important insights into Mark's message by watching carefully the way he has arranged his material.

Jesus Is the Leader of the New Community

At first sight, the opening paragraph of this section of the Gospel of Mark appears to be merely a list of names (Mark 3:13-19). This is one of those sections (like the genealogies) which we tend to skip when reading the Gospel. Yet it is much more than a list of names. Like all stories in the Gospel, it has an important theological message. It not only tells us what happened once upon a time in Palestine, but also tells us what happens each time people are encountered by God in Jesus Christ. Indeed, this account is a powerful antidote to the excessive individualism of Western Christianity. It tells us that the call to discipleship is not an individual matter, that Christianity has never been simply a question of "one man and his God, one woman and her God." Christianity involves the whole community of the people of God.

The call to discipleship is, in fact, determinative for the new community: those who have been called into discipleship have been called into the community of God. Without the call of God, there can be no community of God. Without the community of God, there has been no call of God. To follow the Messiah is to live in solidarity with the messianic community.

As in the stories of the call of the first disciples (Mark 1:16-20; 2:14), so also here Jesus takes the initiative. He is the subject of almost every verb in this section (3:13-19). We are told that *he* goes up on the mountain (3:13), *he* calls those whom he wants (3:13), *he* appoints twelve (3:14), *he* gives the name Peter (3:16), *he* gives the name Boanerges (3:17). Certainly, we are told that the twelve "came to him" and joined him (3:13), but it is stressed that they do this only in response to the previous call of Jesus. As with discipleship, so also Christian community begins with the call of Jesus. We do not first of all choose to follow Jesus in a life on the road, and we do not out of the blue choose to belong to the messianic community. Rather, our membership in that community presupposes and is a response to the gracious call of the Messiah.

"The mountain" (Mark 3:13) had a wide range of religious associations in Israel. It is a place of revelation (Exod. 19:20) and worship (1 Kings 18:42) related to ancient understandings of the nearness of God in the high places. Elsewhere in Mark, "the mountain" serves as a place of solitude and prayer (Mark 6:46), and of the revelation of the messianic glory of Jesus as the Son of God (9:2-8). Here it continues its sacred significance as the place where the representative leaders of the new people of God are chosen.

We are told that the new leaders are chosen "to be with" Jesus (Mark 3:14) as he is on the move in his messianic ministry. They are called to travel with him as he moves from Bethsaida to Bethany, from Capernaum to Cana. They have now been enrolled in the traveling school of mission. As they travel with Jesus, they are to learn the important lessons of life on the road, and they are to learn these lessons together. They soon become well aware that when he is welcomed into a household, for instance, they are also welcomed into that household. When he is rejected, they are rejected. When he is welcomed to the wedding feast in Cana of Galilee, they are also invited (John 2:2). But when the Son of Man has nowhere to lay his head, they have nowhere to lay theirs (Luke 9:58). They are following Jesus, and what happens to him automatically happens to them.

This experience of shared joy and sorrow binds the disci-

ples together as a community of the people of God. They
have been called by Jesus in a supreme act of grace. Because
they all owe their common allegiance to Jesus, they are related to one another in ties which transcend the human. Moreover, because what happens to them is also happening to
their Leader, they care almost nothing about the way they
have to live. They care little about the cost involved in this
revolutionary way of living. They have been brought into a
new community of faith whose focal point is Jesus Christ.

The authority of Jesus as the leader of the wandering
people of God is seen in the way he gives new names to the
people who share leadership roles in the group. "Simon" is
renamed "Peter" or "Rocky"; James and John are to be
known as "Boanerges," fiery apocalyptic preachers (Mark
3:16-17; see Luke 9:54). The act of naming was very important in ancient Near Eastern cultures. In the early story of creation, for example, God gives to humanity the power and authority to name the animals (Gen. 2:19-20). As they are
named, they are placed in their proper order within the created world.

Thus when Jesus calls the twelve, he shows his authority
in renaming the three leaders. This explains the unusual order of the two sets of brothers: Peter, James the son of
Zebedee and John the brother of James, and Andrew. This
sequence differs from Matthew (10:2) and Luke (6:14),
which have Peter and Andrew his brother, James the son of
Zebedee and John his brother. Peter (always mentioned
first), James, and John are the only ones allowed to be present at the raising of Jairus's daughter (Mark 5:37-43). They
alone witness the startling revelation of Jesus as the divine
Son on the mountain of transfiguration (9:2-8). And they are
the only ones with Jesus as he faces the harsh reality of his
impending death (14:32-42).

Peter, James, and John are clearly recognized as leaders
by Mark's church, but the new names which they are given
are intended as promises rather than statements of fact. Peter
is certainly not a "rock" in this Gospel, and James and John
are not yet fiery apocalyptic preachers. Peter is as yet unable
to accept Jesus' teaching about the suffering Son of Man

(Mark 8:32-33), and James and John are still concerned about their status in the kingdom of God (10:33-45). Their new names refer not to their natural gifts and talents but to what they are intended to become under the leadership of the one who had, in turn, called them to leadership in the early church. At this point it is sufficient that they be called "to be with" Jesus (3:14). From him they will receive authority for their messianic ministry (3:15). He is the leader of the messianic community. He will, in turn, lead them out on messianic mission.

An Open Community of Grace and Love

Despite the emphases of a great deal of contemporary Western theology, the Christian church, in its local expression and in its universal manifestation, was never intended to be simply a homogeneous group of middle-class people. It is not enough for church people to meet together because they have similar interests, tastes, and outlooks. The decisive ingredient for the Christian community is not agreement regarding tastes, manners, worldview, political allegiance, or even theology. Like the early disciples, the members of the Christian community are to come together because they have experienced the grace of God in their lives through the call of Jesus to follow him. As Mark emphasizes, Jesus takes the initiative and calls those whom he wants (Mark 3:13). This call of grace brings them together, and this grace holds them together when the pressures of the group threaten to tear the community apart.

Details are sparse about a number of those included in the list of the twelve, though legends abound. Four of their names are Semitic in origin, and two are distinctively Greek. Four of them are fishermen, one a tax collector (Matt. 10:3), and another a Zealot (Luke 6:15). In occupied Palestine of the first century, there was certainly no love lost between tax collectors and Zealots. If they met accidentally in a dark alley in Jerusalem, only one group would emerge to tell of their encounter. The Zealots were totally opposed to the Roman occupation, and the tax collectors were, directly or indirectly, employed by the Gentiles. The tax collector was a collaborator; the Zealot was a loyalist, a freedom fighter, a member of the underground. Yet within the small circle of the disciples, there is a tax collector and there is a Zealot. Better still, there is an ex-tax collector and an ex-Zealot, for in responding to the gracious call of God both have become followers of Jesus.

Mark has already emphasized the superabundance of grace demonstrated in the disciples' call to follow Jesus. Immediately after the call of Levi the tax collector (Mark 2:14), Mark tells us that many tax collectors and notorious sinners shared a messianic meal with Jesus in his house (2:15). In Luke, the meal is located in Levi's house, and Luke emphasizes the celebratory character of the gathering (Luke 5:29-32). In Mark, despite the ambiguities of the text, the meal almost certainly takes place in Jesus' (Greek: his) house, and the stress is upon the communal nature of the undertaking. The tax collectors are eating with Jesus "and his disciples" (Mark 2:15) as the community of his followers find their salvation in Jesus and share the grace which he so freely offers.

The religious authorities object to Jesus' open offer of salvation, but he responds sharply: "Those who are well have no need of a physician, but those who are sick; I have come to call not the righteous but sinners" (Mark 2:17). It is the grace of God which binds together the community of the people of God. The religious leaders' refusal to accept this grace excludes them from the community of salvation.

The three lists of the twelve in the Gospels vary significantly in their location within the ministry of Jesus. Matthew 10:1-4 is part of the missionary sermon. Mark 3:13-19 is an introduction to the second section of the Galilean ministry. Luke 6:12-16 is part of the setting for the Sermon on the Plain. The synoptic Gospels differ marginally in the names included. Many ancient manuscripts of Matthew include Lebbaeus in place of Thaddaeus, while Luke knows of neither and instead has Judas son of James. They all begin with Peter as the first name, however, and end with Judas Iscariot as the last. Before Mark's Gospel is finished, we will be told that Peter denies Jesus in his hour of need (Mark 14:66-72), Judas betrays him to his opponents (14:43-47), and the other ten forsake him and flee (14:48-52). It is a miracle of grace that this particular community survives at all.

We will have many opportunities of looking at the way Peter is portrayed in the Gospels, but we must not overlook the role of Judas in Mark. It must have been an embarrassment to the early church to have to admit that the one who betrayed Jesus belonged to the leadership of the community. According to Matthew, Judas negotiates with the chief priests to hand over Jesus for money and is paid thirty pieces of silver (Matt. 26:14-16). Afterward, he is filled with remorse, repents of what he has done, returns the money, and goes out and hangs himself (27:3-10).

Luke says that "Satan entered into Judas" before betraying Jesus (Luke 22:3) and, through Peter, shows that Scripture foretold his fate and ordered his replacement (Acts 1:15-20). John goes further than any of the others in stressing Judas' hypocritical and mercenary attitude (John 12:4; 13:21-30), practically equating him with Satan: "Did I not choose you, the twelve? Yet one of you is a devil" (John 6:70; see 13:2).

The Gospel of Mark, however, is remarkably circumspect about Judas. The betrayer is mentioned four times, and on three occasions he is described as "one of the twelve" (Mark 14:10, 20, 43; see 3:19). Mark also stresses that he participates in the Last Supper (14:17-21). When Jesus predicts the treachery of Judas, none of the other disciples are aware of whom he is speaking, and they are "too dumbfounded to think of accusing anyone else" (Taylor, 541). The existence of Peter, Judas, and the others among the leadership of the early church demonstrates how important it is for us to realize that the community not only begins and ends as a community of grace, but also continues that way. It is an open community of sinners, not a closed enclave of saints.

The New Family: Those Who Do the Will of God

Immediately following the account of the naming of the twelve (Mark 3:13-19), we encounter an interesting example of Mark's editorial work. He has set one story within the two halves of another in such a way that each is to be interpreted in relation to the other. The Evangelist uses this technique seven times. With one exception (5:21-43, where the arrangement may be traditional), the stories are strategically placed at the beginning of a major section of the Gospel to indicate the leading themes to be developed in the material that follows.

The authority of Jesus in teaching (Mark 1:22, 27) provides the framework for the first story of Jesus rebuking an unclean spirit. That same authority is now also demonstrated by the evident power in expelling demons (1:21-28). Into the account of the healing of a *paralytic,* Mark also inserts material on the authority of Jesus to forgive sins. Now the miracle proves the authority of Jesus in the church (2:1-12). The healing of a woman who has been suffering for twelve years is placed within the context of the raising of Jairus's twelve-year-old daughter (5:21-43), anticipating the suffering and resurrection of Jesus.

Likewise, Mark places the death of John the Baptist at the hands of Herod within the context of the mission of the twelve, thus indicating the costly nature of the church's messianic mission (Mark 6:7-31). The cleansing of the temple is sandwiched between the two halves of the cursing of the fig tree, illustrating God's judgment on Israel (11:12-25). The anointing of Jesus by a woman in preparation for his death is surrounded by the two stories of the religious leaders plotting to kill Jesus. This indicates that throughout the passion narrative, a major emphasis will be the treachery of the leaders and the faithfulness of the women (14:1-11).

Straight after naming the twelve (Mark 3:13-19), Mark tells us that the family of Jesus thinks he has gone mad, and they set out to take him in hand (3:20-21). But before Mark tells us about their arrival, he relates that the religious leaders from Jerusalem attribute his power to Beelzebul and are therefore guilty of an eternal sin which cannot be forgiven (3:22-30). Finally, Mark tells us that the mother and brothers of Jesus arrive and send word that they are outside looking for him. Jesus looks around at those who are with him and declares that his true family is composed of those who do the will of God (3:31-35).

According to Mark, there are two communities. One community is made up of both the natural family of Jesus, whose members think he is mad (Mark 3:20-21), and the religious leaders, who attribute his ministry to Satan (3:22-30). And there is the other community with him at the center; they spend their time listening to Jesus and seeking to do the will of God. The new family of Jesus is a community of grace, but the obverse side of grace is obedience. The community of grace, being conscious of the unmerited favor of God, seeks to do the will of God (3:31-34).

This is the only time Mark uses the Pauline term "the will of God" (Mark 3:35; see Rom. 1:10; 2:18; 12:2; 15:32; and many other places). Matthew (12:50) has altered it to his characteristic expression "the will of my Father in heaven," while Luke (8:21) prefers his designation as "those who hear the word of God and do it." There have been many suggestions as to what Mark means by his expression. Certainly it indicates a need for "unreserved obedience on the part of his followers" (Anderson, 125). In the present context, Mark may be wanting to emphasize again the need for the followers of Jesus to continue his messianic mission. This, after all, is the reason why they are called to be his people (Mark 3:14; see 6:7-13).

Only the mother and brothers of Jesus are involved in seeking to keep Jesus from embarrassing them (Mark 3:31-32). But when Mark describes the new family as "whoever does the will of God," it is notable that Jesus calls them his sisters as well as his brothers and his mother (3:35).

The inclusion of sisters among those who do the will of God is thoroughly consistent with the positive role ascribed to women disciples throughout this Gospel. Here their understanding and faith frequently stand over against the unbelief of the male leaders of the Christian community. Peter's mother-in-law is the first to "serve" Jesus as the ideal disciple (Mark 1:31; see 10:45; 15:41). The faith of the woman with an issue of blood stands in striking contrast to the ridicule of the disciples (5:24b-34). The Syrophoenician woman is the first person to understand the messianic mission of Jesus as involving both Jews and Gentiles (7:24-30), in contrast to the disciples' lack of understanding (8:14-21).

Likewise, the poor widow who gives all her money provides a model for teaching the disciples about commitment (Mark 12:41-44). The woman of Bethany anoints Jesus in preparation for his death and is told that "wherever the good news is proclaimed in the whole world, what she has done will be told in remembrance of her" (14:3-9). But the leaders plot to betray and kill Jesus.

Finally, women standing by Jesus at his crucifixion are in sharp contrast to the twelve: one has betrayed Jesus (Mark 14:43-47), one has denied him (14:66-72), and the other ten have fled (14:50-52). Mark says these women "used to follow him and provided for him when he was in Galilee; and there were many other women who had come up with him to Jerusalem." They view the death of Jesus (Mark 15:40-41) and witness his burial (15:42-47). At the empty tomb, they receive the gracious message from the divine messenger: "Go, tell his disciples and Peter that he is going ahead of you to Galilee; there you will see him, just as he told you" (16:7).

Thus Jesus displayed an outrageously open attitude toward women, but the early church struggled to follow his example. They remembered the names of the brothers of Jesus, but do not mention the names of his sisters (Mark 6:3). They recalled the name of the person in whose house Jesus was anointed, but omitted the name of the woman who did it— even though he had promised that "wherever the good news is proclaimed in the whole world, what she has done will be told in remembrance of her" (14:3-9). Mark seeks to redress the balance of contemporary Christian chauvinism and stresses the faithfulness of the women disciples in the ministry of Jesus. It would be impossible for him to speak about people doing the will of God without making sure that readers understand that women are included.

Obedience is the obverse side of grace. Mark's final "whoever" (Mark 3:35) demonstrates how radically open is the Christian community. Whoever does the will of God belongs to the family of God. Sex roles and status symbols play no role in the Christian community. The twelve have been called to form the nucleus of the new people of God, but this is not to be thought of in a hierarchical sense. Their call to community is not an elitist one. Everyone who does the will of God is admitted on the same basis, not only as brothers and sisters of one another, but even of Jesus himself. The one who is their leader is also their brother. They journey together as the wandering family of God.

Let's Keep Together (Matthew 18:10-22)

Mark's interest in the reality of the new community of the people of God is carried further by Matthew. Writing to a church facing the bitter potential of division, he repeatedly stresses the need for continual reconciliation within the community. He incorporates into his Gospel many sayings and stories on this subject, drawn from other sources and traditions. Harnack suggested that Matthew has, in fact, written an expanded edition of Mark as a "community book." Certainly, he has added to Mark more than a chapter of sayings on the nature of community relationships (Matt. 17:24—18:35), but the community dimension is not restricted to this one chapter. The whole Gospel is imbued with the corporate spirit.

Matthew is writing to a conservative Jewish-Christian community which considered itself the true Israel. He repeatedly stresses the need for a spirit of openness and forgiveness to take the place of an attitude of legalism and paternalism. The leaders of the conservative section of the church understood themselves to belong to the tradition of the teachers of Israel (Matt. 23:1-12). They expected their people to observe the Law right down to the smallest details (23:23-24). The leaders of the charismatic section of the church gloried in their miraculous powers and daring prophecies, while adopting a libertine view of the legal tradition (7:13-23).

Over against both of these groups, Matthew repeatedly emphasizes that in the royal law of love, Jesus has fulfilled the Law and the Prophets (5:17-20; 7:12; 22:34-40). Throughout his Gospel, he calls for the same messianic ethic to be demonstrated in the life of the community (5:21-48; 7:7-29; and many places). More than any other Gospel writer, Matthew continually asserts that the love of God must always be accompanied by a corresponding love of one's neighbor. This dominates his understanding of the church.

[Jesus said,] "Take care that you do not despise one of these little ones; for, I tell you, in heaven their angels continually see the face of my Father in heaven. What do you think? If a shepherd has a hundred sheep, and one of them has gone astray, does he not leave the ninety-nine on the mountains and go in search of the one that went astray? And if he finds it, truly I tell you, he rejoices over it more than over the ninety-nine that never went astray. So it is not the will of your Father in heaven that one of these little ones should be lost.

"If another member of the church sins ["against you" is not in key early manuscripts], go and point out the fault when the two of you are alone. If the member listens to you, you have regained that one. But if you are not listened to, take one or two others along with you, so that every word may be confirmed by the evidence of two or three witnesses. If the member refuses to listen to them, tell it to the church; and if the offender refuses to listen even to the church, let such a one be to you as a Gentile and a tax collector. Truly I tell you, whatever you bind on earth will be bound in heaven, and whatever you loose on earth will be loosed in heaven. Again, truly I tell you, if two of you agree on earth about anything you ask, it will be done for you by my Father in heaven. For where two or three are gathered in my name, I am there among them."

Then Peter came and said to him, "Lord, if another member of the church sins against me, how often should I forgive? As many as seven times?" Jesus said to him, "Not seven times, but, I tell you, seventy-seven times [or: seventy times seven]."

(Matt. 18:10-22)

Using materials drawn from a number of sources, Matthew edits and arranges them into a coherent whole. He develops another of his sermons on the sermons of Jesus. These are characteristic of his presentation of the ministry of Jesus: Sermon on the Mount (Matt. 5—7); missionary discourse (10); parables of the kingdom (13); the messianic community (18); and parables of the end (24—25). Through his account of Jesus teaching the disciples, Matthew addresses himself to the church of his day. He seeks to commend to his rather conservative (Jewish Christian) church a less legalistic, more gracious and forgiving approach to Christian community.

A Church Characterized by Grace and Love

Matthew begins his sermon on pastoral relationships within the Christian community with a question on the nature of true greatness (Matt. 18:1). Then he develops it through a series of sayings about a child (18:2-5) and about "little ones" (18:6, 10, 14). Into this sermon Matthew inserts the parable of the lost sheep, to illustrate the responsibility Christians have toward fellow believers who have gone astray (18:12-14).

The truly great in the kingdom of heaven, says Matthew, are those who have repented, those who have returned to childlike thought, will, and action. Such disciples are living out their lives with a childlike trust and lack of concern. They are the ones who have learned to pray "Abba, Father" (Luke 11:2; Gal. 4:6; Rom. 8:15) and to trust God to supply all their needs (Matt. 6:25-34). They are "the poor in spirit" of the Beatitudes, to whom Jesus has promised the kingdom of heaven (5:3).

Discipleship involves a reversal of value judgments about people, status, and titles. In Judaism, children had no rights, smallness was despised, and their teachers were called "rabbis" or "great ones." "He who learns from the small," said the rabbis, "is like one who eats sour grapes or drinks wine before it has matured." Elsewhere they declare: "A girl who is a devotee, and a widow who goes around idly, and a little one whose mouth is not yet filled, lo, these ruin the world." Not so, says Matthew! Small is beautiful!

The small, the little ones, are those who trust in God (Matt. 18:1-5), who believe in Jesus (18:6, the only time the first three Gospels speak directly of faith in Jesus!). They should never be despised, for they have guardian angels in heaven (18:10), and it is not God's will that any of them should be lost (18:14). The disciples are therefore warned against causing them to stumble (18:6) and are encouraged to do all in their power to win back any of them who have gone astray (18:12-14).

These principles are illustrated in the parable of the lost sheep (Matt. 18:12-14), which has a poetic structure, perhaps in three stanzas. Using Luke's version of the parable, Kenneth E. Bailey has sought to outline the structure of what he considers to be the original form of the parable:

A   What man of *you*, having a hundred sheep
B   and having lost *one* of them
C   does not leave the *ninety-nine* in the wilderness
  1   and go after the *lost* one
    2   until he *finds* it, and having *found* it
      3   he places it upon his shoulders *rejoicing*
        4   And coming *to the home*
        4^1 he calls *to the friends* and neighbors
      3^1 saying to them, *rejoice* with me
    2^1 because I have *found* my sheep
  1^1 which was *lost*
A^1 I say to *you* that there is more *joy* in heaven
B^1 over *one* sinner who repents
C^1 *than over ninety-nine righteous persons who need no repentance.*

(Bailey, 144-145)

While there are some difficulties in this analysis of the first and third stanzas, the central section is clearer and heightens the climax on the "joy at restoration," the major emphasis of the original parable.

Matthew has adapted the parable so that it now speaks more directly to his own church situation and fits more appropriately in the context in which he has placed it. The sheep is not "lost" (as in Luke 15:4), but has merely wandered or "gone astray" (Matt. 18:12). It is not God's will that any of "these little ones" should be "lost" (18:14). He is clearly talking to the pastoral situation within his church. Three times in the first part of this chapter, Matthew speaks of "these little ones" (18:6, 10, 14). The designation "who believe in me" in the first instance (18:6) indicates that he is referring to members of the Christian community.

The use of the term wander or "go astray" (Matt. 18:12c, 12e, 13) is instructive. This is the very term used to describe those who wander away after the false teachers, in the eschatological discourse describing conditions in the end-time (24:4-5, 11, 24). Three of the references have been taken over from Mark, but in the one found only in Matthew we are told:

"Then many will fall away, and they will betray one another and hate one another. And many false prophets will arise and lead many astray. And because of the increase of lawlessness, the love of many will grow cold" (24:10-12).

Matthew believed that his church was living in the end-time and therefore calls on them to be particularly careful in their approach to people who have been led astray by false teachers. Try to win them back! "It is not the will of your Father in heaven that one of these little ones should be lost" (18:14). If God is unwilling to lose one of these little ones, then someone in the community had better get up and go after the one who is going astray. If you see your brothers or sisters wandering off, for heaven's sake, go and discuss the matter with them—and if they can't walk, carry them home!

The parable originally told of God's gracious activity in seeking the outsider, the one who has gone astray and who has been written off as lost. It told of God's joy over the restoration of one who had been separated from his own people. Matthew applies the parable to his community situation. There were some who were astray, and no one from the community was even bothering to do anything about it.

The original parable had a definite communal context. A peasant family might own ten to fifteen sheep, at most forty. But when we are told that a person has a hundred sheep, we are aware that the reference is to a flock which belongs to the extended family or perhaps even to the village. It would have been cared for by more than one shepherd. The loss of the sheep would therefore have been a loss sustained by the whole community. The same is true of the wandering brother or sister. If a wandering brother or sister is lost, the loss is sustained by the whole people of God. Should they be found, the whole community rejoices! For the whole community has regained a brother or sister.

When the apocryphal Gospel of Thomas (an early non-biblical collection of 114 sayings and parables of Jesus with some Gnostic tendencies) retold this parable, it said: "The kingdom is like a shepherd who has one hundred sheep. One of them went astray, which was the largest. He left behind the ninety-nine, he sought for the one until he found it.

Having tired himself out, he said to the sheep, I love you more than the ninety-nine" (G. Thomas 107). Note the difference! Thomas says that the shepherd went after the sheep because it was the most valuable one. Jesus says he went after the sheep simply because it was lost.

Matthew underlines this necessity of searching out even the least of the little ones and carrying them back to the fold. In the Christian community, the emphasis is not upon status, size, and importance. It is a community of grace and love. If there is a priority, it is the priority of the little ones! It is not the will of the heavenly Father that one of these little ones should be lost (Matt. 18:14).

Pastoral Care Through Forgiveness and Reconciliation

Matthew's church was already engaged in a kind of pastoral care among the erring and had, in fact, developed a four-stage rule of church discipline: (1) The person aware of the offense should first of all speak to the offender privately. (2) If that fails, the aware person should speak with the offender before witnesses. (3) If that produces no effect, the matter should be reported to the church. (4) If the offender refuses to listen even to the church, that one should be excommunicated.

The first three steps in the procedure are intended to express direct brotherly and sisterly pastoral care and to bring the sinner back into the fold. But if all these measures fail, the offender is lost as a brother or sister and is no longer regarded as a member of the community. The burden of responsibility is on the person who knows that the fellow member is sinning (Matt. 18:15), and who is then required to "go" and take the initiative with the offender.

The "two or three witnesses" may have originally been included in order to strengthen "the reproof with a view toward restoration" (Gundry, 368). However, note the background of the Old Testament injunction that "only on the evidence of two or three witnesses shall a charge be sustained" (Deut. 19:15). Thus it is probable that this second stage has at least the overtones of being undertaken in a manner that would facilitate possible later exclusion, even if this action is not yet finally contemplated.

The community meeting would no doubt be seeking to win back the wandering member. But when called in response to such a situation, there is again at least a threat of less conciliatory action being undertaken shortly unless, one hopes, the offender sees the error of sinning and repents. The concluding declaration of excommunication has a note of finality: "Let such a one be to you as a Gentile and a tax collector" (Matt. 18:17). The declaration shows the Jewish origin of this community rule and indicates that Matthew the tax collector was probably not the author of this originally anonymous Gospel. From the perspective of his experience, the designation of "tax collector" would have served as a sign of openness for the gospel, a symbol for inclusion rather than exclusion! If the church follows Jesus' style of ministry, tax collectors are part of the mission opportunity for the gospel.

The Jewish community at Qumran had a similar type of community rule: "When anyone has a charge against his neighbor, he is to prosecute it truthfully, humbly, and humanely. He is not to speak to him angrily or querulously or arrogantly or in any wicked mood. He is not to bear hatred [toward him in the inner recesses] of his heart. When he has a charge against him, he is to proffer it on the selfsame day and not to render himself liable to penalty by nursing a grudge. Furthermore, no man is to bring a charge publicly against his neighbor except he prove it by witnesses" (Community Rule: 1QS 5.24—6.1).

The author of the First Gospel was happy that his church was at least exercising some pastoral responsibility toward members who were going astray. They were at least given a number of opportunities to return to the fold. However, because of Matthew's understanding of the nature of grace and the corresponding necessity of forgiveness and reconciliation, he pushes the matter much further and finally redirects their pastoral intentions. He adds the story of Peter (Matt. 18:21-22) and the parable of the unforgiving servant (18:23-35). Thereby he transfers the threat from the erring member who continues in sin (18:17) to the righteous brother or sister who wants to draw a line on forgiving the lost (18:35).

The original text in Matthew says, "If your brother sins, go and discuss the matter with him privately" (18:15). But later scribes added the words "against you" so that it read "if your brother sins against you." Thus they related it only to personal slights and indignities. This is the emphasis of Peter's question (18:21). But the community rule originally had a wider perspective. In this context it would have included those who had wandered off after false teachers, those who had begun to lead lawless lives, and others. The care for the brother or sister is more loving, comphrehensive, and outgoing than just being concerned over a slight to oneself (compare Ezek. 3:16-21).

Peter, the representative leader of the community, has at least learned that forgiveness must take the place of vengeance (Matt. 5:21-48). Yet he is still asking about the limits and is still counting the offenses (18:21). He has not learned what forgiveness and reconciliation are all about. You can set no limits on Christian forgiveness, for in God's mathematics seventy times seven does not amount to four hundred and ninety! Members of the Christian community must be willing to go on forgiving their brothers and sisters, forever, if needed.

In rabbinic discussions it was sufficient that you forgive your brother four times. Peter's question may represent an attempt to go beyond Judaism and to offer what might well be considered perfect forgiveness, signaled by the number seven. But even that is not sufficient in the Christian community. There may also be an allusion here to the story of Cain and Lamech: "If Cain is avenged sevenfold, truly Lamech seventy-sevenfold" (Gen. 4:24). "The unlimited revenge of primitive man has given place to the unlimited forgiveness of Christians" (M'Neile, 268).

The apocryphal Gospel of the Nazarenes (a second-century Aramaic Gospel closely related to Matthew, but known only from fragments in other writings) has an interesting variation: "Jesus said, 'If your brother has sinned with a word and has made you reparation, receive him seven times in a day. Simon his disciple said to him: Seven times in a day? The Lord answered and said to him: Yes, I say to you, until seventy times seven times. For in the prophets also after they were anointed with the Holy Spirit, the word of sin was found' " (in Jerome, *Against Pelagius* 3.2).

Matthew is being quite pastoral in the way he has arranged his material at this point. His church has long since adopted a community rule about how they should treat sinners. It is not unduly harsh: at least, persons have to be given three chances before they can be excommunicated. But Matthew recognized the danger of legalism in the operation of such rules. Instead of making a frontal attack on the tradition of his church, alongside that tradition he places Peter's question and Jesus' answer. By so doing he ensures that the church will think seriously before using the rule of excommunication again.

"Matthew is well aware of the danger that besets the little ones of Jesus in their lives; many have already been lost. And so he can only warn against causing offense, appeal to men to go after those who have gone astray, to exert every effort to help those who have fallen into sin come back, but never to be vindictive about insults or injury, remembering always the great forgiveness of God and extending such forgiveness to others. For when forgiveness that has been received is shown to others, it no longer has meaning for the heart and God takes it back" (Schweizer, *Matthew*, 379).

The Secret Is Jesus at the Center

At least ten adult males must be present for corporate worship in Judaism, but the presence of Jesus is promised to even the smallest group meeting in the name of Jesus (Matt. 18:20). No distinction is made between male and female, small and great! It is the presence of Jesus among the little flock which constitutes the group into a Christian community. It is also the presence of Jesus, the incarnate love and grace of God, that makes reconciliation possible (18:23-35).

Again, the word of Jesus may have been formulated against the background of a Jewish saying: "If two sit together and the words of the Law [are spoken] between them, the Shekinah (the presence of God) rests between them" (Mishnah Aboth 3.2; see also 3.3, "three"; 3.6, "ten").

If this is the situation which gave rise to the saying of Jesus, then the emphasis is that Jesus has taken the place of the Law, and the Christian church has replaced the Jewish community as the location of the divine presence.

For Matthew, the importance of the presence of Jesus in the midst of the community can be seen in the prominence given to this idea in both the introduction and the conclusion of his Gospel. An angel of the Lord declares that the birth of Jesus fulfills what the Lord had spoken through the prophet: " 'The virgin shall conceive and bear a son, and they shall name him Emmanuel,' which means, 'God is with us' " (the explanation was added by the Evangelist; Matt. 1:23). The great commission concludes with the promise of the risen Christ: "I am with you always, to the end of the age" (28:20). With these words, the Gospel ends. The presence of God in Jesus Christ at the heart of the community is the decisive element in the Christian community. It is the presence of Jesus as incarnate grace and love that makes forgiveness and reconciliation possible.

Because of the presence of Jesus in the community, the little flock is even promised that their prayers will be answered (Matt. 18:19) and that their judgments will be binding (18:18). Matthew, however, delights in the prayer of forgiveness (6:9-15) and in the decision of reconciliation (18:23-35). The possibilities of forgiveness and of reconciliation are, on this occasion, granted to the entire community, and not merely to the leaders. In Matthew 16:19 this authority is given to Peter only. Yet Peter is the representative leader of the church (10:2), and all members are called upon to exercise this ministry within the Christian community and to bind and loose (in 18:18 "you" is plural).

Matthew does not want the community to be tempted to ignore his teaching on the absolute necessity of forgiveness. Hence, he concludes his sermon on communal relationships with the parable of the unmerciful servant who is condemned to torture by the king (Matt. 18:23-35). The last words are: "So my heavenly Father will also do to every one of you, if you do not forgive your brother or sister from your heart" (18:35).

What Are Friends For, Anyway? (Acts 2:42-47; 4:32-37)

Mark's emphasis on the reality of the Christian community and Matthew's portrayal of the possibilities of continuing reconciliation within the community are carried further by Luke by his second volume. In Acts, he again seeks to instruct Christians in the way of the Lord and to demonstrate to pagans the superiority of the Christian way of living.

Like the Gospel of Luke, which Acts presupposes and without which it cannot be understood, Acts is a theological work telling of the Christian way and encouraging people to join forces with it. This means that in his second volume, as in his first, the Evangelist is not primarily interested in what happened once upon a time. Instead, he pursues what can happen time and time again as the risen Lord is proclaimed by the apostolic missionaries and the church moves forward in the power of the Spirit. Speeches, narratives, and summary statements are arranged and edited to display the mighty outward movement of the church. This expansion is attested by God (through divine miracles and other charismatic manifestations) and applauded by the people (with only the Jewish opponents hardening their hearts).

> They devoted themselves to the apostles' teaching and fellowship [Greek: *koinōnia*], to the breaking of bread and the prayers.
>
> Awe came upon everyone, because many wonders and signs were being done by the apostles. All who believed were together and had all things in common; they would sell their possessions and goods and distribute the proceeds to all, as any had need. Day by day, as they spent much time together in the temple, they broke bread at home and ate their food with glad and generous hearts [AG: unaffected joy], praising God and having the goodwill of all the people. And day by day the Lord added to their number those who were being saved. . . .
>
> Now the whole group of those who believed were of one heart and soul, and no one claimed private ownership of any possessions, but everything they owned was held in common. With great power the apostles gave their testimony to the resurrection of the Lord Jesus, and great grace was upon them all. There was not a needy person among them, for as many as

owned lands or houses sold them and brought the proceeds of
what was sold. They laid it at the apostles' feet, and it was distributed to each as any had need. There was a Levite, a native of
Cyprus, Joseph, to whom the apostles gave the name Barnabas
(which means "son of encouragement"). He sold a field that
belonged to him, then brought the money, and laid it at the
apostles' feet.   (Acts 2:42-47; 4:32-37)

Luke writes quite some time after the destruction of Jerusalem by the Romans. He describes the life of the early
church in that city, not as an antiquarian would, but as an
apologist and teacher seeking to commend its life and work
to others. This interest can be seen most clearly in the summary statements of community life in the Jerusalem church
(Acts 2:42-47; 4:32-35; 5:12-16). He is obviously intent on
commending this style of life to his contemporaries. As he
presents it in these summary statements, the Jerusalem
church was an ideal community with a remarkable life of
prayer and table fellowship, complete harmony, and sharing
of material possessions, attested by God and respected by
people.

A Vibrant Spiritual Life

According to the stories and summaries of the opening chapters of Acts, the spiritual life of the new community of believers has two focal points: the temple, center and symbol of the
old order which is even then passing away; and the home,
center and symbol of the new which is shortly to replace the
old. The early church in Jerusalem is presented as one that is
aware of both its traditional roots within Judaism and of its
developing life as a new community of the people of God.

The new community gathers in the temple at the hours
prescribed for prayer (Acts 2:46; 3:1; 5:12) and meets together in private homes, breaking bread and sharing meals (2:46;
5:42). The form of communal prayers, even in private houses, probably follows Jewish customs at this early stage. How
ever, there is intimate awareness of God and childlike relationship, which they have entered into through Jesus Christ.
Undoubtedly, these are transforming their praying.

As they come to learn more of the unique position which they occupy, they can address God as "Abba, Father" (Gal. 4:6; Rom. 8:15). This intimate term, used every day by Palestinian children in addressing their fathers, was unknown in the prayer literature of Judaism and contrary to all they understood of the nature of God. Yet it is Jesus' favorite term (Mark 14:36), which he teaches also to his disciples (Luke 11:2). This family relationship with God through Jesus soon marks the Christian community off from society around them, even from the people of Israel.

Similarly, the Christian community is to become distinctive through their shared meals and the unaffected joy that marks these occasions (Acts 2:46). In the early church of Acts, the breaking of bread seems to have be the term used to describe both the liturgical celebration on Saturday evening (20:7) and also the communal meals (2:46). Whether in liturgical acts or communal meals, the breaking of bread has a special significance. It reveals not only the Last Supper (Luke 22:14-19), but also the salvation meals which Jesus shared with the tax collectors and sinners (5:29; 7:37). It also builds on the feeding miracles with the four and five thousand (Mark 6:30-44; 8:1-10, the most frequently recorded miracle in the Gospel tradition!).

All of these are understood as divine anticipations of the messianic banquet to be celebrated in the kingdom of God (Matt. 8:11). In sure hope of this final salvation, symbolized in the messianic banquet, the early community "shared their meals with unaffected joy" (Acts 2:46, AG).

In all of the community's activities, whether in the temple or in private homes, the apostles, the representative leaders of the new people of God, play an important role. We are told that the believers devote themselves to the apostles' teaching (Acts 2:42). The apostles give powerful testimony to the resurrection (4:33), perform many wonders and signs (2:43; 5:15-16), and form the nucleus of the community (4:32). The twelve have been with Jesus throughout his ministry (1:22) and thus guarantee the authenticity of the Jesus tradition and the continuity of salvation history. They link the time of the church in the power of the Spirit with the time of Jesus. The centrality of Jesus in the life of the community continues through the presence of its Spirit-filled leaders and this ensures a vibrant spiritual life.

Fellowship in a Shared Lifestyle

In the early church, the koinonia (Acts 2:42) linked together all members in a brotherly and sisterly fellowship, which found expression in mutual help, shared suffering, and common ownership of property (2:45; 4:32-35). According to Luke's first summary, the believers "devoted themselves to . . . fellowship" (2:42). "[They] had all things in common [and] they would sell their possessions and goods and distribute the proceeds to all, as any had need" (2:44-45). In the second summary, we are told that "the whole group of those who believed were of one heart and soul, and no one claimed private ownership of any possessions, but everything they owned was held in common" (4:32). "There was not a needy person among them, for as many as owned lands or houses sold them and brought the proceeds of what was sold. They laid it at the apostles' feet, and it was distributed to each as any had need" (4:34-35).

In the second summary statement (Acts 4:32-35), Luke is seeking to show that the lifestyle of the early church fulfilled "both the Hellenistic ideal of friendship and the Jewish expectation of a land free of need" (Crowe, 30). The statement that "they were united in heart and soul and not one of them considered anything his private property" (4:32, AG) fulfills the Greek ideal of friendship.

Thus Aristotle taught, "All the feelings that constitute friendship for others are an extension of regard for self. Moreover, all proverbs agree with this; for example, 'Friends have one soul between them.' 'Friends' goods are common property' " (*Nicomachean Ethics* 9.8.2). Cicero wrote, "Nothing, moreover, is more conducive to love and intimacy than compatibility of character in good men; for when two people have the same ideals and the same tastes, it is a natural consequence that each loves the other as himself; and the result is, as Pythagoras requires of ideal friendship, that several are united in one" (*On Moral Obligation* 1.17.26).

In appealing to Jews, the statement "there was not a needy person among them" (Acts 4:35) is to be understood as the fulfillment of the sabbatical year regulations of Deuteronomy 15:4-5. In the Greek Septuagint version (tr. by AG), that text says, "Let there be no one in want among you then. For the Lord will bless you in the land the Lord your God gives you for your inheritance only if you pay careful attention to the voice of the Lord your God, keeping and observing all these commandments that I command you this day." The pious representatives of Israel, Jesus, and the early church, as Luke describes them, observe all the commandments. They care for the poor, and there is no one in need.

Luke cites the example of Barnabas in selling his land, not because it is an exceptional case, as has often been argued, but because he was one of the well-known leaders of the church in Antioch and a fellow worker with Paul (Acts 11:30; 13:1—15:35; 1 Cor. 9:6; Gal. 2:1-10; Col. 4:10). The reference to Barnabas as "Joseph, whom the apostles named Barnabas (which means 'son of Exhortation')" (Acts 4:36, AG) is interesting in this regard, particularly since the name "Barnabas" does not literally mean "son of exhortation." Throughout Acts, Luke provides the second names for persons who could otherwise be confused with others bearing the same name.

It is natural, therefore, that in our present story, Joseph should also be named "Barnabas" to avoid confusion with "Joseph called Barsabbas, who was also know as Justus" (Acts 1:23). However, this is the only time we are told of someone being given a name in this way by the apostles (4:36), and on only one other occasion in Acts are we given the interpretation of a person's name (13:8). The giving of the name by the apostles (a sign of authority) is consistent with the role of the apostles in the Lucan summary statements (2:42-43; 4:33, 35; 5:12, 14).

The parallel interpretation of the name of Elymas (Acts 13:8) indicates that Luke has in mind the *role* of the person rather than the literal meaning of the name, the part Barnabas plays in the present story. The name Barnabas is interpreted as meaning "son of Exhortation" or "son of Encouragement," "one who exhorts or encourages." He sells a field and presents the money to the apostles (4:37) so that it can be distributed to any who might be in need (4:35). Thus Barnabas is fulfilling his role as an encourager or exhorter to faithfulness in the Lord, even as he does later at Antioch (11:22-24). Ananias and Sapphira (5:1-11) are the antitype!

It is difficult to be certain of the exact form of community ownership practiced by the early church and commended by Luke. At one point he speaks of a complete sharing of goods (Acts 2:44; 4:32), but elsewhere it appears that individuals like Barnabas (and Ananias and Sapphira) sell their land and bring the proceeds from the sale to the apostles (4:34—5:11). Was it that they resigned their personal possessions to a common fund? Or did they merely give up (or relativize) private ownership while retaining personal possessions unless (or until) they were needed to relieve the poverty of fellow members? Our difficulty at this point may be theologically significant.

Among the Essenes, the sharing of goods was strictly organized and fixed by law. The Qumran community demanded that every novice who entered the community had to leave his possessions with the overseer. If, after his year of probation, he was accepted as a full member of the order, he had to hand them over to the community. The rules were strict, and the needs of the community were met from these resources and from their work in various crafts and in agriculture. Josephus wrote of the Essenes, "Riches they despise, and their community of goods is truly admirable; you will not find one among them distinguished by greater opulence than another. They have a law that new members on admission to the sect shall confiscate their property to the order, with the result that you will nowhere see either abject poverty or inordinate wealth; the individual's possessions join the common stock and all, like brothers, enjoy a single patrimony" (*Jewish War* 2.122; see Manual of Discipline: 1QS 1.11-13; 6.19-22; 9.8-9, 22).

The early church's communal arrangements were certainly different from the Essenes, and from this arises difficulty. As Luke records the story, these sharing patterns are not strictly organized and not fixed by laws and regulations.

It is a spontaneous "love communism" of the community, and they seek to live out all aspects of their life under the guidance of the Spirit. At this point they are simply continuing Jesus' carefree attitude toward material possessions. Their service to God and their church family fellowship take priority over their concern for the things of this age. As their concern for one another is heightened through their community relationships, so their concern for the future retreats into the background. Their security is in God and in the new community of the people of God. They freely place their property at the disposal of the community, to be used as their leaders determine. In their fellowship, social distinctions are abolished and poverty destroyed.

The twentieth-century church has largely overlooked the community example left by the early Christians. On one hand, the Roman church has tended to restrict its relevance to the religious orders. On the other hand, the contemporary Protestant church has tended to ignore, or cavalierly dismiss, this "spontaneous love communism." The dismissal is based on a number of rationalizations, beginning with the fact that the spontaneity of love and sharing did not last. Indeed, it failed, according to this view: wasn't this the reason Paul had to make a collection among the Gentile churches for the poor saints in Jerusalem?

Second, objectors reason that such sharing is only possible in a church that believes in the imminent return of Jesus Christ; their resources would soon evaporate if they had to live like that for too long. Third, the accounts of such sharing are merely descriptive of a historical event and are not in any way prescriptive or significant for others. Finally, in an attempt to dismiss the possibility of the sharing of the early Christian community as being an example for Christians today, many claim that it was only Luke's idealized picture of life in the early church. It need not be taken too seriously because it never actually existed as Luke describes it. Just as no utopian writer expects to be imitated in real life, so Luke did not intend the church to follow this way. How comfortable it is for rich Christians if such rationalizations excuse us from serious contemporary sharing!

We should be wary of hasty and superficial judgments in these matters. There is no evidence for the supposed "failure" of the communal experiment. Acts 11:28 describes a severe famine in the time of Claudius. The severe strains on the already depleted Jewish economy are sufficient to account for the collection. Second, even if the early church believed in the imminent return of Jesus Christ, Luke focused on the present mission and did not emphasize that he would come *soon* (Acts 1:8, 11). This was one of the reasons behind the writing of Acts.

Third and most important, like the Gospels, Acts is not merely descriptive, and nor is Luke's theology to be evaluated as holding only historical significance. Just as we would grant Paul's theology a broader application into our contemporary situation, so Luke's theology deserves serious consideration. Finally, the example of Ananias and Sapphira (Acts 5:1-11) indicates that this is not a utopian picture. Though it is to some extent idealized, the positive example of Barnabas (4:36-37) and the overall purpose of Luke-Acts indicates that Luke is hoping that his church will adopt a similar lifestyle.

In our churches the level of fellowship rarely goes beyond that of a Rotary luncheon or a local hangout, being able to call a person by the first name, slapping one on the back, and telling a joke about another. We may well ponder the truth Luke is seeking to express—Christian fellowship needs to find concrete expression in the lives of its members. We may wonder whether in today's world, material possessions can stand beyond the perimeter of that fellowship even if the form of sharing necessarily differs from that of the early church.

Approved by God and by the People

The "Good Housekeeping Seal of Approval" was awarded the early community both by God and by the people. The first summary of their corporate life assures us that the believers enjoyed the favor of all the people (Acts 2:46). The third says quite simply that "the people held them in high esteem" (5:13). Divine approval is attested by the many miracles and signs wrought by the apostles (2:43; 5:12) and by the fact that "day by day the Lord added to their number those who were being saved" (2:47). Indeed, when persecution created a situation in which "none . . . dared to join them," God added more and more "believers" to the community, "great numbers of both men and women" (5:13-14). Such is the style of communal life that Luke commends to his readers. It is not merely an ideal: it is an ideal which Luke hopes will be realized in his day, so that his own church might win the approval of God and of the people.

Revolutionary Friendships

The communal dimension is one of the characteristics of early Christianity. All of the Evangelists recognize that to be a follower of Jesus is to be a member of a community committed to a life on the road. However, as we have already seen, each Evangelist's situation and theological emphasis is different.

Mark was writing to a church which was enjoying a powerful success theology and had structured its life around an oppressive hierarchical ministry. He deliberately uses the image of the family when speaking of relationships within the Christian community. The new family of the people of God has Jesus at its center and spends its time listening to his teaching and seeking to do the will of God (Mark 3:31-35). Although Mark recognizes the historical significance of the twelve and realizes that they were all male (3:13-19), sex roles and status symbols are to have no place in the community of faith. Everyone who does the will of God is admitted on the same basis, as sisters and brothers of one another and of Jesus himself.

The one who is their Leader is also their brother, and he is the one who has established forever the obedient family of grace. Mark repeatedly reminds his people of the inherent weakness of the powerful while stressing the faithfulness of women disciples. The new family of God is a community of costly grace, and the powerless are models of sacrificial service (Mark 1:31; 10:45), serving Jesus and following him to the very cross itself (15:41).

Matthew wrote at a later stage to a rather conservative

Jewish Christian church which was always strong on discipline. He repeatedly stresses the need for a less legalistic, more gracious and forgiving approach to Christian community. It is a time of persecution, when members are apparently being led astray by false teachers (Matt. 24:10-12). Yet he urges the church to take the initiative and to go out after them and bring them back to the fold (18:10-14).

To a divided community, Matthew stresses the necessity for repeated forgiveness and reconciliation; members are to go on forgiving their sisters and brothers forever, if need be (Matt. 18:21-22). The presence of Jesus in the midst of the community assures them that their prayers will be answered and their decisions binding (18:18-20). But they must always remember that they are intended to be a community of grace. If they refuse to forgive one another, they will not be forgiven by God. By their own actions, they will have left themselves open to the judgment (18:23-35).

Luke was seeking to commend Christianity to God-fearing Gentiles (Luke 1:1-4). He was troubled by the changes that had been made in his community through the entrance of a prominent group of rich Christians (6:20-26). Luke presents the early church in Jerusalem as an ideal community with a remarkable life of prayer and table fellowship, complete harmony, and sharing of material possessions. The group is attested by God and respected by people (Acts 2:42-47; 4:32-35).

The Jerusalem church is a community aware of its roots within Judaism and of the new life developing in its midst through the ministry of the Holy Spirit. The apostles exercise strong leadership and guarantee the authenticity of the Jesus tradition and the continuity of salvation history. The lifestyle of the community fulfills Hellenistic ideals of friendship and Jewish expectations of equality as they spontaneously share their possessions so that no one is in need. The miracles are seen as evidence of divine approval, and the large number of converts joining the church is indicative of their high standing among the people.

It is somewhat different today. Theodore Roszack has commented that "alienation is the disease from which our age is dying." This deep alienation and pervasive individualism of our culture has invaded our churches and robbed us of much of our courage and enthusiasm. It has frequently stripped us of our families and friends and left us broken and wounded on the side of the road. The gospel provides a powerful antidote to these destructive tendencies.

The French writer Paul Valery once said, "Alone we are always in bad company" (quoted by Soelle and Steffensky, 59). But together we may find God in our midst. It is both sobering and encouraging to realize that, for Christians, God has always existed in community—Father, Son, and Holy Spirit. This is the deep and relevant truth of the Trinity, that the being of God and the development of faith is always a communal activity.

Following Jesus on the road always brings us into new relationships with sisters and brothers who are on the same journey. God knows that it would be a terrible journey to undertake on our own, for so few of us are people of vision and courage. Alone we are easily discouraged and diverted into less-demanding enterprises. But together we are able to dream dreams and plan and scheme and work toward the kingdom of God, where God's will is done on earth as it is in heaven. When we remain fragmented and isolated, the powerful of the earth are able to beat us every time. Together with Jesus, we may become a force that is able to defy the demonic and overthrow the physical and spiritual oppression that is rampant in so many places. We can offer the liberating power of the gospel to women and men groaning under the weight of their oppressors.

The church is beginning to recognize the need for community and to realize its potential for human liberation. The widespread popularity of small groups in the churches demonstrates the need and the potential for a renewal of the church through community. However, we are seeing the most dramatic signs of a new reality emerging in the poor communities of Latin America (the base communities), and in the communal experiments of the West, and in the renewed Catholic orders. They can be variously described as prophetic "Abrahamic minorities," as Dom Helder Camara likes to call them, as subversive cells, as parables of the kingdom. They transcend class and cultural boundaries, ignore racial division, and express a new internationalism. They are opposed to dominating ideologies and are working for justice and peace throughout the earth.

On the road with Jesus we enter into solidarity with the poor and oppressed and develop revolutionary friendships with power to transform the world. We are traveling together, and together we can work for the liberation of those who suffer injustice. In this process of the liberation of others, we continue to work out our own salvation through the liberation that comes from the life and ministry, the death and resurrection of Jesus Christ. In following Jesus and in traveling with him, we journey together with sisters and brothers on a pilgrimage of liberation and life, working for the salvation of all humanity. Life on the road is a journey from death to life, from alienation to reconciliation, from oppression to liberation, from injustice to peace. It is a journey that can only be made by friends traveling together.

Questions for Discussion

1. Why can't one be a solitary Christian, an individual disciple?

2. Why has community become such an optional extra for Western Christianity?

3. Do you have any revolutionary friendships? What makes them revolutionary?

4. Who are the outsiders today? What would you have to do to make room for them within your group?

5. Can a radically open community survive? Doesn't it have to protect itself?

6. How far can we go in forgiving other people? Are you able to forgive yourself?

7. How might churches or Christian communities offer the liberating power of the gospel to people today?

8. In what ways do the members of your church, community, or group share life together? Would you prefer to share more? Or would you prefer to share less?

5

Jobs Along the Way

Discipleship and Mission

Working for All the People

The call of Jesus which brings the disciples together as the messianic people of God is also the call which sends them out on messianic mission in the world. In each of the stories about discipleship which introduce the first three sections of the Gospel of Mark, discipleship leads on to mission. This is by design, not by chance. Mark took it for granted that the gospel had to be proclaimed and to be lived out in daily obedience, and that the church had to be on mission. The early communities lived through the mission and for the mission. To follow Jesus on the road is to share in his messianic mission.

The distinctive feature of the ministry of Jesus is that, while it is directed primarily toward Israel, it is directed toward *all Israel*. No one is excluded. In fact, he seems to deliberately direct his mission especially toward those who are traditionally regarded as being beyond the fringes of respectability. Jesus associates with the nobodies of society. He pronounces God's blessing on the poor and demonstrates his presence with the persecuted (Matt. 5:3-12) He declares forgiveness of sins to people struggling under the weight of their own past (Mark 2:1-12; Luke 7:36-50). And he invites the outcasts and marginalized people to join him in the kingdom of God (Mark 2:15-17; Luke 14:15-24).

What a strange collection of people Jesus regards as his special friends! He responds openly to lepers, whose physical appearance and supposed danger of contamination have led to their ostracism from society. They are forced to live outside the camp, regarded as "unclean," and denied fellowship with others (Mark 1:40-45; Luke 17:11-19). Jesus enjoys the affection and loyalty of women and children, whose physical powerlessness is being exploited by a male-dominated legal system that has robbed them of their rights (Matt. 8:14-17; 9:20-26; and many places throughout all the Gospels).

Jesus publicly welcomes into his community the despised tax collectors, whose grubby employment and shady business practices have earned them the reputation of being notorious sinners (Matt. 11:19; Mark 2:16-17; Luke 7:37-50). He includes the drunkards and prostitutes, whose habits and morality mean that they can never be admitted by the culture that has created them. He shows an equally open attitude to the spurned Samaritans (Luke 9:52; 10:33; 17:16; John 4:1-42) and Gentiles (Matt. 8:5-13; Mark 7:24-30), whose ethnic backgrounds have resulted in their relegation to second-class status by Israelites of the day. "His following consisted predominantly of the disreputable, the uneducated, the ignorant, those whose religious behavior and moral life stood in their way of access to salvation according to the convictions of the time" (Jeremias, *Theology*, 112).

What is really striking about the mission of Jesus is the way he proclaims forgiveness and salvation through the powerful symbolic action of sharing table fellowship with "sinners." Jesus invites them into his house (Mark 2:15). He reclines at table with them at the festivals (Luke 5:29; 7:37) and promises them places of honor at the messianic banquet of the people of God (Mark 2:17; Matt. 5:5-13).

In the East, even today, family and festival meals are occasions of great social and religious significance. To invite a person to share in this way is regarded as an offer of peace and community. Jesus' meals with tax collectors and sinners are therefore not simply expressions of social generosity and sympathy toward the despised. They are symbolic representations of his mission and message to the world. They are pictorial portrayals of the redeeming grace and love of God. Jesus himself expresses this to the religious leaders who are indignant at his free offer of salvation to the disreputable: "I have come to call not the righteous but sinners!" (Mark 2:17).

The majority of the parables of Jesus are addressed to his opponents who continually criticize him for his openness to all sorts and conditions of people. "Again and again they ask: 'Why do you associate with this riffraff, shunned by all respectable people?' And he replies: 'Because they are sick and need me, because they are truly repentant, and because they feel the gratitude of children forgiven by God. Because, on the other hand, you, with your loveless, self-righteous, disobedient hearts, have rejected the gospel. But, above all, because I know what God is like, so good to the poor, so glad when the lost are found, so overflowing with a father's love for the returning child, so merciful to the despairing, the helpless and the needy. That is why!' " (Jeremias, *Parables*, 146).

The three texts which we will explore in this chapter underline the significance of the mission of the disciples as one of costly grace (Mark), describe the worldwide mission of the Christian community (Matthew), and emphasize the gospel as good news to the poor and oppressed (Luke).

The Work Isn't Easy (Mark 6:7-30)

It is significant that the Gospel of Mark, the first to be written, is the product of the church's missionary endeavors. As such, the book sets out in narrative form the story of the mission of Jesus. Mark does this in a way that conveys to the Christian community the Evangelist's own distinctive understanding of the mission in which he believes they should be engaged. The mission of Jesus and the mission of the disciples have become paradigms for the mission of the church. Mark counters the excitement of those who consider the (imminent) destruction of Jerusalem to be the beginning of the end of the age (Mark 13:1-4). He declares that, although the disciples will undoubtedly undergo persecution in the process, the gospel must be preached to all nations (13:10). Their mission is to follow the one who freely gave his life for the salvation and liberation of all humanity, dying upon the cross for all. This is a mission of costly grace.

The structure of Mark's writing indicates his missionary intention in presenting "the good news of Jesus Christ, the Son of God" (Mark 1:1; 15:37-39). In Galilee (1:14—8:26), Jesus' ministry of preaching (1:14-15), healing (3:7-12), and teaching (6:6) receives a great response from the common people (1:28, 32-34, 45; 2:2; 3:7-12; 4:1; 5:21; 6:31, 53-56; 8:1). The disciples are called to follow Jesus (1:16-20), to be part of the messianic community (3:13-19), and to go out on mission throughout the world (6:7-13). The journeys around the Sea of Galilee (6:30—8:21) are designed to demonstrate how the mission is to incorporate both Jews and Gentiles in the one community of faith.

Yet the disciples fail to understand the significance of the mission of Jesus (Mark 8:14-21), repeatedly misunderstand his teaching (8:27—10:52), sleep through the struggle in Gethsemane (14:32-42), and flee from the final conflict (14:50-52). Despite all this, after the resurrection they are called back to Galilee to continue the universal mission of Jesus (16:7). "The community is to be regathered in the very territory where Jesus had first collected them and given them a share in his boundary-breaking kingdom ministry. The community is not to remain in Jerusalem, but to move with renewed awareness and power back to Galilee where the universal mission of the church beckons" (Senior and Stuhlmueller, 218). Jerusalem is falling, and Mark warns his community that the end is not yet. "The good news must first be proclaimed to all nations" (13:10). To this task his community has been called.

[Jesus] called the twelve and began to send them out two by two, and gave them authority over the unclean spirits. He ordered them to take nothing for their journey except a staff; no bread, no bag, no money in their belts; but to wear sandals and not to put on two tunics. He said to them, "Wherever you enter a house, stay there until you leave the place. If any place will not welcome you and they refuse to hear you, as you leave, shake off the dust that is on your feet as a testimony against them." So they went out and proclaimed that all should repent. They cast out many demons, and anointed with oil many who were sick and cured them.

King Herod heard of it, for Jesus' name had become known. Some were saying, "John the baptizer has been raised from the dead; and for this reason these powers are at work in him." But others said, "It is Elijah." And others said, "It is a prophet, like one of the prophets of old." But when Herod heard of it, he said, "John, whom I beheaded, has been raised."

For Herod himself had sent men who arrested John, bound him, and put him in prison on account of Herodias, his brother Philip's wife, because Herod had married her. For John had been telling Herod, "It is not lawful for you to have your brother's wife." And Herodias had a grudge against him, and wanted to kill him. But she could not, for Herod feared John, knowing that he was a righteous and holy man, and he protected him. When he heard him, he was greatly perplexed; and yet he liked to listen to him. But an opportunity came when Herod on his birthday gave a banquet for his courtiers and officers and for the leaders of Galilee. When his daughter Herodias came in and danced, she pleased Herod and his guests; and the king said to the girl, "Ask me for whatever you wish, and I will give it." And he solemnly swore to her, "Whatever you ask me, I will give you, even half of my kingdom." She went out and said to her mother, "What should I ask for?" She replied, "The head of John the baptizer." Immediately she rushed back to the king and requested, "I want you to give me at once the head of John the Baptist on a platter." The king was deeply grieved; yet out of regard for his oaths and for the guests, he did not want to refuse her. Immediately the king sent a soldier of the guard with orders to bring John's head. He went and beheaded him in the prison, brought his head on a platter, and gave it to the girl. Then the girl gave it to her mother. When his disciples heard about it, they came and took his body, and laid it in a tomb.

> The apostles gathered around Jesus, and told him all that they had done and taught. He said to them, "Come away to a deserted place all by yourselves and rest a while." For many were coming and going, and they had no leisure even to eat.
> (Mark 6:7-31)

We notice in Mark 6:7-13 that discipleship leads into mission. This is also true of the other two sections about discipleship in the first major section of the Gospel (Mark 1:16-20; 3:13-19). The first disciples are called to follow Jesus with the promise that, as his disciples, they will "fish for people" (1:17). They are called to be the nucleus of the people of God, "to be with him, and to be sent out to proclaim the message, and to have authority to cast out demons" (3:14-15). Finally, they are sent out to continue the mission of Jesus in the world (6:7-13). Clearly, for Mark, then, mission is the crown of discipleship. Without involvement in mission, the call to discipleship must be considered truncated and incomplete. Those who have experienced the grace of God in their lives through the call of Jesus, and have been brought together into the new community of grace and forgiveness, are also called to share this grace with the world.

Continuing the Mission of Jesus

At the commencement of his ministry, as we have seen, Jesus takes the initiative and calls disciples to follow him (Mark 1:16-20). When he brings the twelve together as the nucleus of the community of the people of God, he again takes the initiative and summons those whom he wants to be with him and to send out on mission (3:13-19). Now as he prepares to send them out on mission in the world, he again takes the initiative and calls them to messianic ministry. This action of Jesus in repeatedly taking the initiative in this way is without parallel in the ancient world and indicates the radical nature of the authority exercised by Jesus.

This authority, so different from that of the scribes (Mark 1:22), is the theme of the opening chapters of the Gospel of Mark. It is demonstrated, first of all, in the opening miracle story of the ministry of Jesus, as he casts out an unclean spirit and teaches (1:21-28). In the initial conflict story, Jesus' authority to forgive sins is subjected to intense scrutiny. Yet his authority is again displayed convincingly in the healing of the paralytic: "They were all amazed and glorified God, saying, 'We have never seen anything like this!' " (2:1-12).

Then Jesus calls the twelve together for the first time (Mark 3:14-15) and is about to send them out on mission (6:7). He endows them with this same authority, for he is the source and power of the ministry and mission of the disciples, and through them, of the church to which Mark is writing.

In the first mention of the mission of the disciples, Mark tells us that they are called to preach and to cast out demons (Mark 3:15). In their commissioning, he says that Jesus "gave them authority over the unclean spirits" (6:7) and relates that "they went out and proclaimed that all should repent. They cast out many demons, and anointed with oil many who were sick and cured them" (6:12-13). On return from the mission, they reported to Jesus "all that they had done and taught" (6:30).

So then, according to Mark, the mission of the disciples is to persuade people to change their way of living, and to teach them how they might live in a proper relationship with God and with one another. They are also to heal the lives of individuals and change or destroy the demonic system that holds people captive—the system of dehumanizing forces and institutions from which so many believe there can be no escape. The mission of the disciples is thus depicted as being essentially a continuation of the mission of Jesus.

As T. W. Manson so eloquently expressed it, "There is only one 'essential ministry' in the Church, the perpetual ministry of the Risen and Ever-Present Lord Himself. . . . All other ministries are derivative, dependent and functional. . . . The Church's ministry is a continuation of the Messianic Ministry of Jesus" (Manson, *Ministry*, 100).

Traveling up and down Palestine with Jesus, they had witnessed his healing ministry to the sick (Mark 1:29-31, 32-34, 40-45; etc.) and demon possessed (1:21-28, 32-34; etc.), and his open hospitality to tax collectors (2:13-17) and notorious sinners (2:15-17). Grace is the first word and grace the last.

Thus where the message or the messengers are rejected, the disciples are told to perform an act of prophetic symbolism, shaking the dust off their feet as a testimony against them (Mark 6:11). Pious Jews returning to their homeland carefully removed the dust of heathen lands from their feet and clothing. The disciples are to declare as heathen those Jewish towns which reject them.

This testimony that they have rejected the grace of God will be used against them at the day of judgment (see also Mark 13:9). According to Matthew, "it will be more tolerable for the land of Sodom and Gomorrah on the day of judgment" than for those towns which have rejected the disciples and their message (Matt. 10:15). Luke pronounces judgment on the Galilean towns of Chorazin and Bethsaida for the rejection of the mission and the miracles of the seventy-two (Luke 10:13-15). The mission of the disciples as a continuation of the mission of Jesus is a mission of grace, but those who reject God's free offer of salvation place themselves in a perilous position.

The Mission of Costly Grace

The grace which the disciples received is costly grace, and costly is the grace they are to impart to others. The one who extended this grace to them has done so at the cost of his own life, and this was to be their experience as well.

When Jesus sends his disciples out on mission, he places strict limitations on what they might take with them. Although these restrictions vary slightly from Gospel to Gospel, they are certainly an indication of the cost and the urgency involved in the mission of Jesus and his disciples. Only the basic essentials are permitted—nothing except a staff, no food, no pack, no money in their belts, a pair of sandals but not a second tunic (Mark); no bag, no second tunic, no sandals, no money in their belts, no staff (Matthew); no staff, no bag, no food, no money, and no second tunic (Luke). "The particular instructions apply literally only to this brief mission during Jesus' lifetime; but in principle, with the necessary modifications according to climate and other circumstances, they still hold for the continuing ministry of the Church. The service of the Word of God is still a matter of extreme urgency, calling for absolute self-dedication" (Cranfield, 200).

Wandering Cynic preachers also traveled light in the first century, though the begging bag was an indispensable part of their missionary equipment, for they lived on the charity of others. The disciples, however, are not even permitted to take a bag or knapsack for their provisions since they are expected to rely on sympathizers for their basic food and shelter. They have left their families and their professions to be involved in the mission of Jesus. Though they are assured of receiving a hundred times more in return (Mark 10:28-30), there are strict limitations on the way they may respond to the typically generous Eastern hospitality.

They are not to move around from house to house in an attempt to secure better lodgings as their reputations for preaching and casting out demons becomes well-known. Instead, until they leave the district, they must remain with the first people who offer them hospitality, no matter how frugal the fare that may have been offered them (Mark 6:10). Self-aggrandizement must not be allowed to bring the gospel into disrepute, and the disciples must avoid giving the impression that the grace of God is more readily available to those who can afford to pay a higher price for it.

The Didache (a Christian manual of instruction from about 120 C.E.) reflects a further development of this tradition when it teaches the church to receive apostles and prophets "as the Lord." But it adds, "He shall stay one day, and, if need be, the next also, but, if he stay three, he is a false prophet. And when the apostle goes forth, let him take nothing save bread, till he reach his lodging; but if he asks for money, he is a false prophet. . . . And any prophet that orders a table in the spirit shall not eat of it, else is he a false prophet. . . . But whosoever shall say in the Spirit, Give me money, or any other thing, you shall not listen to him; but if he asks you to give for others who are in need, let no one judge him" (Didache 11:1-2).

Mark brings out the costly nature of the mission of the disciples through the use of one of his typical theological sandwiches. He inserts the story of the death of John the Baptist (Mark 6:14-29) between the two halves of the story of the mission of the disciples, after they have been sent out (6:7-13) and before they return (6:30-31). Chronologically, there is no necessary connection between the stories, but theologically the relationship is very important for Mark's understanding of the church's mission.

Readers of the Gospel were well aware that the Messiah had met his death as a result of his mission. The preceding story alludes to this in telling of the rejection of Jesus at his hometown (Mark 6:1-6). By his arrangement of the material, Mark reminds us that John, the forerunner of the Messiah, met a similar untimely death (6:14-29). If the forerunner of the Messiah lost his life in carrying out his mission, and if Jesus was put to death because of his mission, can those who have been called to continue the Messiah's mission of costly grace expect any less?

John the Baptist, as Elijah who is to come, plays a quite significant role in the development of Mark's narrative theology of the costly nature of the divine mission in which the disciples have been invited to share. As the messianic forerunner foretold by Old Testament prophecies, he has come to prepare "the way of the Lord" (Mark 1:2-3). In doing that, he prepares the way for a discipleship of following Jesus to Jerusalem—the place of suffering, rejection, and death (8:27; 9:33-34; 10:17, 32, 46, 52). When Jesus is baptized by John, the divine voice declares that he is both Son of God and suffering servant (1:11), with a combination of Old Testament allusions (Psalm 2:7; Isaiah 42:1). All this again anticipates the crucifixion, where the Gentile centurion sees how Jesus "breathed his last" and then makes his confession of faith, "Truly this man was God's Son" (Mark 15:39).

Therefore, Mark has a design in his theological chronology: John the Baptist is arrested just before Jesus begins his kingdom mission, preaching the gospel in Galilee, calling on people to repent and believe (Mark 1:14-15). The technical term which Mark uses to describe John's arrest is precisely the term which he uses for the "handing over of the Son of Man" in the passion story (9:31; 10:33; 14:10-11, 18, 21, 41-42; 15:1, 10, 15). The same term is employed to warn the Christian missionaries of a coming time of persecution of the church: "They will hand you over to councils" (13:9). For Mark, the death of John (the messianic forerunner), the death of Jesus (the Messiah), and the trials of the disciples (the messianic missionaries)—these are all intimately related in the drama of salvation history.

Many of the first disciples apparently lost their lives in the continuation of the mission of Jesus. Mark's application is wider still, however, for as he indicates later, anyone wishing to become a disciple of Jesus must deny himself, take up his cross, and follow him (Mark 8:34). By giving ourselves away for the sake of Jesus and the gospel, we find both ourselves and life itself (8:35—9:1). Again, this teaching is affirmed by John the Baptist when "Elijah and Moses," the two great martyrs of the faith (Rev. 11:1-8), appear with Jesus on the mountain of transfiguration. There God declares once again that Jesus is his Son, whose message of suffering discipleship we must heed (Mark 9:2-8).

Jews and Gentiles in the One Church

Thus Mark has introduced his section on messianic mission (Mark 6:6—8:21) with the sandwich arrangement of the mission of the disciples (6:6-13, 30-31) and the death of the messianic forerunner (6:14-29). Next he carefully edits the material in the major section so that its meaning is abundantly clear to his church. The key-word is "bread" or "food" (6:37-38, 41a, 41c, 44, 52; 7:2, 5, 27; 8:4-6, 14, 16-17, 19). The journeys of Jesus and his disciples across the lake and back (6:32, 45, 53; 8:10) provide the interpretative framework. And the final discussion between Jesus and the disciples (8:10-21) underscores the theology of the section. The story of the Syrophoenician woman (7:24-30) provides the turning point in the narrative.

The initial feeding of the people of God in the wilderness, the feeding of the five thousand (Mark 6:34-44), is located in a Jewish environment. Jesus has compassion on the crowd and teaches them many things (6:34), but later in the day when the crowds are hungry, the disciples tell Jesus to send them off to "buy something for themselves to eat" (6:36). When he tells the disciples to feed the crowd, they consider it an impossibility (6:37). Jesus commands his disciples to ascertain how much food they have, and to have the crowd sit down in an orderly fashion on the grass. After he says the blessing, he breaks the bread and gives it to the disciples to feed the crowd (6:38-41). They are learning from Jesus that the mission to the Jews is his first priority. Significantly, when the task is over they gather up twelve baskets full of the fragments that are left over (6:43).

With the story of the walking on the water (Mark 6:45-52), Jesus and the disciples cross to a Gentile side of the Sea of Galilee. Their reluctance is indicated by the way Jesus "made his disciples get into the boat and go on ahead to the other side" (6:45). At Gennesaret he performs many miracles (6:53-56). Then "the Pharisees and some of the scribes who had come from Jerusalem" attack them for not observing a law of ritual purity. Jesus explains how some traditions of the Pharisees are only human and lead to rejecting the commandment of God. He declares to his disciples that all foods are clean (Mark 7:1-15)—a necessary precondition for any Gentile mission (see the story of Peter's vision and the Gentile mission in Acts 10:1-48).

The disciples are not able to understand the significance of the feeding of the five thousand (Mark 6:52). But the Syrophoenician woman (a Gentile!) perceives the truth that "the children" have already been fed (in the first great feeding of the people of God in the wilderness). There is such an abundant supply that the scraps from the table will be enough for the Gentiles, she claims. Her word is endorsed by Jesus (7:24-30).

Following the healing of a deaf-and-mute man (Mark 7:31-37), Mark tells the story of the second great feeding of the people of God in the wilderness. The disciples are not able to understand what is happening and ask incredulously, "How can one feed these people with bread here in the desert?" (8:4). But, if Jesus has just fed five thousand, why should four thousand provide a problem? Because they are Gentiles! Jesus again gives food to the disciples so that they can feed the people. This time, of course, there are seven loaves and seven baskets full of pieces left over (8:1-9)!

As the disciples are about to cross back over the sea again, they discover that they have no bread—except "only one loaf with them in the boat" (8:14). In the discussion which follows, Mark underlines yet again the missionary message that he has been seeking to communicate to his church. Jesus begins by warning his disciples to watch out for the leaven of the Pharisees, who have just been opposing him (Mark 8:11-12). Beware of the leaven of Herod, who at the beginning of this section of the Gospel has killed John the Baptist because of his prophetic mission in the world (6:14-29).

Jesus then draws attention to the missionary significance of the two feeding miracles (8:16-21): first the Jews, and then the Gentiles. The "twelve" (tribes) and the "seven" (completeness)! Israel and the whole world! By the time of Mark, the Jews have already been fed, and the gospel has moved out among the Gentiles. The Christian community has all the resources they will ever require—with one loaf in the boat symbolizing the Eucharist in the midst of the people of God. Jews and Gentiles—one church! "Do you not yet understand?" asks Jesus (8:21).

There Is No End to the Work (Matthew 5:13-16; 28:16-20)

The worldwide messianic mission of the new community of the people of God occupies an even more important place in the Gospel of Matthew than in Mark. Matthew uses materials drawn from a wide variety of sources, even wider than for the Sermon on the Mount: some sayings have been taken from three chapters of Mark, others have parallels in another five chapters of Luke, others have been drawn from his own special tradition. Matthew edits and arranges them into a coherent whole, and thus develops an extensive sermon on mission (Matt. 9:35—10:42). He gives this sermon precedence over his sermon on the parables of the kingdom (13:1-

52) and even over his sermon on relationships within the messianic community (17:24—18:35).

Even more strongly than Mark, Matthew emphasizes that the twelve have been called for the purpose of the messianic mission. In Matthew 10:2-4, the names of the twelve are actually incorporated into the missionary discourse itself. He also emphasizes that the mission of the church is a continuation of the mission of Jesus: in 10:7-8 the description of their activity is exactly that of the mission of Jesus in 9:35. The church's mission is also a mission of grace: 10:8 is the only place we find the words: "You received without payment; give without payment."

Above all, however, Matthew includes in his missionary discourse a series of sayings, which in Mark related to the final persecution destined to descend on the faithful in the last days. Thus he stresses the costly nature of the mission (Matt. 10:16-25). Matthew therefore goes on to exhort the disciples to fearless confession (10:26-33), to warn them of the cost of involvement in messianic mission (10:34-39), and to assure them that even the most menial tasks will not go unrewarded (10:40-42).

According to Matthew's presentation, Jesus' first words of exhortation to the community of the disciples (Matt. 5:13-16) and his last words to them (28:16-20) are concerned with the worldwide mission of the Christian community. These sayings on mission are for Matthew the alpha and the omega of discipleship, the beginning and the end, the context in which all of his teaching is to be interpreted.

[Jesus said,] "You are the salt of the earth; but if salt has lost its taste, how can its saltiness be restored? It is no longer good for anything, but is thrown out and trampled under foot.

"You are the light of the world. A city built on a hill cannot be hid. No one after lighting a lamp puts it under the bushel basket, but on the lampstand, and it gives light to all in the house. In the same way, let your light shine before others, so that they may see your good works and give glory to you Father in heaven." (Matt. 5:13-16)

Now the eleven disciples went to Galilee, to the mountain to which Jesus had directed them. When they saw him, they worshiped him; but some doubted. And Jesus came and said to them, "All authority in heaven and on earth has been given to me. Go therefore and make disciples of all nations, baptizing them in the name of the Father and of the Son and of the Holy Spirit, and teaching them to obey everything that I have commanded you. And remember, I am with you always [AG: all the days], to the end of the age."   (Matt. 28:16-20)

As we have noted, the structure of the Gospel of Matthew is dominated by the five great "sermons on the sermons of Jesus": the Sermon on the Mount (Matt. 5—7), missionary discourse (10), parables of the kingdom (13), responsibilities within the Christian community (18), and parables of the end-time (24—25). Within this structure, the Sermon on the Mount is ascribed pride of place as the opening discourse, which sets the tone for the rest of the teaching of Jesus. The Sermon is set within the framework of grace, following as it does the first proclamation of the gospel (4:17) and the call of the first disciples (4:18-22). It depicts the lifestyle required of those who have heard the good news of the kingdom and have responded to the call to follow Jesus. The Sermon prevents the call to discipleship from becoming cheap grace, and the call prevents the life of discipleship from becoming legalism. Matthew's theme is responsible grace, as discipleship issues in mission to the world.

Salt of the Earth and Light of the World

The Sermon begins with a triumphant declaration of the terms of entry into the kingly reign of God: poor in spirit, meekness, mercy, pure in heart, peacemaking, persecution for the sake of justice (Matt. 5:3-12). Matthew then goes on immediately to outline the missionary function of the Christian community (5:13-16). In so doing he protects the Beatitudes from pietistic misinterpretation whereby the disciples could simply wallow in their weakness and withdraw from the world.

The disciples are emphatically declared to be the salt of the earth: "You, and only you who have heard the good news of the kingdom and have responded positively to this grace, recognizing your poverty and dependence upon God, are the salt of the earth!" In the first century, salt was the primary form of preservative, used to preserve foodstuffs from putrefaction. The first disciples (Matt. 4:18-22) would have understood the metaphor well as they packed their catch in salt before shipping it to market. "You, the little people of society, society's nobodies, are the only ones capable of preventing the world from rotting!" Humanity's continued unpolluted existence depends upon those who recognize their poverty and dependence upon God, work for peace, and are persecuted because of justice.

The rabbis likened the Law to salt, and originally this saying may have been formulated against this background. Likewise, the promise, "Where two or three are gathered in my name, I am there among them" (Matt. 18:20), may have been framed against the background of a Jewish saying: "If two sit together and the words of the Law [are spoken] between them, the Shekinah (the presence of God) rests between them" (Mishnah Aboth 3.2; see also 3.3, "three"; 3.6, "ten"). Writing against the background of Pharisaic Judaism, Matthew emphatically declares that it is the Christian community, and not the Law, which is the salt of the earth.

But be warned: if salt loses its salinity, it will end up on the rubbish heap! In Palestine, salt was not artificially prepared, but was simply dug from evaporated pools near the Dead Sea and so was never pure. It contained many impurities, and if drenched by rain on the way to market, the salt dissolved, and what remained was useless. It was then simply thrown into the street, the first-century dump, and trampled underfoot.

The Talmud preserves a story about Rabbi Joshua ben Chaniah (ca. 90 C.E.) in which the rabbi makes fun of this saying. Someone asked him, "If the salt loses its savor, with what will it be salted?" He replied, "With the afterbirth of a mule." When the retort was made that since the mule is barren, it cannot have an afterbirth, he answered, "Neither can salt lose its savor!" This is the rabbi's response to the idea that Judaism has been replaced by the Christian community. Certainly, it is true that salt—as long as it remains salt—cannot lose its salinity! The operative statement, however, is "as long as it remains salt." Let the community beware lest it lose its status before God! Privilege involves responsibility.

The missionary function of the community is not only hidden and all-pervasive, it is also open and illuminating. The spiritually poor who acknowledge their dependence upon God are "the light of the world" (Matt. 5:14). In the Old Testament "light" is the most meaningful manifestation of God's activity in the world. Apart from the light created by God, the world would still be in chaos and darkness; so light is one of God's greatest gifts to humanity. Israel was illuminated by the light of God and was to become a light to the nations (Isa. 49:6; 60:3-5; 62:1). Again, Matthew takes a promise to Judaism and applies it to the Christian community, to those who have responded to the call of grace and become disciples of Jesus.

They are like a city set on a hill which cannot be hidden (Matt. 5:14b). They should take heart, for although the community may appear weak and insignificant, its light will go on shining in the darkness. It will never be overcome (16:18). According to the Gospel of Thomas (32), "Jesus said, 'A city which is set on the summit of a high hill, and on a firm foundation, cannot be brought low, nor can it be hidden.' " Almost certainly "the city on the hill" was originally a reference to Jerusalem (Isa. 2:2-4; Mic. 4:1-3; Ps. 122:3). Again Matthew takes Jewish images and promises and applies them to the Christian community.

It is absurd to light a lamp and immediately extinguish it by placing it under a bushel-measure (Matt. 5:15). "If a bushel-measure were placed over the small clay lamp, it would extinguish it. In the little, windowless, one-roomed peasants' houses which have no chimney, this might well have been the customary method of putting out the lamp, since blowing it out might cause unpleasant smoke and smell, as well as the risk of fire through sparks (see Mishnah Shabbath 3.6). A free rendering, then, would be: "They do not light a lamp in order to put it out again immediately. No! Its place is on the lampstand, so that it may give light to all the inmates (all through the night, as is still customary among the Palestinian fellaheen)" (Jeremias, *Parables,* 120).

The Gospel of Thomas relates the saying of the lamp and the lampstand to the preaching of the gospel (G. Thomas 33a). Mark emphasizes that Jesus is the ultimate source of light (Mark 4:21). Matthew would not wish to exclude these emphases, but his perspective is somewhat broader. The preceding saying on "salt" (Matt. 5:13) and the following exhortation (5:16) indicates that he has in mind a discipleship which proves itself to the world by its good works. Jesus encourages his disciples by emphasizing their status as "the salt of the earth" (5:13) and "the light of the world" (5:14). In addition, he throws out the challenge to be salt and to be light for all the world. "Without the challenge, Jesus' metaphors would engender isolationism and arrogance. The disciples are to be a church that retains firm contours and is far from identical with the world, but they are still a 'church for the world' " (Schweizer, *Matthew,* 103).

In the succeeding passages, Matthew leaves us in no doubt as to the way in which the Christian community is to perform its mission: through the observance of the royal law of love. Immediately after the salt and light sayings is Jesus' statement on fulfillment of the Hebrew Scriptures. "Do not think that I have come to abolish the law or the prophets; I have not come to abolish but to fulfill" (Matt. 5:17).

The six antitheses provide examples of the way the teaching of Jesus fulfills the Law and the Prophets: "You have heard that it was said to those of ancient times, . . . but I say to you." The emphasis rests on the last in the series: "Love your enemies and pray for those who persecute you" (Matt. 5:43-48). Later in the Sermon on the Mount, Jesus teaches that the Law and the Prophets are fulfilled when we do unto others as we would have others do to us (6:12). When Jesus is asked "Which commandment in the law is the greatest?" Jesus replies by citing the commands to love God and to love one's neighbor, and then adds, "On these two commandments hang all the law and the prophets" (22:40).

Matthew's distinctive emphases are to be seen in the fact that the lifestyle mission of the community is for the benefit of the whole world. The light is for "all" who are in the house (Matt. 5:15), and the glory belongs not to the disciple, nor to the community, but to the heavenly Father (5:16). After all, those who have heard the call of God in Christ know that they stand before God not on the basis of their own merits, but on the basis of the grace of God (4:17-22). They are aware of their own spiritual poverty, and they are always willing to acknowledge their dependence upon God (5:3-12). To God belongs the glory!

The Worldwide Mission of the Disciples

The Gospel of Matthew reaches its climax in the great commission (Matt. 28:16-20), a climax which can only be understood in the context of all that precedes it and prepares for it. It is the key for understanding the whole book. On the mountain of revelation, Jesus collects the remaining members of the messianic community and encounters them as the exalted Lord present among his people. He thrusts them forth on worldwide mission, promising his continuing presence to all those who are obedient to the command on which the promise rests.

The commission contains "a compendium of important Matthean themes: Jesus as the greater Moses and lawgiver, the deity of Jesus, the authority of his commands, the trinitarian associations of baptism, the danger of doubt among disciples, the teaching ministry of disciples, discipleship as keeping Jesus' law, the presence of Jesus with his disciples, and the directing of Christian hope to the consummation. Paramount among these themes, however, is the mission to all the nations" (Gundry, 593).

Nothing happens by chance in the messianic community. The disciples gather on the mountain in response to the command of the earthly Jesus (Matt. 26:32; also 28:7, 10). In this Gospel "the mountain" is a place of revelation (17:1, 9), of prayer (14:23), of healing (15:29), and of survival (24:16). Most important, it is the place of teaching, where Jesus gives the new law for the new community of the people of God (5:1) and sends them out on mission to all the world (28:16).

The mountain is also in Galilee, the scene of Jesus' earthly ministry, as Matthew repeatedly emphasizes (Matt. 4:12, 15, 18, 23, 25; 15:29; 17:22; 19:1; 21:11). The exalted Lord encounters his church at the same place where Jesus of Nazareth first called his disciples to follow him so that they might become fishers of people (4:18-22). In "Galilee of the Gentiles," as attested by Isaiah 8:23—9:1 (4:14-16), the church is commissioned to make disciples of all nations (28:19). While Matthew was certainly a Jewish Christian writing for a predominantly Jewish Christian church, it is clear that the separation of this church from Judaism is complete. Matthew seeks to direct their missionary attention primarily to the Gentiles.

The exalted Lord of the church comes to his disciples with all power and authority, fulfilling the hopes and expectations of the Son of Man. Behind Matthew's presentation stands Daniel's vision of the heavenly council, where the seer views one like a son of man coming to the Ancient of Days. The Greek Septuagint version says, "To him was given authority, and all the nations of the earth by race and all glory were serving him. And his authority is an everlasting authority which shall not be taken away, and his kingdom one which shall not be destroyed" (Dan. 7:13-14, tr. by AG).

Naturally, the eleven disciples bow down in worship before the Lord of the church (Matt. 8:2; 9:18; 14:33; 15:25; 20:22; 28:9). Yet we are told that even here some doubt (28:17). Faith and obedience must never be taken for granted, not even among the disciples standing in the presence of the crucified and risen Lord. Miracles may well evoke worship, but they cannot eliminate doubt—even the miracle of the resurrection cannot guarantee that. Faith is both a gift and obedience a struggle.

In Matthew the stress is on the universal lordship of Christ, which leads to the universal mission of the church. "All authority" has been given to Jesus (Matt. 28:18), and he directs that they go to "all nations" (28:19) and teach them "all" that Jesus had commanded them. Jesus promises that he will be with them "all the days" until the end of the age (28:20). Previously the mission of the disciples was restricted to Israel (10:5, 23), but now the universal reign of Christ calls forth a universal mission and brings into existence a community of disciples stretching across the world and throughout the ages (28:19-20).

Mark depicts John's baptism as "a baptism of repentance for the forgiveness of sins" (Mark 1:4). But Matthew describes it simply as "a baptism of repentance" (Matt. 3:11) and inserts the phrase "for the forgiveness of sins" into his account of the Last Supper (26:28). In his theology, it is the cross which makes possible the forgiveness of sins. In Mark, Jesus refers to the temple as "a house of prayer for all the nations" (Mark 11:17), but in Matthew he calls it only "a house of prayer" (Matt. 21:13). This Evangelist saves the phrase "for all nations" to include in the great commission (28:20), since in his theology it is the cross and resurrection which make possible the church's universal mission.

Missionary proclamation is the responsibility of the whole Christian community, and the formation of community is part of this missionary obligation. The eleven are commanded not only to make disciples, but also to baptize in the name of the Father and of the Son and of the Holy Spirit (Matt. 28:19). Their missionary function includes initiating new converts into the missionary community of the people of God. The trinitarian authority which Matthew provides for this action, in turn, points to the ultimate basis of Christian community. Community exists in the heart of God, in the eternal community of Father, Son, and Holy Spirit.

In contrast to the other Gospels, Matthew makes no mention of the gift of the Spirit to the disciples (Luke 24:49; Acts 1:8; John 20:22-23). Also, he includes no command to preach the gospel (Luke 24:47; Mark 16:15). For him, the important thing is teaching the commandments of Jesus. The sermons which dominate his Gospel indicate the contours of this gospel teaching. They are to teach that discipleship involves an acknowledgment of spiritual poverty and an utter dependence upon God, a willingness to forgive others, and a resolute refusal to be enslaved to material possessions (Matt. 5:1—7:29).

The disciples will not forget to include teaching on the importance of the messianic mission of the people of God as an expression of costly discipleship in the world (Matt. 9:35—10:42), and on the necessity of reconciliation and forgiveness within the Christian community (18:1-35). They will teach, through parables, the nature of the kingly reign of God in which they have been called to share (13:1-35). And they will exhort the community to remain faithful as they await the kingdom's final inbreaking in salvation and judgment (23:1—25:46). Above all else, they are to teach the ways of Jesus and to exhort the community to follow him as "the salt of the earth" and "the light of the world" (5:13-16).

As the Christian community fulfills its missionary obligation to all nations, it is assured of the continuing presence of the crucified and risen Lord (Matt. 28:20), the presence which makes discipleship and mission possible, even in a hostile world.

Working for the Poor and Oppressed (Luke 4:14-30)

The mission of costly grace that was to take the early Christians throughout the world was by its very nature directed primarily toward the poor and the oppressed. These themes are emphasized time and again throughout the Gospel of Luke. Already during the presentation of Jesus in the temple, Simeon sings his song of blessing:

> "Master, now you are dismissing your servant in peace,
>   according to your word;
> for my eyes have seen your salvation,
>   which you have prepared in the presence of all peoples,
> a light for revelation to the Gentiles
>   and for glory to your people Israel."   (Luke 2:29-32)

In Luke, John the Baptist not only prepares the way of the Lord (as in Matthew and Luke), but also makes the rough places smooth so that "all flesh shall see the salvation of God" (3:4-6, continuing Mark's Old Testament quotation so that the emphasis now falls on the concluding words relating to the Gentile mission). There is the mission of the twelve (9:1-6), and the number of disciples involved corresponds to the number of tribes of Israel. Then follows a mission of seventy-two disciples (Luke 10:1-16), with the number of disciples involved corresponding to the number of Gentile nations according to Jewish tradition. The arrangement serves as "a preliminary notice of the two-fold mission among Jews and non-Jews" (Hahn, *Mission*, 130).

It is, however, particularly in the story of Jesus' inaugural preaching at Nazareth (Luke 4:16-30) that the Evangelist unfolds the pattern of the subsequent mission of Jesus and the apostles. This story has an amazing constellation of Lucan themes and introduces the whole of Luke's two volumes: Jesus is introduced as the spirit-filled messenger (4:14, 18) and prophet (4:19, 24-27) who has fulfilled the divine promises (4:18-19). The nature of the mission of Jesus and of the church is anticipated (4:18-19) as the reader is prepared for Jesus' rejection by his own people (4:22-24) and for his acceptance by the Gentiles (4:25-27).

> Then Jesus, filled with the power of the Spirit, returned to Galilee, and a report about him spread through all the surrounding country. He began to teach in their synagogues and was praised by everyone.
> When he came to Nazareth, where he had been brought up, he went to the synagogue on the sabbath day, as was his custom. He stood up to read, and the scroll of the prophet Isaiah was given to him. He unrolled the scroll and found the place where it was written:
> "The Spirit of the Lord is upon me,
>   because he has anointed me
>   to bring good news for/to the poor.
> He has sent me to proclaim release to the captives
>   and recovery of sight to the blind,
>   to let the oppressed go free,
> to proclaim the year of the Lord's favor."
> And he rolled up the scroll, gave it back to the attendant, and sat down. The eyes of all in the synagogue were fixed on him. Then he began to say to them, "Today this scripture has been fulfilled in your hearing [AG: even while you are listening]." All spoke well of him and were amazed at the gracious words [AG: words of grace] that came from his mouth. They said, "Is not this Joseph's son?" He said to them, "Doubtless you will quote to me this proverb, 'Doctor, cure yourself!' And you will say, 'Do here also in your hometown the things that we have heard you did at Capernaum.' " And he said, "Truly I tell you, no prophet is accepted in the prophet's hometown. But the

truth is, there were many widows in Israel in the time of Elijah, when the heaven was shut up three years and six months, and there was a severe famine over all the land; yet Elijah was sent to none of them except to a widow at Zarephath in Sidon. There were also many lepers in Israel in the time of the prophet Elisha, and none of them was cleansed except Naaman the Syrian." When they heard this, all in the synagogue were filled with rage. They got up, drove him out of the town, and led him to the brow of the hill on which their town was built, so that they might hurl him off the cliff. But he passed through the midst of them and went on his way.   (Luke 4:14-30)

In each of the Gospels, the key to the understanding of the church's mission in the world is to be seen in the person and mission of Jesus. In Matthew and Mark, we see the mission of the disciples as a continuation of the mission of Jesus, a mission of costly grace in the world. Jesus is the one who takes the initiative, calls the disciples to follow him (Mark 1:16-20; Matt. 4:17-22), and sends them forth on mission (Mark 6:7-13; Matt. 10:1-42). His presence is crucial for the existence of the community (18:20) and for the success of the worldwide mission (28:20). With Luke's strong emphasis on the mission of the church, it is perhaps not surprising, then, that he should favor the story of Jesus' inaugural sermon in Nazareth (contrast Mark 6:1-6). Luke chooses that dramatic account to introduce Jesus' mission and anticipate the mission of the church, which by Luke's time had reached out and encompassed the pagan world.

It is clear that Luke wants us to understand this Nazareth episode as programmatic for understanding both Luke and Acts. Although it is presented as the first event in the ministry of Jesus, we are told that when the people are astounded at his teaching, Jesus says, "Doubtless you will quote to me this proverb, 'Doctor, cure yourself!' And you will say, 'Do here also in your hometown the things that we have heard you did at Capernaum' " (Luke 4:23). Luke himself knows his readers will recognize that the story has been moved forward in the ministry of Jesus. He therefore adds comments to the opening summary statement taken from Mark 1:14-15: "A report about him spread through all the surrounding country," and "he began to teach in their synagogues" (Luke 4:14-15). These are words drawn from Mark's account of Jesus' ministry in Capernaum (Mark 1:23, 28).

Moreover, the concluding statements reach beyond Jesus' present ministry: Elijah was not sent to any of the widows in Israel, and Elisha did not heal any lepers in Israel, but both exercised ministries to the Gentiles. This theme anticipates the ministry of the church rather than simply that of Jesus, for Jesus was indeed sent to the widows of Israel and healed many lepers in Israel. The Nazareth story, then, relates to both volumes of Luke's writings. We ought not to be surprised to discover that it contains so many Lucan themes.

Fulfilling the Divine Promises to Israel

Jesus commences his ministry as the Spirit-filled messenger of God (Luke 4:1a, 1c, 14, 18). While Mark and Matthew rarely mention the Holy Spirit, Luke's two-volume work abounds in references, all carefully arranged at important points in the development of the story. There are seven references in the infancy narratives (1:15, 35, 41, 67; 2:25-27), six in the opening chapters of Jesus' public ministry (3:16, 22; 4:1a, 1c, 14, 18), and four at the commencement of the travel narrative (10:21; 11:13; 12:10, 12). But none appear in the Jerusalem ministry or in the passion narrative.

In Acts the multitude of references to the Holy Spirit in the opening chapters (42 times in Acts 1—12) gives way to the occasional reference in the later chapters (12 times in Acts 13—18). The time in Jerusalem and the journey to Rome (21:1—28:16) contain no references to the Spirit whatsoever. This is Luke's way of indicating that the commencement of each of the significant stages in the history of salvation takes place under the guidance of the Holy Spirit and with the endorsement and power of the Spirit. The history of salvation is no mere human history, but rather it is the activity of God, divinely conceived and controlled.

After Jesus defeats the power of evil and begins his ministry in Galilee (Luke 4:14-15), he now chooses his hometown of Nazareth for his inaugural sermon (4:16-30). In the Gospel of Matthew is a certain downplaying of the role of

Nazareth, and Capernaum becomes Jesus' hometown (Matt. 4:12-16; 9:1). In contrast, Luke stresses that Nazareth is the town to which Jesus belongs. In the birth stories (again in contrast to Matthew), Joseph and Mary live in Nazareth (Luke 1:26-28) and journey to Bethlehem only because the census requires them to be enrolled in their ancestral town. Jesus is born during their brief sojourn there (2:1-7).

The two Lucan notices about Jesus growing to maturity stress that the family is living in Nazareth all this time (Luke 2:39-40, 51-52). Nazareth is "their own town" (2:39-40), the place where Jesus "had been brought up" (4:16). In this obscure and despised town (John 1:46), never mentioned in the Old Testament or in any Jewish writing prior to Jesus, the revelation of God begins through the One who is empowered by the Spirit from birth (Luke 1:35). Here is all the paradox of the Gospel. The mission which was soon to envelop the known world was launched in an obscure town which would probably never have been remembered had the mission not begun there. The power of God is frequently revealed in very ordinary, unimportant places.

According to Luke, Jesus attends the synagogue on the sabbath "as was his custom" (Luke 4:16). This is an important Lucan emphasis. Throughout the birth narratives (Luke 1—2), all of the characters are portrayed as models of Jewish piety, diligent in their attendance at worship and devout in all they do (1:9-11; 2:22-24, 37-42). Similarly, the leaders of the early church are depicted as regular and devout in their attendance at the temple (Acts 2:46; 3:1; 4:1; 5:12, 42). Jesus himself is a model of devotion, attending both synagogue (Luke 4:15-16, 33, 44; 6:6; 13:10) and temple (19:47-48; 21:37-38), and being diligent in prayer (3:21; 5:16; 6:12; and many places).

The Third Gospel opens and closes with the faithful community worshiping in the temple (Luke 1:8-25; 24:52-53). The book of Acts commences with the community worshiping both in the temple and in private houses (Acts 2:46-47), and it ends with worship in private houses only (20:20; 21:8; also 28:30-31). By Luke's time the house church has replaced temple and synagogue as the center of Christian worship, but throughout his ministry Jesus is a loyal Jew, as are the apostolic leaders. In Luke and Acts, the church rejects Judaism only after Judaism has rejected Jesus and the apostolic missionaries.

The mission of Jesus is launched with the triumphant declaration that the Old Testament Scriptures are being fulfilled *this very day* in Jesus (Luke 4:21). He is inaugurating the mission of the church through his preaching. The adverb "today" plays an important role in the Lucan eschatology. The angel of the Lord tells the shepherds, "To you is born this day [today] in the city of David a Savior, who is the Messiah [Christ], the Lord" (2:11). Jesus speaks of Zacchaeus, "Today salvation has come to this house, because he too is a son of Abraham. For the Son of Man came to seek out and to save the lost" (19:9-10). When the thief on the cross asks Jesus to remember him in his kingdom, Jesus replies, "Truly I tell you, today you will be with me in Paradise" (23:43).

Similarly, in our story Jesus tells the people of Nazareth, "Today this Scripture has been fulfilled even while you are listening" (4:21, AG). This note of promise and fulfillment, of fulfillment and anticipation, is characteristic of Luke's understanding of the importance of Jesus. He is the center of the history of salvation; he fulfills the old and inaugurates the new. The mission of the church, anticipated in the mission of Jesus, can only be interpreted within the context of the mission of the people of God through the ages. Its focal point is Jesus.

Determined by the Mission of Jesus

At first sight the quotation from Isaiah appears to dominate the text, and it might appear that the nature of the mission of Jesus (and thereby of the church) is determined by the Old Testament; but this is not so. Luke does not quote the Old Testament. He *interprets* the Old Testament—through his understanding of Jesus Christ.

Luke likely used Isaiah 61:1-2 from the Greek text:

"The Spirit of the Lord is upon me
   for he has anointed me;

he has sent me
> to bring good news to the poor,
> to heal the brokenhearted,
> to proclaim liberty to captives,
>> and recovery of sight to the blind;
> to proclaim a year of favor from the Lord
>> and a day of vengeance [recompense],
> to comfort all who mourn."   (translated by AG)

This passage is used a number of times in the New Testament in connection with the ministry of Jesus (Matt. 11:5; Luke 7:22; Acts 4:27; 10:38; see Matt. 5:4). Luke adds to Isaiah 61:1-2 the line "to let the oppressed go free" (words taken from Isa. 58:6), and he omits "to heal the brokenhearted." Most important, Luke closes the text early so as to exclude the mention of "the day of vengeance of our God" (Hebrew text) upon heathen nations oppressing Israel. Luke perhaps alludes to the first Servant Song of Isaiah as well: "I am the Lord [Yahweh], I have called you . . . to open the eyes that are blind, to bring out the prisoners from the dungeon" (Isa. 42:6-7). Luke's understanding of Jesus, then, determines his reading of the Old Testament. Jesus is the center of salvation history. The Old Testament points to Jesus and is interpreted through him. The mission of the church is anticipated by Jesus and determined by him.

Isaiah 61:1-3 is a proclamation of salvation made by a person aware of being especially authorized by God for this particular message. Taking up themes from the earlier Servant Songs (Isa. 42:1-4; 49:1-6), the prophet proclaims the arrival of the promised salvation for the faithful within Israel, "the poor" and "the brokenhearted." He looks for the liberation of the oppressed, especially of people imprisoned for debts. He proclaims "a year of favor from the Lord," the reintroduction of the Jubilee Year. Such a year requires that the fields lay fallow, people return to their ancestral homes, land is given back to its original owners, debts are canceled, and slaves are set free (Lev. 25:1-55). For the prophet, this is symbolic of a guaranteed period of salvation for Jerusalem, with a corresponding judgment on nations in "the day of vengeance for our God."

For Luke, the promises will ultimately be reversed, with judgment coming upon Israel and salvation coming to the Gentiles (Acts 28:23-28). Yet for the moment, it remains "a gracious word," an open offer of salvation for Israel. And Jesus indicates that this salvation will also be an open possibility for the Gentiles as well (Luke 4:25-27; and his hint at 4:19 by not reading about "the day of vengeance"). Israel's rejection of Jesus, and especially of the apostolic missionaries, finally results in salvation bypassing most of Israel. But the Gentiles "will listen" (Acts 28:24-28).

The mission of Jesus, and of the church, is good news for the poor, the captives, the blind, and the oppressed. Society's nobodies, those who are despised, rejected, and abused by the world's powers are marked out for God's special attention, for the Gospel which Jesus proclaims and embodies is good news of grace (Luke 4:22). Those who have no hope in this world are singled out as the recipients of grace: "the poor" (6:20; 14:13, 21; 16:19-31), "the blind" (7:21-22; 14:13, 21; 18:35), and "the oppressed." These include "Samaritans" (9:52-55; 10:33; 17:16), "children" (7:7; 8:54; 9:42), and "women" (8:1-4; 10:38; 11:27; and many places), forgiven by Christ (7:36-50). The "rich and powerful," as long as they cling to their riches and oppress the poor, will be excluded (6:24-26; 16:19-31; and many places).

The mission of the church, anticipated in the mission of Jesus, is a mission of grace in the world. It is seen to be such because of its special interest in those who have no standing in the eyes of the world, those whose status is dependent upon God and upon God alone. The extent to which the church is involved in the mission of liberation, or salvation, of the poor and the oppressed is indicative of the extent to which it is willing to be led by Christ, the Spirit-filled messenger of salvation.

Not Always Welcomed by the People of God

The presence of the Spirit and the fulfillment of the Old Testament indicates that this mission of Jesus is attested by God. The people of God, however, are offended, especially when they come to an understanding of its implications. When Jesus is teaching in the synagogues throughout Galilee, he is "glorified by all" (Luke 4:15); when he indicates that the Old Testament prophecy is being fulfilled, they "spoke well of him" and wondered that such "words of grace" should come from his mouth" (4:22). Yet, they soon reject him. Some are offended at the weakness of the incarnate Lord, whom they think they know only too well (4:22). Others are offended when they realize that his mission has been more successful in other areas (4:23).

Jesus responds with the proverb, "No prophet is accepted in the prophet's hometown" (Luke 4:24), introduced by the solemn assertion, "Truly I tell you." Luke usually avoids the use of Aramaic words ("amen" or "truly"), and the fact that this introductory formula is used only five times elsewhere in this Gospel (12:37; 18:17, 29; 21:32; 23:43) indicates the importance of this saying for Luke (found also in Mark 6:4; Matthew 13:57; John 4:44; Oxyrynchus Papyri 1; Gospel of Thomas 31).

The identification of Jesus as a "prophet" is a favorite Lucan theme (Luke 7:16; 9:8, 19; 13:33; 22:64; 24:19). It is reinforced in this present story through the way Jesus applies to himself the words of the prophet (4:19) and has drawn a parallel between his own ministry and that of Elijah and Elisha (4:25-27). The proverb has been taken over from Mark's account of the rejection of Jesus in Nazareth (Mark 6:4). But Luke has deleted the words "among their own kin, and in their own house." Luke has a more positive attitude to the relatives of Jesus, and he wishes to present the contrast as one between "his hometown/country" and others. The Gentiles will ultimately embrace his message (Acts 28:28).

Soon the implications of Jesus' mission of grace become clear through the references to the widow of Sarepta and to Naaman the Syrian (Luke 4:25-27). Then the religious of his day ("all in the synagogue"!) rise up and try to kill Jesus, thereby excluding themselves from the community of grace. The deletion of "the day of vengeance of our God" (Isa. 61:2) was already bad enough, for it removed any thought of the destruction of the Gentiles and indicated their basic equality with Israel in the history of salvation. With the references to the widow of Sarepta (1 Kings 17:9) and Naaman the leper (2 Kings 5:1-19), the ultimate priority of the Gentiles is anticipated.

But the purposes of God are not to be frustrated. Jesus "passed through the midst of them and went on his way" (Luke 4:30)—the way that will finally lead him to Jerusalem. In the Gospel of Luke, the ministry of Jesus is depicted primarily in terms of a journey of salvation (4:42; 9:51-52; 24:28; and many places). This theme is continued in the second volume as the apostolic missionaries carry the message from Jerusalem to the ends of the earth (Acts 1:8), with the gospel going to the Gentiles (18:6; 28:26). The journey cannot be frustrated by the people of God, or by anyone else.

As disciples we have been called by grace. This call has brought us into the community of grace and has thrust us out into a mission of grace in the world. If we do not receive the word of grace, however, and we remain unconcerned about the needs of the oppressed, we stand in danger that the word of grace will become a word of judgment. Then Jesus will go on his way without us.

Working for a New World

The Synoptic Gospels are all products of missionary churches. Although they differ in their emphases, they all consider that involvement in God's mission in the world is of the essence of life on the road. Emil Brunner wrote, "As fire exists by burning, so the church exists through its mission in the world" (Brunner, 108).

When Jerusalem was falling to the Romans in the war of 66-70 C.E., many early Christians interpreted it as the beginning of events that would usher in a new age with the return of Jesus Christ. Mark sought to counter such excessive excitement by any group within his church by stressing that before Christ's return, the gospel had to be preached to all the nations (Mark 13:10). He structured his Gospel in such a way as to reinforce this missionary emphasis.

The disciples, says Mark, are called to follow Jesus (Mark 1:16-20), to belong to the Christian community (3:13-19), and to go out on mission throughout the world (6:7-13). In his day, Mark sees the church's mission reflecting the mission of Jesus and the trials of the earliest church; mission is to be understood as a mission of costly grace (6:14-29). With the eucharistic meal at the center of the community, the disciples had all the resources they needed. Jews and Gentiles were able to celebrate together in a liberated community in which all social, racial, and religious barriers had been abolished (8:14-21).

For Matthew, too, it was impossible to speak of discipleship without emphasizing the community's missionary responsibilities. He accepts the strong priority which his church accorded the mission to the Jews (Matt. 10:23). Nevertheless, he concludes his Gospel by stressing the universal significance of the death and resurrection of Jesus and of the mission which they inaugurated; "all nations" are to be called (28:16-20).

In the midst of persecution, Matthew exhorts his community to fearless confession and assures them that their work will not go unrewarded (Matt. 10:16-42). By living according to the royal law of love, a love extending even to one's enemies, the community fulfills its missionary obligations and serves as salt and light for all the world (5:13-16). The community is to preach the gospel to all humanity, bring them into the community of faith through baptism, and teach them to obey all of the commands of Christ. In so doing, the disciples will fulfill their responsibility to the risen Christ. And they are promised his presence forever (28:16-20).

Luke's church was struggling with the problem of the delay of the return of Jesus Christ and the lethargy resulting from unfulfilled hopes. He reinterprets the history of salvation so that they can understand the importance of the time of the church in the power of the Spirit fulfilling its God-given mission throughout the world.

Through his programmatic presentation of Jesus' inaugural sermon in Nazareth (Luke 4:16-30), Luke shows his church that Jesus is the center point of salvation. He fulfills and reinterprets the divine promises to Israel, while preparing the way and marking out the direction for the church's mission throughout history. For Luke, the mission of Jesus, and of the church, is to be understood primarily in terms of good news for the poor, the captives, the blind, and the oppressed. Those rejected and abused by the world's powers are marked out for God's special attention. The gospel which Jesus proclaims and embodies is good news of grace.

Despite their many obvious differences, all of the Gospel writers agree that when we want to talk about the mission of the church, the starting point must always be the mission of Jesus. He has called us to this life on the road, and he will let us know the jobs he has for us on the way. The supreme characteristic of his life was his radical openness to all people, especially to those whom society had relegated to the edges. The despised of the world were the special friends of Jesus. He began and ended his life on the underside of history. Jesus grew up in the obscure, insignificant, and despised town of Nazareth. He worked among the fishermen, the tax collectors, the prostitutes and notorious sinners of Galilee. He ended his life on the rubbish dump of humanity, driven out of the city and put to death on the very edge of society.

The epistle to the Hebrews has expressed it this way: "Therefore Jesus also suffered outside the city gate in order to sanctify the people by his own blood. Let us then go to him outside the camp and bear the abuse he endured. For here we have no lasting city, but we are looking for the city that is to come" (Heb. 13:12-14). Jesus suffered outside the gate, and he calls on us to go to him outside the camp to find our place with the outcasts and lepers of society, among the marginalized and downtrodden. He calls on us to bear society's abuse with the outcasts and to work with them for the city that is to come. Remember, too, that it is only a few verses earlier that we are told, "Jesus Christ is the same yesterday and today and forever" (13:8). The message is clear. Jesus does not change—nor do his message and his mission.

From the perspective of life on the road with Jesus, the "homogeneous principle" of some branches of the church growth school appears as nothing short of blasphemy. It likewise seems to be dangerous heresy to separate the unified mission of the church into evangelism, social action, and political involvement, and to ascribe an absolute priority to one or other of them. The mission of the church insists on breaking down all artificially constructed barriers—especially those which support oppression and marginalization. The good news of the kingdom addresses people and societies at every level of their existence. There is no area of life untouched by its challenge.

The gospel is to be preached and lived out by the Christian community. The demons are to be denounced and overthrown, and new patterns of Christian living have to be developed in which justice and grace are the dominant factors. We can understand the anguish of Dom Helder Camara, Archbishop of Brazil's poorest diocese, when he says, "When I feed the poor, they call me a saint, but when I ask why some are poor they call me a communist." Following Jesus in his life on the road inevitably leads us into conflict with the power brokers of the day, but in that struggle Jesus promises to be with us. We can therefore go forth in courage and faith.

Questions for Discussion

1. What might happen if our churches decided that their mission was essentially a continuation of the messianic ministry of Jesus?

2. What are the most important aspects of the church's mission?

3. What are the most important resources that the church has for carrying out its mission?

4. How can we be salt and light today?

5. Why is the understanding of the gospel of Jesus as good news to the poor not always welcome in our churches?

6. How can we enter into solidarity with the poor?

7. In what ways have you experienced the gospel as a liberating power in your life and in the lives of others?

8. Does Jesus still live on the other side of the tracks? Why? Why not?

6

Road Under Repair

Discipleship and Power

A Poor Man As Liberator of the Poor

Jürgen Moltmann has written: "A poor man as a liberator of the poor, a vulnerable man as a saviour of the helpless—that seems like a contradiction in terms." But the crucifixion and resurrection have given a new definition to these terms and have drawn the community of Jesus' followers into "his self-surrender, into his solidarity with the lost, and into his public suffering" (Moltmann, *Church*, 82).

The Gospels repeatedly remind us of the difficulty which the early church experienced in following the way of Jesus. The believers had trouble recognizing that the same one who claimed that "all authority in heaven and on earth has been given to me" (Matt. 28:18), was also the one who "emptied himself, taking the form of a slave [servant]. . . . He humbled himself and became obedient to the point of death—even death on a cross" (Phil. 2:7-8).

Raised in the obscure and despised village of Nazareth, Jesus from the beginning takes his stand with the despised and dispossessed people of Galilee. People recognize that his teaching contains an authority unknown among his contemporaries (Mark 1:21-28) and that with divine power he performs miracles (Matt. 11:20, 13:54; 14:2). Yet he still associates with the powerless poor, who are shunned by the religious and political leaders of the day.

Jesus claims authority to forgive sins (Mark 2:1-12), to exercise lordship over the Sabbath (2:23-28), and to ignore the stringent food regulations (7:14). He cures the sick (1:28-45), casts out demons (1:21-28; 5:1-17), calls disciples to follow him (1:16-20; 2:14) and expels traders and pilgrims from the temple (11:15-17). Jesus has the power to defeat the forces of evil (3:22-30; Luke 11:14-23), yet he is crucified outside the camp (Heb. 13:11-13), rejected by the power elite, and even in his death is found in the company of the despised, the rejected, and the tortured outcasts of society (Mark 15:21-39).

Jesus' contemporaries looked for a messianic leader of great power and glory who would restore the political fortunes of Israel, defeat the Gentiles, and establish his kingdom in Jerusalem. Jesus refuses to fulfill these hopes and ambitions for political domination; he deliberately identifies with the plight of the powerless. At the beginning, the temptation stories portray in a dramatic way Jesus' renunciation of the way of the powerful, ascribing such thoughts to the devil himself (Matt. 4:1-11; Luke 4:1-13). At the end, the soldiers mockingly salute him "King of the Jews" (Mark 15:18), and the religious leaders jeer the Messiah who could save others but could not save himself (15:31-32)—not knowing the truth they proclaim. And so it is that as Jesus is most helpless, nailed to a cross, a Gentile centurion sees how he died and confesses, "Truly this man was God's Son!" (15:39).

Jesus is our motivation for sacrificial service. However, James and John, the disciples who want positions of honor and glory in the kingdom of God (Mark 10:35-45), stand as a stark warning to us. They are the embodiment of a temptation always present: to seek the way of earthly power and glory rather than the way of suffering and service.

To follow the way of Jesus demands a radical detachment from the ways of the world and a corresponding commitment to the community of the people of God. The call of Jesus brings disciples together as a community of the people of God distinct from the world. Yet that same call sends them out to a life of obedience in the world. Discipleship involves mission. While following Jesus, the early church was a community on a mission which especially embraced the poor and the oppressed, the outcasts and the marginalized. All those who were traditionally excluded from the people of God were particularly welcome.

This life of community and mission involved the voluntary renunciation of power and privilege and the acceptance of a new role as servants of God and of humanity. The kingdom does not depend on the prestige, power, and authority of the disciples. It is the work of a gracious and loving God, revealed in humility and powerlessness in Jesus of Nazareth, who was born in a stable and crucified on a cross.

This chapter explores three examples of the way the Evangelists sought to reinterpret for their communities the significance of Jesus and the disciples as it related to the power structures of their day: the priority of the oppressed as seen in the incidents relating to women and children (Mark), the presentation of the humble and merciful Messiah in his entry into Jerusalem (Matthew), and the overthrow of the powers of structural evil in the defeat of the demonic (Luke). The road we travel in following Jesus is a road under repair.

The Priority of the Oppressed (Mark 10:1-16)

The central section of the Gospel of Mark is devoted to the significance of Jesus and the meaning of discipleship (Mark 8:27—10:52). Three times Jesus tells of his impending death (Mark 8:31; 9:31; 10:33-34), but on each occasion his followers misunderstand the significance of what he is saying (Mark 8:32-33, Peter; 9:32-34, the disciples; 10:35-37, the sons of Zebedee). Jesus has to take them aside and teach them about the real nature of discipleship.

At Caesarea Philippi, near the start of his fateful journey to Jerusalem, Jesus begins to tell his disciples that the Son of

Man must suffer and die (Mark 8:27-31). Peter does not understand (8:32-33). After that, Jesus teaches his community that those who follow him must do so by way of the cross (8:34—9:1). This now is public proclamation; the crowd as well as the disciples must hear this because it has significance for anyone who would follow Jesus. Six days later, Elijah and Moses, the suffering righteous ones, stand with Jesus on the Mount of Transfiguration, and the divine voice affirms the truth of Jesus' message about the suffering Son of Man and the need to take up the cross and follow him (9:2-8). Even then they fail to understand (9:9-13), and Jesus has to teach them that discipleship involves dependence upon God (9:14-29).

As they continue their journey through Galilee, Jesus speaks the second time of his coming rejection and death (Mark 9:31). Again, they fail to understand and become involved in fruitless discussions about their own importance (9:32-34). Jesus seeks to show them that discipleship must cover the whole of life: human priorities (9:30-50), social relationships (10:1-16), and material possessions (10:17-31). The life of discipleship involves a renunciation of false views of status, of tyrannical use of power, and of reliance on material security. The kingdom brings a complete reversal of values—those who "are first will be last, and the last will be first" (10:31).

When it becomes clear that Jerusalem is their destination, Jesus tells them a third time that he is to suffer and die (Mark 10:32-34). But they fail to understand yet again as James and John ask for the first and second positions in the kingdom of God (10:35-40). Jesus seeks to tell them that discipleship involves sacrificial service—not exalted authority—and again uses the example of the suffering Son of Man to illustrate the essential nature of discipleship (10:41-45).

Mark has carefully arranged his material in 8:27—10:52 so that we will not miss his intentions. When he wishes to begin a fresh subsection, he provides a new geographical location. When he wishes to bring it to a conclusion, he does so with an "amen" saying about discipleship: "Truly I tell you" (Mark 9:1, 41; 10:15, 29). The one exception is at the end, where he returns to a saying about the Son of Man so that the start and finish of the section, the total context of discipleship, is seen to be christological (10:45).

Mark's whole focus is on teaching the disciples the meaning of following Jesus. Some of the stories originally centered on others, such as the healing of the epileptic boy (Mark 9:14-27), and the Pharisees asking their trick question about divorce (10:2-9). Now in Mark these stories focus on the disciples as Jesus goes indoors and explains to them the meaning of what has happened (9:28-29; 10:10-12). The rich young man who asks the important question about the meaning of life (10:17-22) quickly disappears from view, and Jesus gives extended teaching to the disciples on the vexing question of material possessions (10:23-31). The crowd appears only at those points where Mark wishes to draw attention to the universal significance of the teaching of Jesus. Our present story is a case in point:

[Jesus] left that place and went to the region of Judea and beyond the Jordan. And crowds again gathered around him; and, as was his custom, he again taught them.

Some Pharisees came, and to test him they asked, "Is it lawful for a man to divorce his wife?" He answered them, "What did Moses command you?" They said, "Moses allowed a man to write a certificate of dismissal and to divorce her." But Jesus said to them, "Because of your hardness of heart he wrote this commandment for you. But from the beginning of creation, 'God made them male and female.' 'For this reason a man shall leave his father and mother and be joined to his wife, and the two shall become one flesh.' So they are no longer two, but one flesh. Therefore what God has joined together, let no one [Greek: *anthrōpos*; AG: man] separate."

Then in the house the disciples asked again about this matter. He said to them, "Whoever divorces his wife and marries another commits adultery against her; and if she divorces her husband and marries another, she commits adultery."

People were bringing little children to him in order that he might touch them; and the disciples spoke sternly to them. But when Jesus saw this, he was indignant and said to them, "Let the little children come to me; do not stop them; for it is to such as these that the kingdom of God belongs. Truly I tell you, whoever does not receive the kingdom of God as a little child will never enter it." And he took them up in his arms, laid his hands on them, and blessed them.   (Mark 10:1-16)

Once again Mark has arranged his material carefully so that the context and extent of his teaching are immediately apparent. As is his pattern in this section of the Gospel, he begins his new subsection with a geographical notice (Mark 10:1). Then he concludes it with an "amen" or "truly" discipleship saying, which has clearly been inserted into the narrative at this point (10:15). The Pharisees provide the setting for the story (10:2), and the crowds are present (10:1) because what takes place here is of universal significance. At the end, however, Jesus moves indoors and gives to the disciples a private explanation of the meaning of what he has just said publicly (10:11-12). This explanation is for the church, and Mark's primary interest lies in the church.

The story about the disciples' attempt to stop the children being brought to Jesus (Mark 10:13-16) follows immediately, without geographical notice. It is to be read together with the preceding story (10:1-12). The climax is reached in the discipleship saying which Mark has inserted, "Truly I tell you, whoever does not receive the kingdom of God as a little child will never enter it" (10:15). The kingdom of God brings with it a truly remarkable reversal of values.

The traditional division of material in our printed Bibles ignores Mark's careful arrangement of his material. Their headings, "Teaching About Divorce" (Mark 10:1-12) and "Little Children Blessed" (10:13-16), miss the point Mark is trying to make. This is not just a story of what happened once upon a time, and it doesn't simply deal with the questions of divorce and children. It is a unified presentation on the priority of the oppressed in the kingdom of God—an eternal gospel theme.

Rejection of the Abuse of Privilege

Old Testament Law, unlike the legal codes of Mesopotamia, contains no explicit regulation about divorce (Ewald, 13-34). However, in the Law prohibiting the restoration of a previously annulled marriage, it obviously permitted a man to dismiss his wife, provided he gave her a certificate of divorce to protect her interests (Deut. 24:1-4).

The formula of divorce was simply, "She is not my wife, and I am not her husband" (Hos. 2:2). The husband himself administered this, simply with an oral statement in Arab Muslim practice and ancient custom. However, Mosaic Law required a written document (Deut. 24:1-4), which would deter rash action, especially if the husband had to find someone else who could write. Unlike our Western legal system, no judicial authority was involved. Thus when Jesus says, "What God has joined together, a man [Greek: *anthrōpos*] must not separate" (Mark 10:9, AG), the reference is to the husband, not to a legal or civil official.

Since the Old Testament has no explicit rules governing divorce, it does not explain legal grounds for divorce. Deuteronomy 24:1 uses an obscure statement which means literally "because of the nakedness of a thing." This is variously translated: "because he has found some indecency in her" (RSV); "something objectionable" (NRSV); "shameful" (NEB); "offensive" (REB). It may simply be a summary reference to legal causes which were well-known at the time but which have not been recorded.

In the first century the matter was still not settled. The school of Shammai interpreted Deuteronomy as only permitting dismissal on the ground of the wife's sexual immorality. First-century practice, however, tended to follow the school of Hillel, which was more liberal in giving permission to husbands to divorce their wives. The Hillelites claimed that the "shameful" thing (Deut. 24:1) could not mean adultery because that was punishable by death (Deut. 22:22; Lev. 20:10). So they expanded the grounds for discharge to include any aspect of life in which the wife no longer found favor in her husband's eyes—if she burned his food or if he found another woman more attractive (Mishnah Gittin 9.10)!

In our text, "Pharisees" approach Jesus as he is in the midst of teaching the crowds. When they ask him the trick question (Mark 10:2), they represent, for Mark, not so much the Jewish religious authorities in the time of Jesus as certain

Christian religious leaders in his own church (as Mark 10:10-12 suggests). The Pharisees seek to trap Jesus by bringing him into conflict with the Law. They want to uphold the Law, but they show little concern for the real questions of justice and oppression involved in husbands dismissing their wives. They are like the Sadducees, who are so involved in the little trick question they had worked out that they show no compassion for the woman whom seven brothers "had to wife" (12:18-27, KJV).

Jesus refuses to become involved in a debate about stricter (Shammaite) or more broad-minded (Hillelite) interpretations. He answers their questions not on the basis of what is permissible, but on the basis of the will of God—even though this means setting aside the Mosaic Law (Mark 10:5-9). They keep on asking what is permitted/lawful/allowed (10:2, 4), but Jesus keeps referring to what is commanded (10:3, 5). They are concerned about their rights; Jesus is concerned about their responsibilities. They are seeking loopholes in the regulations that they might exploit to their own advantage. Jesus, however, lifts the discussion out of the context of legalistic interpretation and exploitation by speaking of first principles.

It is of fundamental importance to understand, says Jesus, that God has joined the married couple together as "one flesh" (Gen. 2:24). Therefore, it is not permissible to separate them (Mark 10:8-9). In dismissing his wife, the husband is refusing to accept the work of God in his life and arrogates to himself rights which belong to God. He then proceeds to exploit these rights to his own advantage.

Among the Jews of the first century, the right of dismissal belonged solely to the husband. Only in a few well-defined exceptions could a woman achieve the dissolution of her marriage, and then only with the consent of her husband, who was under no obligation to grant it. According to rabbinic law, a man could be held to commit adultery against another married man, a wife could be held to commit adultery against her husband, but a husband could not be held to commit adultery against his wife.

In all matters relating to Jewish women, whether of legal

or social status or of religious responsibility, women were relegated to a secondary position. Any of the few and limited rights they did enjoy were always mediated to them through a man—first through the father, and then, if married, through the husband. As the first-century Jewish historian Josephus expressed it, "A woman is in every respect of less worth than a man" (Josephus, *Against Apion,* 2.201). The Eighteen Benedictions, a Jewish prayer compiled before the destruction of Jerusalem in 70 C.E., contains this note of thanksgiving: "Blessed art thou, O Lord our God, King of the Universe, who hast not made me a heathen. Blessed art thou, O Lord our God, King of the Universe, who hast not made me a bondman. Blessed art thou, O Lord our God, King of the Universe, who hast not made me a woman."

The ways of humanity involve the exploitation of others through the fraudulent, even if legal, abuse of privilege. The way of God involves accepting the work of God in our lives, acknowledging our responsibilities to others, and living out those responsibilities.

Reciprocal Relationships Within the Community of Faith

Jesus' teaching is quite explicit, but when he goes indoors, the disciples ask him to explain it to them (Mark 10:10). In Mark, the place of private instruction for the church is indoors. Here the disciples' questions show that they cannot understand why discipleship should involve such an absolute refusal to use power and privilege to one's own advantage. They do not understand that many of the rabbinic rules, which they are eager to defend, were drawn up by males in a male-dominated society and were, so often, designed to protect the position of the powerful. To make things worse, the male leaders are looking for loopholes so the law will be even more in their favor.

What about the wife? Does she not have any rights? Jesus' first explanation to his disciples (Mark 10:11) would have shocked his Jewish contemporaries, for it speaks of the husband committing adultery *against his wife.* For Jesus, the woman is a person in her own right and is in no way inferior to her husband. She is neither his possession nor his chattel.

Marriage is a relationship of reciprocal rights, for both husband and wife.

The second explanation (Mark 10:12), however, shows that this new freedom for the woman carries with it a corresponding responsibility. If she gains the right to divorce her husband (as under Hellenistic or Roman law, or under Jewish law in rare cases), then she stands under the same restrictions as her husband. From this perspective, marriage is a relationship of reciprocal responsibilities, for both husband and wife.

But, as we have seen, Mark is not only speaking about relationships within marriage. He is concerned about domination and oppression in all human relationships and is calling for fundamental justice to replace superficial legality. Hence, the story of the children follows immediately because it is also concerned with the questions of power and oppression.

Rejection of the Abuse of Power

The story of the disciples' attempt to prohibit the children being brought to Jesus comes directly after his teaching on divorce. It demonstrates once again that the disciples are unable to understand the way of God in Jesus Christ.

In this story, Mark strikingly has no interest in biographical details whatsoever. He gives not the slightest indication of the time or the place of the incident; there are no geographical details. Mark does not tell us who the children are and says nothing about their age. The same word is used in Mark 5:39-42 to describe Jairus's daughter, who is reported to be twelve years old. Mark does not even bother to tell us who brought the children to Jesus!

The text says nothing at all about the disciples wishing to protect Jesus because he was tired, or about parents coming with wrong motives. It doesn't say anything about the children being from families outside the community of the committed, or about them being too immature to make responsible decisions about Jesus. The text says nothing at all about infant baptism or even of how the church should treat children. This saying of Jesus knows nothing about the pseudo-psychological suggestion that we should strive to develop personal characteristics such as purity and humility so we might be able to enter the kingdom. Indeed, that would make entrance into the kingdom dependent upon a human work rather than upon the grace of God—the very attitude Jesus is seeking to combat.

Rather, the story about the disciples and the children again deals much more simply and profoundly with one of the basic issues of discipleship. Once again the ways of God are differentiated from the ways of humanity as Jesus rejects the abuse of power, privilege, and prestige.

At Capernaum Jesus was obliged to teach the disciples that the question of who is the greatest is quite inappropriate for them. Discipleship is concerned with service rather than with position and privilege (Mark 9:33-37). Immediately afterward, however, John demonstrates his lack of understanding—and the denseness of the other disciples and of the church through the ages.

John reports that they have just seen someone casting out demons in Jesus' name, but they tried to stop him because he did not belong to their circle (Mark 9:38-41). Thus John is an example of exclusive ecclesiastical authority. The grossness of his action can be seen when we remember that just a little while earlier he and the other disciples were unable to cast the demon out of an epileptic boy (9:14-29). They couldn't do that, and yet they think they have the authority to stop someone who can! Jesus seeks to teach them about the need for open community: "Do not stop him; for no one who does a deed of power in my name will be able soon afterward to speak evil of me. For whoever is not against us is for us" (9:39-40). Do not try to stop them!

Later Jesus teaches the husbands within the community that they are to stop claiming for themselves rights which belong to God. Husbands are not to use their privileged legal position to their own advantage. Yet the disciples again immediately demonstrate their lack of understanding by seeking to prohibit the children from coming to Jesus (Mark 10:13-16; the same word for "stop" is in 9:38 and 10:14).

Again, we must recall that in first-century Jewish community, children had even less status and power than women.

The rabbis frequently referred to "the deaf and dumb, the weak-minded, and people under age." The disciples must be thinking: Perhaps now Jesus is the wonder-working Messiah of our hopes and dreams, who is to restore the political fortunes of Israel, defeat the Gentiles, and establish his kingdom in Jerusalem. Surely he has no time for the little people and the powerless ones of society.

For Jesus, however, the kingdom of God belongs especially to the poor, the powerless, the outcasts, and the dispossessed—all those who have no standing within the community (see Matt. 5:1-12). Those who count for nothing in the eyes of their fellows are the very ones to whom the kingdom of God is promised. They come empty-handed, with no power or position of their own. Their only hope is in God, and that hope will not go unrewarded. No matter what the leaders may think, Jesus will not be deterred; he takes the little ones into his arms and blesses them.

Those in positions of power and privilege, even those nearest to Jesus, find this lesson so hard to understand. The disciples try to stop the children from coming to Jesus (Mark 10:13-16), even as they try to stop Jesus from going to his death (8:32). But, just as Jesus has to rebuke Peter in the strongest possible ways (8:33), so here he is indignant at such a blatant misunderstanding of the way of God and at such an offensive abuse of power. Only here in the Gospels is Jesus said to be "indignant"—a harsh word! The disciples still have to learn that the kingdom of God does not depend on them, their talents, and their status. It is the work of a gracious and loving God, a work which knows no boundaries save our willingness to receive God's grace as a gift.

Making Room for the Little People (Matthew 20:29—21:17)

As we observed, the Gospel of Matthew was probably addressed to a rather conservative middle-class community of Jewish Christians living in an urban situation somewhere outside Palestine, possibly in Syria. It was obviously a church that was zealous in its pursuit of the Law (Matt. 5:17-48). Its members were still diligently observing the strict Sabbath regulations (24:20), tithing carefully (23:23), and praying regularly (6:5-8).

The Matthean Christians were, however, prone to a rather harsh legalism and were guilty of sitting in judgment on others (Matt. 7:1-5) as they attempted to maintain a "pure church" (13:24-30). In this connection, they adopted the old synagogue rule outlining the procedure for excommunication of those who refused to conform (18:15-17). They were confident that these decisions would be confirmed in heaven (18:18). Throughout his Gospel, however, Matthew presents Jesus as the merciful Christian Messiah and develops his teaching on discipleship and community relationships. He seeks to show his fellow believers a broader perspective and to engender in them a more loving and accepting spirit.

Thus in his opening genealogy, the Evangelist inserts references to four women (Tamar, Rahab, Ruth, and the wife of Uriah), all of whom had an unfortunate past. Yet they come to play a significant role in the ancestry of Jesus Messiah (Matt. 1:1-17). These women are representative of only some of the marginalized people for whom Matthew is concerned.

Matthew watched for such persons as he collected the miracles of Jesus and arranged them in a systematic presentation of the *works* of the Messiah (Matt. 8—9). Reports of these works follow his exposition of the *words* of the Messiah in the Sermon on the Mount (Matt. 5—7). Matthew deliberately introduces the works with stories of marginalized people in contemporary society: a leper, a Gentile, and a woman. The Evangelist gives this systematic presentation of Jesus' works programmatic status by concluding with an Old Testament quotation (Isa. 53:4). That text emphasizes that in the healing of these sorts of people, Jesus, their model, is fulfilling the exalted role of the suffering servant (Matt. 8:1-17).

To the same end, Matthew emphasizes in the Beatitudes that mercy will be shown to the merciful (Matt. 5:7, a beatitude formulated by the Evangelist himself). In his teaching on the Lord's Prayer, he states that only those who forgive will be forgiven (6:14-15, where the emphatic concluding statement has been added to the verse taken from Mark 11:25). Twice Matthew teaches that mercy is more important than sacrifice, on both occasions inserting the quotation of Hosea 6:6 into a Marcan story (Matt. 9:13; 12:7). He stresses that the whole of the Law and the Prophets (thus referring to the whole Old Testament) is summed up in the commandment to love God and to love your neighbor (22:34-40, adding this statement to Mark's text). And his golden rule of doing to others what you would like them to do for you is given as a one-line summary of the Law and the Prophets (7:12).

As we discovered in chapter four, Matthew has skillfully softened the effect of the old harsh synagogue rule of excommunication (Matt. 18:15-20). He places alongside it the story of Peter being told that he is to forgive his brothers and sisters seventy times seven (18:21-22). Then Matthew continues with the parable of the debtor, which concludes: "And in anger his lord handed him over to be tortured until he would pay his entire debt. So my heavenly Father will also do to every one of you, if you do not forgive your brother or sister from your heart" (18:34-35). Matthew attempts to engender a more loving spirit in his rather legalistically minded church members. He allows the regulation of church discipline to stand to represent brotherly and sisterly care, but makes sure that the church will think seriously before using the rule of excommunication again!

Behind the difficulties of discipleship experienced in Matthew's church was a tendency to understand Jesus in terms of "the Jewish Messiah," an earthly potentate of great power and glory. Throughout his Gospel, he seeks to correct this false Christology, even as he seeks to correct the false view of the church which has developed out of it. For instance, according to Matthew's story line, when Jesus predicts his death for the third time (Matt. 20:17-19), the mother of the sons of Zebedee asks for positions of honor and glory for her boys in the kingdom of God (20:20-23). Jesus denies the request and marks out the way of discipleship as the road of sacrificial service (20:22-28). He carries through this theme with the story of the healing of the blind men (20:29-34), the entry into Jerusalem (21:1-11), and the cleansing of the temple (21:12-17).

As they were leaving Jericho, a large crowd followed [Jesus]. There were two blind men sitting by the roadside. When they heard that Jesus was passing by, they shouted, "Lord, have mercy on us, Son of David!" The crowd sternly ordered them to be quiet; but they shouted even more loudly, "Have mercy on us, Lord, Son of David!" Jesus stood still and called them, saying, "What do you want me to do for you?" They said to him, "Lord, let our eyes be opened." Moved with compassion, Jesus touched their eyes. Immediately they regained their sight and followed him.

When they had come near Jerusalem and had reached Bethphage, at the Mount of Olives, Jesus sent two disciples, saying to them, "Go into the village ahead of you, and immediately you will find a donkey tied, and a colt with her; untie them and bring them to me. If anyone says anything to you, just say this, 'The Lord needs them.' And he will send them immediately." This took place to fulfill what had been spoken through the prophet, saying,

"Tell the daughter of Zion,
Look, your king is coming to you,
humble, and mounted on a donkey,
and on a colt, the foal of a donkey."

The disciples went and did as Jesus had directed them; they brought the donkey and the colt, and put their cloaks on them, and he sat on them. A very large crowd spread their cloaks on the road. The crowds that went ahead of him and that followed were shouting,

"Hosanna to the Son of David!
Blessed is the one who comes in the name of the Lord!
Hosanna in the highest heaven!"

When he entered Jerusalem, the whole city was in turmoil, asking, "Who is this?" The crowds were saying, "This is the prophet Jesus from Nazareth in Galilee."

Then Jesus entered the temple and drove out all who were selling and buying in the temple, and he overturned the tables of the money changers and the seats of those who sold doves. He said to them, "It is written,

'My house shall be called a house of prayer';
but you are making it a den of robbers."

The blind and the lame came to him in the temple, and he cured them. But when the chief priests and the scribes saw the amazing things that he did, and heard the children crying out in the temple, "Hosanna to the Son of David," they became angry and said to him, "Do you hear what these are saying?" Jesus said to them, "Yes; have you never read,

'Out of the mouths of infants and nursing babies
   you have prepared praise for yourself'?"

He left them, went out of the city to Bethany, and spent the night there.   (Matt. 20:29—21:17)

Matthew is using the Marcan account as the basis of his story, but as elsewhere in his Gospel, he rearranges and rewrites the material so that his message comes through clearly. It will help us in understanding his message if we compare his account with Mark's, not in an attempt to harmonize them, but rather to see the distinctive emphases he is making. He relocates the story of the cursing of the fig tree (Matt. 21:18-22) after the incidents in the temple (contrast Mark 11:12-14, 20-25). He also deletes the references to Jesus going in and out of Jerusalem (21:11-12, 15) so that the story is presented as a single unit within the ministry of Jesus.

Matthew adds the Scripture quotations (Matt. 21:5 from Zech. 9:9; Matt. 21:16 from Ps. 8:2, NIV). He includes the stories about the whole city going wild with excitement (Matt. 21:10-11), the healing of the blind and the lame (21:14), and the children crying their hosannas in the temple (21:15-16). Thus he has carefully edited the story as a unified presentation of Jesus, the Christian Messiah, who uses his power on behalf of the outcasts. This Messiah is greeted with enthusiasm by the little people of society, but he incurs the indignation of the powerful.

The Messiah Shows His True Colors

Mainstream Jewish messianic hopes in the first century centered on the prophecies that one day a descendant of David would arise and restore the kingdom of Israel to its former glory. This understanding of the Messiah seems to have received only minor modifications before the apostles transferred the center of destiny from Israel to the church. It influenced Matthew's church in their interpretation of the person and work of Christ.

However, Matthew's presentation is a radical reinterpretation of this messianic hope. Four times within these stories, Jesus is greeted as "the Son of David" (Matt. 20:30-31; 21:9, 15; the first two taken over from Mark, the third and fourth added by Matthew). Indeed, precisely the acclamation of Jesus as the Son of David binds the stories together. This theme is reinforced by the Evangelist as he emphasizes that the entry into Jerusalem fulfills the prophecy of Zechariah 9:9 (in 21:4-5). To bring out the "Son of David" theme, Matthew also reinterprets the story of the cleansing of the temple (21:12-13) against the background of Zechariah 14:21, where it is said that "there shall no longer be traders in the house of the Lord of hosts on that day."

Zechariah 9:9 belongs to the opening oracle of the messianic promises which make up the second half of that book, and Zechariah 14:21 is the last verse of that collection of prophecies. By stressing the fulfillment of the first and last of Zechariah's majestic predictions, Matthew is indicating to his readers that the totality of messianic expectations have found their fulfillment in Jesus. At this point he would have received an enthusiastic response from even the most conservative members of his church. Matthew is particularly interested, though, in showing exactly *how* these majestic predictions were fulfilled in Jesus.

In the healing of the blind men near Jericho (Matt. 20:29-34), nonessential details have been omitted so that the story can be told in 77 words, compared to Mark's 118 (Mark 10:46-52). All attention is focused on Jesus. The name of the blind man is no longer given (in Mark it is found in both Aramaic transliteration and Greek translation), but in the brief space of five verses the name "Jesus" occurs three times (Matt. 20:30, 32, 34), and he is addressed as "Lord" three times (20:30-31, 33) and "Son of David" twice (20:30-31). Strong messianic testimony indeed!

That there are now two blind men (only one in Mark) strengthens their messianic testimony. According to Old Testament law, every word is to be established by the mouth of two or three witnesses (Deut. 17:6). This is the third time Matthew has done this: two demoniacs testified to the Gadarenes that Jesus was "Son of God" (Matt. 8:28-34; only one demoniac in Mark). And two blind men called him "Son of David" (9:29-31). There can be no mistaking Matthew's intention.

When the crowd attempts to silence the testimony of the blind men, this only serves (as in Mark) to heighten their appeal for mercy (Matt. 20:31). Jesus responds with "compassion" and touches their eyes. The blind men can see again, and they become followers of the Messiah (20:34). We know Matthew wants us to understand that they became disciples of Jesus: in this Gospel only disciples "follow" Jesus and address him as "Lord." All this sets the scene for his entry into the temple. There he will show his true colors!

Matthew's account of the entry into Jerusalem (Matt. 21:1-11) is dominated by the Old Testament quotations which he adds to the Marcan story. He combines two messianic passages (Isa. 62:11 and Zech. 9:9) and interprets the prophecy as requiring two animals. He also rewrites the whole story in such a way that it now provides a literal fulfillment, with Jesus riding into Jerusalem on a donkey and its foal (Matt. 21:2, 5, 7).

Yet Matthew does not simply quote the Old Testament: he *interprets it through Jesus.* Zechariah 9:9 says:

> Rejoice greatly, O daughter of Zion!
>   Shout aloud, O daughter Jerusalem!
> Lo, your king comes to you;
>   triumphant and victorious is he,
> humble and riding on a donkey,
>   on a colt, the foal of a donkey [AG: beast of burden].

Matthew has deliberately omitted the line "triumphant and victorious is he" so that the emphasis now falls on the words "humble and riding on a donkey, on a colt, the foal of [a beast of burden]."

Zechariah was looking for a mighty king who would lead the mighty men of Israel in a victorious battle, "trampling the foe in the mud of the streets" (Zech. 10:5). The first-century B.C.E. pseudepigraphical Psalms of Solomon show that this was still the dominant expectation, among the Pharisees at least. Psalm of Solomon 17 speaks of "the Son of David" who will "purge Jerusalem," "shatter unrighteous rulers," and break Israel's enemies "with a rod of iron."

In direct contrast, Matthew deletes the reference to triumph and victory and emphasizes the lowliness, the humility of the king of the little people. Many in Matthew's day would have recognized the royal and messianic significance of the act of riding into Jerusalem on a donkey, as ancient rulers traveled (see Gen. 49:10-11; Gardner, 312). Yet the one who is to be the judge of all the world disclaims worldly power, glory, triumph, and victory, entering Jerusalem in lowliness and humility on the way to the cross. He is the Christian Messiah, the king who is to be crucified.

The crowds who lead the way and the disciples who follow understand the gospel message and shout their hosannas to "the Son of David" (Matt. 21:9, with the title added to the Marcan acclamation). When Jesus enters Jerusalem for the first time, the whole city goes wild with excitement, and he is identified as "the prophet Jesus from Nazareth in Galilee" (21:10-11).

What an unexpected message for the people of the national and religious capital, the economic center of the country! The "Son of David" is a truly charismatic figure, but he comes from Nazareth. Nazareth of Galilee! That insignificant and despised place (John 1:46) never mentioned in the Old Testament or in any other literature prior to the Gospel tradition! Truly, this is a pointer for those looking for a mighty ruler who would set up his kingdom in Jerusalem. Here is a sure sign that religious hopes and political ambitions are about to be reinterpreted. And it is in Jerusalem, at the very temple itself, that this reinterpretation is about to take place.

He Uses His Power on Behalf of the Outcasts

Zechariah's prophecies of the day of the Lord looked forward to the time when there would no longer be any traders in the house of the Lord (Zech. 14:21). All possible space would be required for the nations who would come to Jerusalem to "worship the King, the Lord of hosts" (14:16). All of the pots and bowls in Jerusalem and Judah would have to be collected so there would be enough for all who would want to come and "boil the flesh of the sacrifice" in them (14:21). It was to be a mighty celebration—and Matthew builds on Zechariah.

Matthew also describes a mighty celebration in the temple, but again there is a striking difference. When Jesus cleanses the temple of the traders in fulfillment of Zechariah's prophecy, the blind and the lame come to him, and the children worship him there. Not the nations, but the nobodies! Matthew even has a reason for omitting Mark's reference to the temple being "a house of prayer for all the nations" (Mark 11:17). Unfortunately, in Zechariah's picture, the coming of the nations to worship had become part of Israel dominating the Gentiles, now an integral part of their nationalistic heritage. In Matthew's presentation, Jesus comes as the liberator of the oppressed—not as the oppressor of the nations.

The blind and the lame who come to Jesus in the temple (Matt. 21:14) do not often come together in Scripture, but one important Old Testament story refers to them. It provides the key to their significance in this passage. Second Samuel 5:6-10 tells, briefly and with some obscure references, the story of David's capture of Jerusalem. Until that time it had been a Jebusite (Canaanite) fortress, strong and naturally fortified. Its inhabitants boasted that even the blind and the lame could ward off any attack that might be mounted against it; perhaps the blind and the lame incited Jebusite resistance to David. David's plan of capturing the city was to enter through the water shaft rather than by scaling the walls (according to NRSV and some interpreters). David and his men were successful.

As he took the city, David remembered the taunts by or about the blind and the lame and ordered his men to attack them (NRSV). Or he commanded his men to deliver only fatal blows, striking at the throats of any resisting Jebusites, so that David would not be left with a city of crippled people (Anchor Bible, vol. 9; Deut. 20:10-18 gives a ban, for all to be put to death). The blind and the lame either hate David (NRSV note), or David hates them (NRSV text); probably from religious scruple, David deems killing better than mutilating living human beings. The writer adds, "Therefore it is said, 'The blind and the lame shall not come into the house of the Lord' " (2 Sam. 5:8, from the Greek).

In keeping with the spirit of that passage, the Levitical law forbade blind and crippled priests from offering sacrifices in the temple (Lev. 21:18). In certain cases, a mutilated person was barred from public worship (Deut. 23:1). The monks of the Qumran community, in developing their model of "a pure church," excluded the crippled, the blind, the deaf, the mute, the insane, and the deformed (Messianic Rule: 1QSa 2.5-7; Damascus Rule: CD 15.15-17).

On that first occasion when David came to Jerusalem, he killed the blind and the lame. But when the Son of David comes to Jerusalem for the first time (in Matthew), he heals the blind and the lame (Matt. 21:14). There is the difference, says Matthew. The Christian Messiah, the one that his church should be following, uses his power on behalf of the blind and the lame. Jesus champions all who have been legally excluded from the presence of God by the power elite of the day. And people on the fringes of society, whom the majority frequently want to silence (20:31), who have been marginalized and have no power to help themselves (21:14)—those are the very ones on whose behalf the Christian Messiah intervenes as he is on his way to his own rejection, suffering, and death, "outside the camp" (Heb. 13:11-12).

The Powerful Are Indignant, the Little Ones Shout His Praise

At Jericho the crowds first want to silence the cries of the blind men for help (Matt. 20:31). But when Jesus responds with compassion, even the crowd is won over. As he is entering Jerusalem, the people spread their coats on the road and shout their hosannas to "the Son of David" (21:8-9). But inside Jerusalem there is a different response at the temple (21:12-13). The religious are absolutely indignant when they see "the amazing things" he is doing in the temple. Wonderful acts of liberation are not always welcome, especially by the powerful whose privileged position is threatened! The children (those without status, power, or glory), however, rush to greet the liberator of the poor and oppressed, once more shouting, "Hosanna to the Son of David" (21:15).

Again, Matthew stresses the importance of reinterpreting Zechariah's prophecies of messianic triumph. The prophet had declared that Israel would "be like warriors in battle, trampling the foe in the mud of the streets. . . . Their children shall see it and rejoice" (Zech. 10:5, 7). As it turns out in fulfillment, the children shout their praise when they see Jesus healing the blind and the lame and restoring them to their rightful place in society (Matt. 21:15).

Jesus finally silences the opposition with a word from Scripture. The psalmist rightly understood that it would always be the little people who see God's greatness in the world and who sing his praises (Matt. 21:16 from Ps. 8:2). Yahweh is their God, Jesus their king! "O Lord, our Sovereign, how majestic is your name in all the earth!" (8:1, 9).

The Psalms sung in that very temple testify to the truth of what is happening in its midst; but to no avail, as far as the religious authorities are concerned. The people of power nail Jesus to the cross; the little people shout, "Hosanna to the Son of David!" This is the gospel truth, says Matthew to his community, which is being trapped in its own web of power! Jesus is the humble Christian Messiah who uses his power on behalf of the marginalized people of society. They are the ones who recognize him and worship him, but those who are powerful cannot understand the truth. They are indignant at his acts of mercy and liberation and will finally nail him to the cross. Yet, it is at the cross that final liberation takes place. The powerful cannot stop the process of salvation history.

The Defeat of the Demonic (Luke 11:14-28)

A strong fear of demons was widespread in the ancient world. Illnesses of various kinds, particularly mental disorders, were attributed to demons, which were thought to have taken over the victims in such a way that the people were no longer in control of their own affairs. Healing miracles, particularly expulsions of demons, were seen as victory for the miracle worker over the demon which had previously held the sick person under its control. The Gospel stories depict Jesus regarding demons as the underlings of Satan, the ruler of the powers of evil. In healing and casting out demons,

Jesus sees himself locked in battle with the ultimate power of evil. His victories are a sign of the inbreaking of the kingly reign of God, the beginning of the defeat of Satan, an anticipation of final victory, in which Satan would be stripped of all power.

Luke records more miracles of Jesus than any other Evangelist. From Mark, he has taken over the stories of the cleansing of the demoniac in Capernaum (Luke 4:33-37), the healing of Peter's mother-in-law (4:38-39), the cleansing of a leper (5:12-16), the healing of a paralytic (5:17-26), the healing of a man with a withered hand (6:6-11), the stilling of the storm (8:22-25), the freeing of the Gerasene demoniac (8:26-39), the healing of Jairus's daughter and the woman with a hemorrhage (8:41-56), the feeding of the five thousand (9:10-17), the rebuking of the unclean spirit of the epileptic boy (9:37-43), and the healing of a blind man (18:35-43).

Together with Matthew, Luke has the story of the dumb demoniac (Luke 11:14-15) and the healing of the servant of the centurion from Capernaum (7:1-10). He is the only one to record the miraculous catch of fish (5:1-11; see the similar story in John 21:1-8), the raising of the widow's son at Nain (Luke 7:11-17), the healing of a man with dropsy (14:1-6), the cleansing of the ten lepers (17:11-19), and the healing of the ear of the high priest's servant (22:51). In all, Luke has nineteen saving "deeds of power" (10:13), not counting the many indirect references to Jesus' healing ministry (4:18-19, 40-41; 6:17-19; 7:21-23; 8:2; and many other places).

When John the Baptist has second thoughts about Jesus and sends two of his disciples to ask Jesus if he really is the true Messiah after all, Jesus replies: "Go and tell John what you have seen and heard: the blind receive their sight, the lame walk, the lepers are cleansed, the deaf hear, the dead are raised, the poor have good news brought to them. And blessed is anyone who takes no offense at me" (Luke 7:22-23).

For Jesus and his followers, the miracles are not simply seen as displays of mighty power. They are regarded as evidence that God is with him and that the promised kingly reign of God is about to break into human history, with salvific and creative dynamite (Luke 10:13, NRSV: "deeds of power"; Greek: *dunameis*). Jesus' miracle-working power is part of the early church's testimony to Jesus, and so Peter is reported as telling Cornelius "how God anointed Jesus of Nazareth with the Holy Spirit and with power; how he went about doing good and healing all who were oppressed by the devil, for God was with him" (Acts 10:38). The miracles play a more important role in the writings of Luke than in those of the other Evangelists.

But, as the New Testament itself indicates, there were many other miracle workers in the first century (Luke 11:15; Mark 9:38-40). Hence, Jesus' miracles are signs of God's presence only to those who have faith. They do not and can not have the character of an indisputable proof of God's presence with Jesus. The religious opponents reject the idea that Jesus' power came from God. Yet already at an early stage in his ministry, they do not reject his miracles or seek to explain them away. After all, Jesus performs many of them in public with a large crowd present, and he clearly builds up quite a reputation as a miracle worker. The critics however, claim that it is by the power of Beelzebul, the prince of demons, that he performs his miracles (Mark 3:22-30; Luke 11:14-23). His power, they assert, comes not from God, but from God's powerful adversary.

> Now [Jesus] was casting out a demon that was mute; when the demon had gone out, the one who had been mute spoke, and the crowds were amazed. But some of them said, "He casts out demons by Beelzebul, the ruler of the demons." Others, to test him, kept demanding from him a sign from heaven. But he knew what they were thinking and said to them, "Every kingdom divided against itself becomes a desert, and house falls on house. If Satan also is divided against himself, how will his kingdom stand?—for you say that I cast out the demons by Beelzebul. Now if I cast out the demons by Beelzebul, by whom do your exorcists [AG: followers; Greek: sons] cast them out? Therefore they will be your judges. But if it is by the finger of God that I cast out the demons, then the kingdom of God has come to you. When a strong man, fully armed, guards his castle, his property is safe. But when one stronger than he attacks him and overpowers him, he takes away his armor in which he trusted and divides his plunder. Whoever is not with

me is against me, and whoever does not gather with me scatters.

"When the unclean spirit has gone out of a person, it wanders through waterless regions looking for a resting place, but not finding any, it says, 'I will return to my house from which I came.' When it comes, it finds it swept and put in order. Then it goes and brings seven other spirits more evil than itself, and they enter and live there; and the last state of that person is worse than the first.

While he was saying this, a woman in the crowd raised her voice and said to him, "Blessed is the womb that bore you and the breasts that nursed you!" But he said, "Blessed rather are those who hear the word of God and obey it!" (Luke 11:14-28)

Luke is not simply writing of a scholarly discussion which took place at some time in the ministry of Jesus when he records this debate about the origin of Jesus' power in the battle with the demonic. As with all of the stories and discussions in his Gospel, he is primarily concerned with the significance of the discussion for the church to which he is writing. The material he is using has parallels to Mark (3:22-27) and Matthew (12:22-30, 43-45). But Luke has reworked it into a consistent passage on the contemporary significance of the defeat of the demonic in the ministry of Jesus and in the mission of the apostolic community. Therefore, he locates this discussion of overcoming the rule of Satan within the context of the journey to Jerusalem, as Jesus instructs his followers on the meaning of discipleship (Luke 9:51—19:48).

Discipleship, too, is the meaning of the final declaration of happiness: "Blessed are those who hear the word of God and obey it" (11:28). The "word of God" is a favorite Lucan term for the preaching of the apostolic gospel (Luke 5:1; 8:11, 21; Acts 6:2, 7; 8:14; 11:1; and many other places). "Listen" is Luke's favorite description of an obedient faith response to the proclamation of the gospel (Luke 9:35; 16:29; Acts 28:28; and many other places). The discussion is therefore presented as one which has significance for the people of God in all ages.

The Inbreaking of the Kingdom

In Luke's setting to the discussion, we are told of the crowd being amazed when Jesus casts a demon out of a mute person, who then speaks. But some attribute it to magic, while others are not convinced and want some definite and unmistakable proof as a further sign from heaven (Luke 11:14-16). In Matthew, the dispute takes place when Jesus heals a blind and mute demoniac and all the crowds are amazed and say, "Can this be the Son of David?" (Matt. 12:22-23). The Pharisees accuse Jesus of collusion with the leader of the demons (12:24). In Mark, it is "the scribes who came down from Jerusalem" (Mark 3:22).

In Luke, however, the critics are simply "some of them" (Luke 11:15). Luke was aware that this sort of objection was often made against Jesus and his apostolic missionaries and was in no way restricted to the Jewish leaders in the time of Jesus. It was still being made against the charismatic prophets and preachers in Luke's own day. It was a real-life issue for his church in its proclamation to the pagan world.

Later, Luke will return to the waverers who want further signs from heaven (Luke 11:29-30). Here Jesus addresses himself to the opponents who charge that he is in collusion with Beelzebul (11:17-20). Beelzebul was but one of the many Jewish names for the ruler of the demonic world; elsewhere he is called Mastema, Sammael, Asmodaeus, and Belial. Jesus gives two refutations of their charge of collusion with Satan. First, says Jesus, Satan is no fool; he and everyone else knows that the welfare of his kingdom, like all other kingdoms, requires unity. Why would he work against himself by giving his power to Jesus so that Jesus could drive out Satan's underlings and eventually challenge the ruler himself? And anyway, what about the many Jewish exorcists, some of whom were their followers? Are they also inspired by Beelzebul? The conduct of their own disciples destroys their argument. Their charge is clearly without foundation.

After Jesus silences his critics, he goes on to teach that he casts out demons as a sign that he is at war with Satan. Instead of being in an alliance with Satan, he casts out demons as a sign of the inbreaking of God's kingly rule into a world dominated by the forces of evil (Luke 11:20). Psalm 8:3 says that the creation of the heavens is the work of God's fingers. The covenant law is said to have been written on tables of stone by "the finger of God" (Exod. 31:18; Deut. 9:10). Even more important, "the finger of God" brought forth the plagues which confounded Pharaoh and his magicians and eventually led to the liberation of the Israelites (Exod. 8:19). Against this background in the Exodus story, the finger of God (Luke 11:20; compare Matt. 12:28, "the Spirit of God") is a symbol of God's power freeing women and men from the power of Satan. God's power is active in liberating men and women from the destructive and dehumanizing forces that control them. This act of liberation revealed in the ministry of Jesus is a sign of the inbreaking of God's kingly rule, an anticipation of that day when all dehumanizing forces will be destroyed in the age of grace and love.

Neutrality Is Impossible

In the battle with the demonic, neutrality is an impossible stance. Those who have not united with Jesus in his battle against Satan have in fact taken their stance against Satan. Even those who refuse to become involved are against Jesus because they are allowing Satan to accomplish his demonic purposes in the world (Luke 11:23). Not to decide between the two is nevertheless to make a decision, and not to be involved is to allow the forces of evil to triumph.

The picture of the two opposing kingdoms (Luke 11:21-22) is based on Isaiah 49:24-26, a prophetic poem to Jerusalem announcing God's restoration following judgment. In 586 B.C.E. Nebuchadnezzar (or Nebuchadrezzar) captured Judah, destroyed Jerusalem, and took leading people of Israel in chains to Babylon. The prophets interpreted this action as the judgment of God upon a sinful nation. Now Isaiah is sitting in Babylon, exiled with his people, and begins to tell them that their time of judgment is almost over. Salvation is at hand. In scenes of horror and destruction, the prophet predicts how the all-powerful God of Jacob will smash the mighty tyrant Babylon and snatch back his people who had been taken captive by Nebuchadnezzar's armies.

In Luke, the story of deliverance is reinterpreted: the mighty one is Satan, his armor is the demons, the spoils are his victims, and the more powerful one is Jesus. The background in Isaiah, however, shows that Luke is thinking, not only of personal evil, but of corporate evil as well. The demonic had manifested itself in the mighty tyrant Babylon, who, through superior military power, had crushed the whole nation of Israel. The liberation of the enslaved, which the prophet predicts, is also corporate, and for this reason the poem is addressed to Zion rather than to individual Israelites.

The Bible takes seriously the existence of corporate evil, its destructive powers, and its ability to enslave whole nations. The preexilic prophets saw structural evil at work in Israel, acting predominantly through its religious and political leaders. Isaiah 49 pictures structural evil in the Babylonians enslaving the people of Israel, Daniel in the oppression by the Greeks, and the book of Revelation in the tyranny by Rome. The Bible also takes seriously the liberating power of Jesus Christ, the stronger one, who by the finger of God is able to defeat the demonic and inaugurate the kingly reign of God. The deliverance of which the Bible speaks is both personal and corporate, involving humanity in all its many dimensions, the personal and the social, the religious and the political.

In the struggle between oppression and liberation, "whoever is not with me is against me," says Jesus (Luke 11:23). Elsewhere, however, he tells his disciples, "Whoever is not against us is for us" (Mark 9:40). These seemingly contradictory statements are in fact complementary. In the other Marcan story, John had told Jesus that they had seen another person driving out demons in his name, and they had stopped him because he did not belong to their group. According to Jesus, they must learn that group or party affiliations are not the important thing.

The only criterion for acceptability is involvement in the battle with the demonic. In that battle there is solidarity between people of many different groups (Mark 9:39-40). Indeed, it is possible that the strange one casting out demons was not even a disciple of Jesus: "He was not following us" (9:38). We know that some non-Christian exorcists used the name of Jesus along with names of other gods in their incantations of exorcism (on Simon Magnus, see Acts 8:9-24). In the Old Testament story of the liberation of Israel from exile in Babylon, the action of God is accomplished through the pagan Cyrus, who is designated the Lord's "anointed" (Isa. 45:1). Thus also the church is called to join hands in a practical way with all others who are working for the liberation of people and nations from demonic oppression.

Conversely, however, those who refuse to be involved in the battle with the demonic know nothing of this solidarity with Jesus and his disciples, no matter to what group they belong (Luke 11:23).

Demons Do Not Readily Accept Defeat

The parable of the person who loses one evil spirit only to be taken over by seven more (Luke 11:24-26) is a graphic portrayal of demonic life in first-century terms. In the Old Testament, demons or unclean spirits are sometimes found in deserted cities (Isa. 13:21; 34:14). As we see in the temptation stories in the Gospel tradition, the wilderness is thought to be one of their favorite haunts. However, their preference is for human habitation, as illustrated in the story of the Gadarene demoniacs (Matt. 8:28-34; Mark 5:1-20).

The expelled demon of the parable (Luke 11:24-26) is pictured as wandering through the waterless wastes of the earth, no longer happy with a bedouin existence after the control it has enjoyed over humans. He is looking desperately for someone to dominate. Disappointed, he returns home, but here the real nature of the demonic is to be seen. Though the demon has no claim at all to the person from whom it has been evicted, it nevertheless regards that person as its home, as its right. "I will return to my house," it says! When a visit of inspection reveals that the person is now in fine shape, fully recovered from the havoc the demon had wrought, the demon refuses to accept this situation as final. With malice aforethought, the demon finds seven others worse than itself, and together they take over. The person is then in a far worse state than before.

The expulsion of the demon and the restoration of the victim is not sufficient in and of itself. Jesus and those engaged with him are in battle against the forces of evil. Casting out demons is a manifestation of the kingly reign of God. The person from whom the demon has been expelled must submit to God's reign. On the personal level, this is a New Testament way of saying that it is not enough for people simply to be liberated from their fears and complexes. They must submit also to the lordship of Jesus Christ if they are to find wholeness and liberation.

We have noticed throughout, though, that Luke is not speaking of the defeat of the demonic simply on the personal level. The same lesson holds true with respect to the social and political dimension of the demonic. Demons allow no easy victories, and they consider that the world, its structures, and its systems belong to them by right. Reforms and revolutions, improvements in social systems, and even overthrows of demonic dictators—these may easily lead to a greater tyranny and oppression. They are signs of the inbreaking of God's kingly reign of grace.

However, the new structures and institutions themselves must come under God's rule if they are truly to result in joy for the downtrodden, the oppressed, the sinners, and the outcasts. Apart from costly grace and sacrificial love, there is always the possibility that reforms will end in slavery rather than liberation, that eventually one tyrant will be replaced by another even worse than the first.

We must have a continuing commitment to the revolution and development of structures in the direction of humanity and justice if the process of liberation is to continue as a sign of the inbreaking of the kingly reign of God. We also need to have a matching commitment to personal conversion if the process of liberation is not to end in a worse tyranny than the first. The story therefore concludes with blessing pronounced on those who hear the word of liberation and obey it. That is the way the seeds of human freedom and justice are sown and nurtured in the blackened earth of demonic degradation.

A Priority for the Church

Once again, in the passages we have studied, the Evangelists have different emphases. In a teaching situation with his traveling companions, the Marcan Jesus instructs the church, especially its leaders, against the abusive use of power. He calls for the development of a community based on reciprocal responsibility in relationships. Leadership is concerned with responsibility, not rights. Leaders are to be particularly careful that nothing is done to exclude the very people whose powerless state in contemporary society is a model of life in the kingdom.

Matthew works with a series of narratives centering on the person of Jesus, whom he seeks to present as the compassionate Son of David. In fulfilling the messianic expectations of his people, Jesus is particularly concerned for liberation of the marginalized people of society, those who have been ostracized because of handicap or powerlessness. He comes as the merciful Messiah, humble and riding a poor man's beast of burden. Thus Jesus himself is the model for the whole Christian community, both in its relationship to the world and in relationships among its members.

Luke is working in a situation of conflict. He confronts the reality of corporate evil, calling for a continuing commitment to the revolution and renovation of social structures in the direction of humanity and justice. In this struggle for liberation, neutrality is impossible, and the church is called to work for the overthrow of all demonic structures of oppression.

The specific issues addressed by the Evangelists are different, but there is no mistaking their unity of direction. The Christian community is to reflect the concern of Jesus for the liberation of the oppressed. They are to work for the day when justice for all becomes a way of life, when church and society embody the ways of the kingdom. Jesus has no time whatsoever for entrenched structural oppression, no matter how hallowed the basis on which it has been established. It does not matter whether or not supporters of the oppressive structure can point back to Moses or to David, the greatest of Israelite leaders, the most noble fountains of tradition within their culture. Justice still has to be established because this is a fundamental aspect of creation and of the kingdom.

Oppression comes from the hardness of people's hearts. It is ultimately a manifestation of the anti-God forces at work in the world, which are therefore antihuman. Any form of oppression, whether it is within the church or within society at large, is demonic, and a primary function of the Christian community is to work for its overthrow. In this battle, the Christian community is called to cooperate with and alongside all other groups who are not against Jesus and who are working for justice, no matter what their religious, social, or political affiliations might be. A neutral stance is impossible, and to refuse to be involved in the struggle for justice—no matter how noble the reason given—is to stand against Jesus and his disciples.

The message of Jesus and the Evangelists is as relevant as it is radical. Examples of situations where these principles should be guiding the people of God at the present time flood into the mind every day as we read the newspaper, listen to the radio, or watch the television reports. They are occurring at all levels of our society. We can see it in churches where sexual discrimination excludes women (and in some cases married men) from the celebration of the eucharist and from leadership in many other areas of its life.

Of course, supporters of this oppression can point to ancient and seemingly noble church tradition. Just the same way, the Jewish opponents of Jesus, and their supporters in the early church, claimed to be able to point back to Moses for their policy of divorce as a male right, and to David as the origin of their discrimination against the handicapped! However, they can never point back to Jesus, the fountain of faith, for support for such discrimination and oppression. Such oppression is counter to the values of the kingdom and, in the final analysis, a reflection of our hardness of heart and of the all-pervading presence of demonic degradation.

Even worse discrimination can be seen enshrined in the law codes of every country. The law is formulated under the influence of the powerful, and in many instances that law is enacted to protect the rights of the powerful. As if that is not enough, it is administered in favor of the powerful, those who are able to engage the services of skillful lawyers and accountants. The disproportionately high percentage of blacks in prison in Australia, the United States, and South Africa is an offense to Christian conscience and to any genuine feeling of humanity. Research in all three countries shows that the legal process at all stages discriminates against these people in favor of powerful white interests.

Study Luke's parable about the expelled demon who goes and recruits seven of his friends to occupy the person's house. This is an apt description of what has happened to the plight of the poor in many parts of the world. Continuing vigilance and liberation is called for. Let us watch for actions such as that which declared apartheid to be heretical. These proclamations unmasking evil must be heralded as evidence of the inbreaking of the kingdom and the defeat of the demonic.

Nevertheless, we have to remember that the demons do not readily admit defeat. They have powerful friends who are always quite willing to help them secure control again. We most clearly see injustice, oppression, and demonic degradation in the foreign policies of the powerful nations of the world. It does not matter whether we are looking at the decades of Soviet domination of Eastern Europe, at the American domination of Central America and the Caribbean, or at destruction in Vietnam, Afghanistan, or the Middle East. The same demonic forces are present. The demons still think they own these houses! Their occupancy results in degrading human conditions.

Every move for the liberation of humanity is met by appalling displays of naked military power by the superpowers. They think that, in the name of so-called "national interest," they are justified in the use of whatever covert or overt force is necessary for them to regain control. These are but examples of many demonic reactionary events which flash on the screen today. Yesterday there were others; tomorrow there will be more.

Despite the ample evidence of demonic degradation, we nonetheless rejoice in the victories of the kingdom, in every case where liberation is taking place even though it will always carry with it the imperfection of our humanity. The development of the base Christian communities in Central and South America, in Africa, and in the Philippines are a source of great encouragement for all people working for liberation.

The courage of the Solidarity Trade Union leaders in Poland, the movement toward more just government in Argentina, the granting of land rights to aboriginals in some parts of Australia, the increasing presence of blacks in the political processes of the United States—these all are signs of the near presence of the kingdom. The growing peace movement around the world, involving people of many different religious persuasions and political affiliations, is another sign of hope. In all of this we can see the road to the coming kingdom of God undergoing necessary repairs, and we see the work of Jesus, who leads us along the road and into the kingdom.

Questions for Discussion

1. What does it mean to follow the Christian Messiah today?

2. Why does Jesus champion the cause of the outcasts and the marginalized?

3. How do you feel about the idea of Jesus as the poor man from Nazareth? Why do you feel like that?

4. Have you ever suffered from discrimination? How did you feel about it?

5. Why do people in positions of power and privilege find Jesus' message so difficult? What power do you have? Are you ever tempted to abuse it?

6. Should Christians get involved in politics? If so, how?

7. Where do you see demons at work in the political world today? What would you like to do about it?

8. Where do you see Jesus at work for liberation today? How can we work with him?

7

Streams in the Desert

Discipleship and Prayer

A Revolutionary Approach to God

As the disciples responded to the gracious call to follow Jesus on the road, their relationships with one another and with the world around them were transformed as they took their stand with the powerless people of Galilee. Through Jesus they learned that involvement in God's mission required the voluntary renunciation of power and privilege. They became servants of the despised and rejected outcasts of society.

At the same time, however, they became aware of a new privilege which was theirs before God, and they became conscious of a new power available to them from God. Their outward journey in the mission of grace and love was to develop its necessary counterpart in the inward journey of prayer and dependence upon God, the very source of that grace and love. The Jesus whom they followed provided the model for this new lifestyle of wholeness and integrated spirituality. He displayed not only a radical attitude toward the world, but also a revolutionary approach to God, daring to address him as "Father," our heavenly parent, and inviting his followers to do the same, even though such intimacy with the divine was unknown among their contemporaries.

Following the first hectic day of mission in Capernaum in the beginning of his ministry, as Mark describes it, Jesus arises early the next morning, leaves the house where he is staying, and goes out of town to a lonely place to spend time in prayer (Mark 1:35). After the feeding of the five thousand, he dismisses the crowd and goes up the hill to pray (6:46). And at the end of his ministry, shortly before his death, he prays in the garden of Gethsemane (14:32-42). Indeed, from the cross itself Jesus prays that those who have crucified him will be forgiven (Luke 23:34), and finally he places his spirit in the care and protection of the Father (23:46).

Raised in a pious Jewish home (Luke 2:41), Jesus apparently follows traditional practices of public and private prayer. He attends the synagogue on the Sabbath (4:16 and many other places), gives thanks before and after meals (Mark 6:41; 8:6; 14:22-23), and possibly joins in prayers three times a day (see Acts 3:1; 10:3, 30). Thus Jesus is reported to follow liturgical traditions of his people—although some of these references may reflect later Jewish-Christian practices.

Nevertheless, the content of Jesus' prayers is completely new and unexpected, especially in the way he addresses God simply as "Abba, Father" (Mark 14:36). His contemporaries love to pile up epithets in their addresses to God, but they studiously avoid the term "Abba"; it is simply too familiar. "Abba" is primarily "a children's word, used in everyday talk" in greeting their earthly fathers, but Jesus seems to use it regularly in addressing God. In a totally new way, Jesus "spoke with God as a child speaks with its father, simply, intimately, securely" (Jeremias, *Prayers*, 97).

However, not only does Jesus do this himself. He also teaches his disciples to pray in the same intimate and confident way. Conscious of the fact that, through him, God has called them to carry on the mission of grace and love in the world, he introduces them in a new way to the source of grace and love, encouraging them to pray confidently and securely, reverently and obediently. As disciples of Jesus, they are God's little ones devoid of power and status, relying solely on his grace and love.

Following his own practice of praying to Abba (Mark 14:36), Jesus teaches his disciples to pray to God as their Abba, Father. Even the Greek-speaking churches retain Jesus' favorite Aramaic word for God (Rom. 8:15; Gal. 4:6). They seek the inbreaking of God's kingdom and confidently ask him to supply all their needs (Matt. 6:9-13; Luke 11:2-4). He alone is their source and strength. In prayer, they come before God as his obedient children, seeking his glory and the inbreaking of his kingdom.

This chapter concentrates on three texts which underline the need to understand prayer as dependence upon God (Mark), the importance of the communal dimension in prayer (Matthew), and the necessity of persistence in prayer (Luke).

Learning to Trust God (Mark 9:14-29)

At the beginning of Mark's Gospel, we have his dramatic description of Jesus praying the morning after a typical day's ministry in Capernaum (Mark 1:21-39). Yet it comes as somewhat of a surprise to discover how little emphasis Mark places upon prayer, particularly when compared with the other Evangelists (contrast, for example, Matt. 6:1-18; Luke 11:1-13; John 17:1-26). Certainly, Jesus spends time in prayer after the feeding of the five thousand (Mark 6:46) and especially in the garden of Gethsemane on the night of his arrest (14:32-42). He says the blessing before and after meals (6:41; 8:6; 14:22-23). But these references have all come to Mark from the early church as part of the original stories, and he lays no stress upon them.

The only words of Jesus' prayers that Mark records are these: "Abba, Father, for you all things are possible; remove this cup from me; yet, not what I want, but what you want" (Mark 14:36). In Mark, Jesus does not teach his disciples how to pray (contrast Matt. 6:5-15; Luke 11:1-4). The only regulations that he gives about prayer are embedded in the traditional sayings attached to the cursing of the fig tree (Mark 11:24-25). Clearly, prayer was not thought to be a serious problem in Mark's church.

In the story of the epileptic boy, because of the father's wavering faith and the disciples' inability to perform a miracle (Mark 9:14-29), Mark breaks his silence and makes his own distinctive contribution to our understanding of prayer as dependence upon God.

> When they came to the disciples, they saw a great crowd around them, and some scribes arguing with them. When the whole crowd saw [Jesus], they were immediately overcome with awe, and they ran forward to greet him. He asked them, "What are you arguing about with them?" Someone from the crowd answered him, "Teacher, I brought you my son; he has a spirit that makes him unable to speak; and whenever it seizes him, it dashes him down; and he foams and grinds his teeth and becomes rigid; and I asked your disciples to cast it out, but they could not do so." He answered them, "You faithless generation, how much longer must I be among you? How much longer must I put up with you? Bring him to me." And they brought the boy to him. When the spirit saw him, immediately it convulsed the boy, and he fell on the ground and rolled about, foaming at the mouth. Jesus asked the father, "How long has this been happening to him?" And he said, "From childhood. It has often cast him into the fire and into the water, to destroy him; but if you are able to do anything, have pity on us and help us." Jesus said to him, "If you are able!—All things can be done for the one who believes." Immediately the father of the child cried out, "I believe; help my unbelief!" When Jesus saw that a crowd came running together, he rebuked the unclean spirit, saying to it, "You spirit that keeps this boy from speaking and hearing, I command you, come out of him, and never enter him again!" After crying out and convulsing him terribly, it came out, and the boy was like a corpse, so that most of them said, "He is dead." But Jesus took him by the hand and lifted him up, and he was able to stand. When he had entered the house, his disciples asked him privately, "Why could we not cast it out?" He said to them, "This kind can come out only through prayer."   (Mark 9:14-29)

Mark has taken over an isolated story of the healing of a boy with a destructive spirit that made him mute (Mark 9:17, 20-22, 25-27). This account had already been adapted in the preaching of the early church to emphasize the dynamic nature of faith (9:19, 23-24). Now Mark places it within the context of his instructions on discipleship (8:27—10:52). To indicate the essential nature of prayer as an expression of ultimate dependence on God, he gives it a new introduction (9:14-15) and conclusion (9:28-29).

The Struggle Takes Place in the World

Mark has provided the story with a fresh introduction (Mark 9:14-15) in order to integrate it into the section of his Gospel dealing with the true meaning of discipleship (8:27—10:52). According to Mark's presentation, Peter, James, and John have been with Jesus on the Mount of Transfiguration and have witnessed the revelation of the divine glory; they have seen Elijah and Moses and have heard the divine voice (9:2-8). On the way down the mountain, they have become engrossed in theological discussions about the meaning of the resurrection and the place of Elijah in salvation history (9:9-13). Suddenly, as they reach the foot of the mountain and rejoin those who had been left behind, they find themselves embroiled in struggle and conflict.

Now they find themselves surrounded by everyone. They are all there in Mark's story: the supporters of Jesus and his movement, the opponents, and the undecided potential converts. There also are the disciples, those who have been called by Jesus in a special way to be with him and to carry on his mission in the world (Mark 1:16-20; 3:13-19; 6:7-13), who have already had outstanding success (6:7-13, 30). Despite this success, however, they are the ones who, in Mark, experience the greatest difficulty in understanding the significance of the ministry of Jesus (6:52).

Thus almost in desperation, Jesus asks them, "Do you still not perceive or understand? Are your hearts hardened? Do you have eyes, and fail to see? Do you have ears, and fail to hear?" (8:17-18). On the way to Jerusalem, Jesus seeks to teach them about the meaning of the cross (8:31; 9:31; 10:32-

33) and of sacrificial discipleship (8:34—9:1; 9:33—10:31; 10:35-45), but they repeatedly make mistakes. Still, they are always keen for a miracle or two. With Jesus away, the epileptic boy provides them with a further opportunity to demonstrate their power.

The crowd is there, a large crowd such as has not been around since the feeding of the four thousand (Mark 8:1-10). These are the people who have been responding so positively to the ministry of Jesus. As soon as his work began in Capernaum, they flocked to see him (1:32-34, 45; 2:2, 13). They came from all over Galilee and Judea, from as far away as Jerusalem, Idumea, Transjordan, and the regions around Tyre and Sidon when they heard of the miracles he was performing (3:7-12). They gathered to hear him teach in parables (4:1-2; 7:14) and flocked to him every time he came ashore on the western side of the Sea of Galilee (4:36; 5:21-42; 6:30-44; 7:14, 33).

Later, in the Jerusalem ministry, the crowd's support of Jesus will repeatedly thwart the religious leaders in their desire to have Jesus arrested (Mark 11:18; 12:12; 14:1-2). Only after Jesus is abandoned do they throw in their lot with his opponents (15:11). But those events are still in the future. Just before our present story, Jesus tells the crowd along with the disciples that if they want to go with Jesus, they will have to take up the cross and follow him (8:34). That is the situation here. The very ones who are on the verge of possibly becoming followers of Jesus are there with the disciples who have been left behind.

But the scribes, the traditional opponents of Jesus and his followers, are also present. These are the very ones who accuse Jesus of blasphemy at the beginning of his ministry (Mark 2:6), claim he is demon possessed (3:22), challenge his disciples about his practice of eating with tax collectors and sinners (2:16), and complain that he is teaching his followers to ignore the traditions of the elders (7:1, 5). Only recently, Jesus predicts that the scribes would enter into an unholy alliance with the other members of the Sanhedrin to put him to death (8:31; 10:33).

During the brief Jerusalem ministry, they will join with

the chief priests (Mark 11:18, 27; 14:1-2) and elders (11:27) in plotting his death. Later in the passion week, they line up with the same groups in arresting Jesus (14:43) and condemning him on false charges (14:53) before finally handing him over to Pilate (15:1). At the crucifixion they stand with the chief priests in mocking Jesus, calling on him to come down from the cross so that they might see and believe (15:31). It is true that on one occasion Jesus assures one of their number that he is not far from the kingdom of God (12:34). But, even then, he immediately goes on to condemn their teaching (12:35-37) and their lifestyle (12:38-40). The leading opponents of Jesus in the Gospel of Mark are at the foot of the mountain, watching.

They watch as a distraught father brings his epileptic son to Jesus in the hope that he might be able to cure him. In Jesus' absence, they see that same father turn to the disciples for help. The struggle between light and darkness is about to happen. It takes place not at the top of the mountain but at the bottom, right there in the midst of the world, with all the potential followers and the opponents crowding around. Here is an opportunity too good to miss. The disciples have taken up the challenge, but they can not meet it. The demon refuses to move. As the boy's father will shortly testify, it is a particularly difficult and destructive demon (Mark 9:17-18, 22), so an easy victory is out of the question. Yet the difficulty of the situation is what provides the possibility for a glorious victory which could silence their critics and win many converts to their cause. If only they could rise to the occasion!

When they reach the point of frustration and helplessness in their mission, when they can do nothing but engage in futile arguments of self-justification, Jesus comes to them from the mountain. The crowds are amazed and enthusiastically run to greet him, but the struggle has taken its toll on the disciples. They wait for him to ask, "What are you arguing about?" Even then, it is the father of the boy who responds.

Faith Is Dynamic, and It Is a Gift of God

The disciples, according to Mark, remain silent. They are humiliated. The father calls from the crowd. Though he is still hopeful that his son will be cured, his faith is uncertain. Like the frightened disciples during the storm on the lake (Mark 4:38) and the rich young man who finally can not answer the challenge to follow Jesus (10:17-22), he is only able to call him "Teacher" (9:17). This father describes his dilemma. From young boyhood, his son was possessed by a destructive spirit keeping him deaf and mute. In desperation, he brings him to be healed, but the disciples are no help at all (9:17-18). He makes his plaintive appeal. Finally, encouraged by Jesus' declaration that God's power is limitless for those who have the courage to expect great things from him, the father cries out, "I believe, help my unbelief!"

The father understands that faith is not static—it is not something that can be exercised as a once-for-all response to the initial call to follow Jesus. It is a dynamic day-to-day reality influencing the whole of life. The father knows that in the particular strains and stresses that they have been through with their boy, there is always the danger of falling from faith. He knows that there is every chance of this happening, if it were not for the sustaining grace of God. Faith is a continuing response to the grace of God; it is called forth by his grace and sustained by his grace. It is not a human achievement, and it provides no ground for boasting self-confidence.

"Whoever dares to say 'I believe' must say, in the same breath, that he can make this assertion only as one who trusts God to help him again and again to believe. . . . Only in the knowledge of his unbelief can one acknowledge the divine gift of faith joyfully and with assurance. It is impossible to be confident unless one is relying on God's action. Therefore, faith is that unconditional receptiveness to the action of God—that constant expectation that as often as one looks to himself he will discover nothing but unbelief. In looking to God, however, he joyously and confidently confesses that God will continue to heal this unbelief" (Schweizer, *Mark*, 188-189).

The disciples, as Mark portrays them, continually fail to understand the meaning of faith. Because of their position as disciples, they feel that they have arrived and that security is theirs. When Jesus speaks of salvation as a human impossibility made possible only by the grace of God, Peter boasts of their noble achievements: "We have left everything and followed you!" (Mark 10:28). After Jesus predicts that they will all forsake him and flee, Peter twice declares that he will never desert him even if it costs him his life. So confident are they that, as Mark emphasizes, all the disciples say the same thing (14:27-31). The treachery of Judas (14:10), the speedy departure of the ten from the garden (14:50), and the ready denial of Peter before a young servant girl (14:66-72)—these all show how fragile is the faith of those who are confident that they can stand in their own strength.

Discipleship Involves Dependence

At the conclusion of the story, the scene changes. The disciples go indoors and ask Jesus why they failed. Again, it is here that Mark's primary interest is to be seen as the scene changes from what happened once upon a time to what happens time and time again in the history of the church.

In the Gospel of Mark "house" or "home" fulfills a wide range of spatial functions with profound social and religious consequences. It denotes a building, a place of residence (Mark 1:29; 2:1, 11; 3:19; 6:10; 7:24; 8:3, 26; 10:29-30; 12:40; 13:15) and family life (3:25; 5:19; 6:4). The house or home also is the location of a number of Jesus' miracles (2:1-11; 5:35-43; 7:24-30), and it provides space for extended meals and celebrations (2:15; 14:3). It is the setting for conflicts about the authority of Jesus to forgive sins and to extend table fellowship to sinners and outcasts (2:1-11, 15-17). Notably, the house functions as the place for Jesus teaching the disciples, especially on contemporary and controversial issues of church practice (7:17; 9:28, 33; 10:10). In all of this Mark, like other New Testament writers, is simply reflecting the fact that the early Christian movement was primarily a house-church movement.

Since Jesus is described as having moved indoors to teach his disciples, the contemporary readers of the Gospel would immediately understand that the message is intended for them as they met in their house churches throughout the empire (see especially Acts 2:2, 46; 5:42; Rom. 16:5; 1 Cor.

16:19; Col. 4:15; Philem. 2). "As they met in their house-churches and as Mark's Gospel was read, they would have been instructed in the true meaning of discipleship; as Jesus, in Mark's presentation, once took his disciples aside into houses to teach them, so now his words as they are read and discussed continue to teach Christians in their house-churches" (Best, 227).

The question to which the disciples all need an answer is quite simple, but it has profound ramifications for the Christian movement. Why were they unable to help? Jesus had given them authority to cast out demons (Mark 3:15) and had sent them out on mission to preach and to expel unclean spirits (6:7-13). They had done it all before, and they had been successful (6:13, 30). The problem wasn't that they were unwilling to help the father, and it wasn't that they did not expect to be able to do it. They thought they could do it; in fact, they were sure they could do it. Why couldn't they? They had such a great opportunity, with a large crowd on hand to witness their triumph—but they had failed, and failed so miserably!

Jesus replies quite simply: "This kind can come out only through prayer" (Mark 9:29). It is not that their technique is wrong, or that they fail because of their lack of pious practices (though the later addition "and fasting" interpreted his word in this way). It is something more basic. The disciples fail to understand that God's grace is not given to them so that they can exercise their ministry in an independent and arbitrary way. The power of casting out unclean spirits does not reside in them. They are disciples, and only as they recognize their dependence upon God are they able to maintain their mission in the world.

Disciples who think they have arrived have not yet begun, and those who think they have the necessary power in themselves are powerless. But some are prepared to acknowledge their own powerlessness and to recognize that everything they are and have comes from God. These are the ones who have power to cast out even the most difficult of demons.

Forgive Your Sisters and Brothers (Matthew 6:1-18)

Matthew has taken over from the Gospel of Mark the story of Jesus going up the mountain to pray after the feeding of the five thousand (Matt. 14:23) and the account of his intense prayers in Gethsemane (26:36-46). From Mark is the assurance that "whatever you ask for in prayer with faith, you will receive" (21:22). The exhortation to "pray for those who persecute you" (5:44) has been taken over from Q (the sayings source used by Matthew and Luke). However, Matthew has not retained Mark's programmatic reference to Jesus' praying at the commencement of his ministry (Mark 1:21-39). He has also omitted the important reference to prayer as an expression of faith and dependence upon God (9:14-29).

Matthew was writing to a Jewish-Christian community whose members were heirs of the rich devotional tradition of Israel and who had learned to pray when they were children. He therefore does not feel the need to encourage his people to pray. They prayed often, and they enjoyed praying (Matt. 6:5-8). Yet there was the danger that their prayers would become routine and that, conscious of the transcendental dimension, they would ignore the horizontal dimension of faith (5:23-24; 6:14-15). They were becoming so concerned about their relationship with God that they were prone to overlook their responsibility to one another and to the world.

Matthew's distinctive teaching on prayer, therefore, is found in the context of discipleship and of Christian community. This is seen in the Sermon on the Mount (Matt. 5:1—7:29) and in Jesus' speech to the disciples on the nature of community (18:1-35). On these occasions Matthew clearly shows that both discipleship and community are gifts of God, and that prayer only takes on real meaning when these two contexts are brought together. Jesus teaches the disciples the joy of prayer (7:7-11). To the community gathered in the name of Jesus, he gives the assurance that their prayers will be answered (18:18-20).

> [Jesus said,] "Beware of practicing your piety before others in order to be seen by them; for then you have no reward from your Father in heaven.

"So whenever you give alms, do not sound a trumpet before you, as the hypocrites do in the synagogues and in the streets, so that they may be praised by others. Truly I tell you, they have received their reward. But when you give alms, do not let your left hand know what your right hand is doing, so that your alms may be done in secret; and your Father who sees in secret will reward you."

"And whenever you pray, do not be like the hypocrites; for they love to stand and pray in the synagogues and at the street corners, so that they may be seen by others. Truly I tell you, they have received their reward. But whenever you pray, go into your room and shut the door and pray to your Father who is in secret; and your Father who sees in secret will reward you.

"When you are praying, do not heap up empty phrases as the Gentiles do; for they think that they will be heard because of their many words. Do not be like them, for your Father knows what you need before you ask him.

"Pray then in this way:
Our Father in heaven,
  hallowed be your name.
  Your kingdom come.
  Your will be done,
    on earth as it is in heaven.
  Give us this day our daily bread.
  And forgive us our debts,
    as we also have forgiven our debtors.
  And do not bring us to the time of trial,
    but rescue us from the evil one.
For if you forgive others their trespasses, your heavenly Father will also forgive you; but if you do not forgive others, neither will your Father forgive your trespasses.

"And whenever you fast, do not look dismal, like the hypocrites, for they disfigure their faces so as to show others that they are fasting. Truly I tell you, they have received their reward. But when you fast, put oil on your head and wash your face, so that your fasting may be seen not by others but by your Father who is in secret; and your Father who sees in secret will reward you."
(Matt. 6:1-18)

Before Matthew came to write his Gospel, his community had already been warned about the deliberate public performance of the good works of almsgiving, prayer, and fasting

(Matt. 6:2-4, 5-6, 16-18). The Evangelist has taken up this theme, inserting the warning against lengthy prayers (6:7-8), adding the Lord's Prayer (6:9-13), and including at this point sayings on the importance of forgiveness (6:14-15). Almsgiving, prayer, and fasting constitute the great trilogy of Jewish piety. Although Matthew's addition to the tradition is confined to the section on prayer, these additions also serve to transform the attitude toward almsgiving and fasting. For Matthew, the human orientation of piety is always at least as important as its divine dimension. Characteristic of this Gospel is the recurring theme: the love of God and the love of neighbor must always accompany one another.

In Private and with Few Words

In the sayings which had come down to Matthew from the early church, the primary concern was the avoidance of the ostentatious use of almsgiving, prayer, and fasting—the public performance of good works to be seen and applauded by others. In Matthew 6:2-4, 5-6, 16-18, the uniform contrast structure of each of these sections draws attention to the fundamental teaching and indicates that they belonged together in the oral tradition:

> 1 When you . . . [give alms, fast, pray],
>   2 Do not [do it] . . . as the hypocrites do . . .
>   so that they may be praised by others.
>   3 Truly I tell you, they have received their reward.
> 1¹ Rather, when you . . . [give alms, fast, pray],
>   2¹ Do [it] . . . in secret . . .,
>   3¹ And your Father who sees in secret
>   will reward you.

The term "hypocrite" indicates that the contrast is being made with the piety of contemporary Pharisaic Judaism, for in Matthew the Pharisees are the hypocrites par excellence (Matt. 15:7; 22:18; 23:13, 15, 23, 25, 27, 29). The tradition calls for the Christian community to replace ostentatious public displays of individual piety with a privatization of practice. Matthew takes up this emphasis in the opening verse, which he provides as a heading for the whole section:

"Beware of practicing your piety before others in order to be seen by them; for then you have no reward from your Father in heaven" (6:1).

In the teaching on prayer, this emphasis is continued: watch out that you avoid the ostentatious self-aggrandizing use of prayer epitomized by the Jewish hypocrites. They love to stand in prominent positions in the synagogue and delight to pray in public places at the hour of prayer, devoutly turning toward the temple. Rather, go into the storeroom where you can't be seen because it is the only room in a Palestinian house which has a door, and there pray to God in private (Matt. 6:5-6).

Watch out, too, says Matthew, that you avoid the Gentile habit of thinking that your prayers will be answered if you pile up many meaningless words. The reference here may be to the way many first-century Gentiles, in their uncertainty concerning the true God, joined together an almost endless list of names and terms for God, hoping not to omit the correct one. Or it may refer to the long list of epithets sometimes ascribed to individual deities to placate them, or to the frequent attempts to wear down the gods and goddesses by endless prayers and promises. Matthew probably has the last in mind, since his motivation for brevity is that "your Father knows what you need before you ask him" (Matt. 6:7-8). Thus he inserts the Lord's Prayer (6:9-13) at this point as an example of a prayer that is short, sharp, and to the point. For Matthew, it is important that in the Lord's Prayer, Jesus "teaches us to pray great things in few words" (Maurer, 546).

True prayer involves a prophetic mystery. In one situation it is of the essence of prayer to bring our requests before God and to have faith to leave it with our loving heavenly Parent, who "knows what you need before you ask" (Matt. 6:7-8); but in another situation persistence is required (Luke 11:5-8). Luke is writing to a church that finds the path of prayer difficult, and he asks them to exercise faith through persistent prayer. Matthew, however, is writing to a church that loves to pray, and he asks them to exercise faith in simply committing matters to God. Avoid arrogant and ostentatious behavior in prayer, as in other aspects of life, and simply trust in your heavenly Parent, says Matthew.

In Trust and with Obedience

"'Word for word, few creations in all the history of literature have received so much attention, and probably no other prayer has wielded as much influence in the history of religious devotion" (Reumann, v). Jesus, the one who makes it all possible, is the author and the content of this prayer. "He is the invisible background of every one of its petitions" (Thielicke, 122). This is the one prayer that he taught his disciples.

There are two versions of the Lord's Prayer in the New Testament (Matt. 6:9-13; Luke 11:2-4), but the form of words best known among Protestants is the extended version with the final doxology found first in the Didache (about 120 C.E.; Didache 8). The Matthaean version consists of an address, "Our Father in heaven," followed by seven petitions. Luke has the simpler address "Father," followed by five petitions.

In seeking the earliest form of the Lord's Prayer, we need to observe several characteristics of Matthew. This Evangelist frequently refers to God as "your heavenly Father" or "your Father in heaven": (Matt. 5:16, 45; 6:1, 9, 14, 26, 32; and many other places). He is partial to sevenfold arrangements: beatitudes, parables, woes against the scribes and Pharisees, forgiveness not seven times but seventy times seven. Matthew inserts the prayer "your will be done" into the prayers of Jesus in Gethsemane (26:42). He often reflects the apocalyptic spirit of the final petition. Thus, it is probable that the original wording of the prayer was as follows, with Matthew's additions in brackets:

> [Our heavenly] Father,
>> May your name be honored,
>> May your kingdom come,
>> [May your will be done
>>> on earth as in heaven].
>> Our bread for tomorrow give us today,
>> And forgive us our debts
>>> as we have also forgiven our debtors.
>> And do not put us to the test,
>>> [but deliver us from the evil one].

Jesus taught his disciples to pray to God simply as "Father" (Luke 11:2) even as he himself did (Mark 14:36). This confident cry of the child came to express the Christian's freedom and security in God (Rom. 8:15; Gal. 4:6). In the Judaism of the rabbis, the term "Abba" was never used as a form of address to God, for it was simply too familiar. There is a relevant saying in the Babylonian Talmud: "When a child experiences the taste of wheat [when it is weaned], it learns to say abba and imma [these are the first sounds that it prattles]." However, even grown sons and daughters addressed their fathers as "Abba" (Jeremias, *Theology*, 66).

Nevertheless, when the modern Western world thinks of God, there is a danger of overfamiliarity and misunderstanding. In first-century oriental culture, the address "Father" conveyed not only feelings of love and protection but also attitudes of obedience and respect. Contemporary references to God as "Daddy" are misleading, for they express only one aspect of the meaning of "Abba.'

Matthew has moved to avoid possible misunderstandings by changing the simple address "Father" to "Our heavenly Father" or "Our Father in heaven." As always, Matthew stresses the essentially corporate dimension of discipleship: it is as members of his family together, not as isolated and independent children, that we are able to pray to God as Father or Parent. Matthew adds "in heaven" to the address and inserts the third petition, "Your will be done on earth as it is in heaven" (Matt. 6:10). Thus he also underlines the notion of authority and obedience. Hence, the Lord's Prayer is the prayer offered by the obedient children of God to their loving and exalted parent.

The first group of three petitions in the prayer is concerned with God: God's name, God's kingdom, and God's will (Matt. 6:9-10). They represent variations on a theme—parallel expressions of the same idea. "These petitions are a cry out of the depths of distress. Out of a world which is enslaved under the rule of evil and in which Christ and Antichrist are locked in conflict, Jesus' disciples, seemingly a prey of evil and death and Satan, lift their eyes to the Father and cry out for the revelation of God's glory. But at the same time these petitions are an expression of absolute certainty. He who prays thus, takes seriously God's promise, in spite of all the demonic powers, and puts himself completely in God's hands with imperturbable trust" (Jeremias, *Prayers*, 99).

Through his addition of the third petition, "Your will be done on earth as it is in heaven" (Matt. 6:15), Matthew bridges the gap between piety and politics, turning the petitions to God into exhortations to the community. In the midst of persecution and suffering (5:1-12; 8:23-27; 10:23; 23:34), the Christian community is called to a life of obedience. Jesus himself is the model for the persecuted community. In Gethsemane, under the pressure of death, he prays "My Father, if this [cup] cannot pass unless I drink it, your will be done" (26:42). Here "My Father" is parallel to "Our Father" in the Lord's Prayer and "your will be done," found only in Matthew (6:10; 26:42; cf. 7:21; 12:50; 18:14; 21:31).

The second group of four petitions is concerned with the needs of humanity: our bread, our sins, and our struggles (Matt. 6:11-13). In Matthew, it is not possible to think of God without also going on to think of one's neighbor. The physical needs of his people are never foreign to the concerns of Jesus of Nazareth, who eats with tax collectors and sinners (9:10-13) and feeds the hungry when they are with him (14:13-21; 15:32-39). Hence, Jesus encourages his disciples to believe that the bread of the kingdom and the needs of tomorrow will be supplied by the loving Father, the one who is willing to forgive their sins.

The disciples need to receive the grace of forgiveness. Likewise, they need to be kept by the sustaining grace of God so that they will not be tested beyond their capacity to respond to his grace. Thus Jesus encourages them in his own time of trial in the garden of Gethsemane: "Stay awake and pray that you may not come into the time of trial; the spirit indeed is willing, but the flesh is weak" (Matt. 26:41).

Again, we notice that this is a prayer which can only be offered by the Christian community or, at least, on behalf of the Christian community. We are instructed to pray for "our bread," not for "my bread." The word normally translated "daily" is notoriously difficult. But there is widespread agreement that it should be translated "Our bread for tomorrow give us today," reflecting the Palestinian practice of baking tomorrow's bread today. Observe that Jesus does not encourage us to pray for a week's food at a time; the Christian life is one of relying on the loving Father day by day.

Of course, for those of us who have the refrigerator and freezer constantly full of food, this petition is superfluous and therefore difficult. Our security so often lies elsewhere, and faith becomes apparently irrelevant. But Jesus is speaking to the poor, who must depend on God for each day's existence. They rely on God to see them through today and tomorrow and through all of their tomorrows. Thus the petition speaks not only of tomorrow's bread, but of "Tomorrow's Bread"—the bread of the kingdom. Frequently in Scripture the messianic age is depicted in terms of a meal (Isa. 49:9-12; Mal. 1:12; 3:10-11; Matt. 8:11; 26:29; Luke 14:15-24; 22:30; Rev. 3:20; 19:9). Those who suffer and hunger look forward not only to having enough food to survive tomorrow, but also to participating in the messianic banquet with God, celebrating the end of all oppression and suffering.

In Luke we are encouraged to pray "forgive us our sins" (Luke 11:4), but Matthew gives the more literal "forgive us our debts" (Matt. 6:12). Behind the two words "sins" and "debts" lies an Aramaic word "which had the literal meaning of monetary debt and the figurative meaning of sin as a moral debt" (Gundry, 108), and both meanings may well be intended. Jesus spoke in Aramaic, and his teaching was translated into Greek, the language of the Gospels. Luke's form is particularly radical when he says that we should pray, "Forgive us our sins, for we ourselves forgive everyone indebted to us" (Luke 11:4). Luke is advocating here that we should seek from God the same measure of forgiveness for our moral debt (sin) that we have shown toward our monetary debtors. What a test for Christians in our capitalistic society!

The final petitions (Matt. 11:13) are prayers of deliverance offered by a community conscious of the suffering and testing of the last days. In this Gospel one of the most graphic pictures of the church is of the disciples in the boat being buffeted by the violent storm on the lake. They are frightened and able only to cry out to Jesus, "Lord, save us! We are perishing!" (8:25). In the midst of its suffering for the faith, the church cries out for deliverance from the power of evil. It knows that apart from God's sustaining grace, it will never survive. God alone is the hope of believers.

Forgive and Forget

Judaism taught that the sacrifice of the Day of Atonement did not atone for the sins of those who were not willing to forgive others. The Lord's Prayer already involves disciples in the forgiveness of others (Matt. 6:12). Now Matthew takes up this theme as he adds, from Mark 11:25, the positive declaration: "If you forgive others their trespasses, your heavenly Father will also forgive you" (6:14). So that his intention might not be missed, he formulates the same thought again, in negative form: "If you do not forgive others, neither will your Father forgive your trespasses" (6:15). This is Matthew's strong emphasis. "The gift of being able to address God as Father which far surpasses anything one might dare to ask; the great hope that one day God's name, God's kingdom, God's will would be victorious; even the pain of hunger, sin and temptation—none of these concerned Matthew and his community as much as forgiveness among men" (Schweizer, *Matthew*, 157).

In the Sermon on the Mount, Matthew has prepared for Jesus' teaching on prayer and forgiveness with two sayings: "You have heard that it was said, 'You shall love your neighbor [friend] and hate your enemy.' But I say to you, Love your enemies and pray for those who persecute you, so that you may be children of your Father in heaven" (Matt. 5:43-45). The second saying is only in Matthew: "So when you are offering your gift at the altar, if you remember that your brother or sister has something against you, leave your gift there before the altar and go; first be reconciled to your brother or sister, and then come and offer your gift" (5:23-24). Matthew repeatedly makes the same emphasis in his chapter on Christian community: the parables of the lost sheep (18:10-14) and the unforgiving servant (18:23-35), and especially in the declaration to Peter of the need to forgive his brother or sister not seven times, but seventy times seven (18:21-22).

The gospel is the good news of God's forgiveness, which knows no limits save our willingness to accept it as a gift. Our forgiveness of others is the outstretched hand by which we are able to grasp the forgiveness of God. Through Jesus, the incarnate grace of God, we are enabled to forgive and forget. Through Jesus, the incarnate Son of God, we are able to pray to God our loving heavenly Parent.

Don't Be Discouraged (Luke 18:1-14)

Forty years after the crucifixion, the Roman legions destroyed Jerusalem, smashing the temple and all that it represented in the religious and political life of Israel. A decade or so later Luke undertook "to set down an orderly account of the events that have been fulfilled among us" (Luke 1:1). The church then was facing two serious theological problems: the relationship of the church to Israel, and the consequences of the delay in the return of Jesus Christ.

Luke began to respond to these questions by developing a story of the history of salvation divided into three periods: (1) the time of Israel centered on the Law, with the faithful people gathered in the temple awaiting the coming of the Spirit-filled Deliverer (Luke 1—2); (2) the time of Jesus as the center of salvation history (Luke 3—24); and (3) the time of the church in the power of the Spirit, beginning with the gospel spreading from Jerusalem to Rome and with the church becoming the new Israel (Acts). In the first century this church has "thousands of believers . . . among the Jews" (Acts 21:20), and by the second century it becomes predominately Gentile. The *continuity* between the new Israel and the old is seen in the worshiping community, the *discontinuity* in many Israelites rejecting the apostolic missionaries. At the end, Paul declares that Isaiah's fearful words of judgment are being fulfilled and that "this salvation of God has been sent to the Gentiles; they will listen" (Acts 28:25-28).

The Gentiles did listen, and by Luke's time many had

flocked to the church. As time went by, however, and the second coming of Jesus did not happen, many of them began to be discouraged. The Gentile believers in these churches did not have a long tradition prayer and worship, and many lacked sustaining power for the long haul through history. It is not surprising, then, that Luke shows considerably more interest in prayer than do the other Evangelists. He wishes his people to experience the riches of the heritage of Israel, to keep on praying, and not to lose heart (Luke 18:1). Thus, when the Son of Man returns, he will find many faithful believers on the earth.

In Luke's account, the time of Israel (Luke 1—2) focuses upon the devout and faithful who gather at the temple. Zechariah and Elizabeth are "righteous" and obedient (1:6). As Zechariah serves in the temple, with the people praying outside at the hour of incense, the angel of the Lord assures him that his prayer has been heard and Elizabeth will bear a son (1:13). Simeon, a "righteous and devout" priest, blesses Jesus and his parents (2:25-35). The prophetess Anna, who worships in the temple day and night, gives thanks for Jesus and speaks to all who are looking for the redemption of Israel (2:36-38).

The time of the early church (Acts), as Luke depicts it, is characterized by the same spirit of prayer and devotion. The apostles gather frequently for prayer (Acts 1:14), and the whole community meets daily for prayer, fellowship, and study (2:42-47). James and John go up to the temple at the hour of prayer (3:1). When the daily tasks become too great, they appoint seven helpers so that the apostles can devote themselves to prayer and the study of the Scriptures (6:4). They pray before the election of Matthias (1:24), after the seven helpers are appointed (6:6), and when commending the newly appointed elders of all the churches (14:23). They pray earnestly when Peter is in prison (12:5, 12), when Barnabas and Saul are sent out on their first missionary journey (13:3), and before Paul goes up to Jerusalem for the last time (21:5). Peter (9:40; 10:9), Cornelius (10:4, 30), and Paul (9:11; 16:16, 25; 28:8) are all represented as people of prayer.

The time of Jesus, however, is the center point of salvation history (Luke 3—24), and the most important moments of his ministry are associated with prayer. We are told that it is his custom to go away to lonely places and pray (5:16). He spends the whole night in prayer before appointing the twelve (6:12). While Jesus is praying, the heavens are opened and the Holy Spirit descends (3:21). Jesus is praying just before Peter's confession of him as the Messiah of God (9:18), and while he is praying, he is transfigured (9:28-29). He prays on the Mount of Olives (22:39-46) and on the cross (23:34, 46). He teaches his disciples how to pray (11:1-13) and tells them a parable so they will keep on praying and not lose heart (18:1-8). Jesus assures them that their prayers will be answered (11:5-13), and that everyone who humbles himself will be exalted (18:14).

> Then Jesus told them a parable about their need to pray always and not to lose heart. He said, "In a certain city there was a judge who neither feared God nor had respect for people. In that city there was a widow who kept coming to him and saying, 'Grant me justice against my opponent.' For a while he refused; but later he said to himself, 'Though I have no fear of God and no respect for anyone, yet because this widow keeps bothering me, I will grant her justice, so that she may not wear me out by continually coming.' " And the Lord said, "Listen to what the unjust judge says. And will not God grant justice to his chosen ones who cry to him day and night? Will he delay long in helping them? I tell you, he will quickly grant justice to them. And yet, when the Son of Man comes, will he find faith on the earth?"
>
> He also told this parable to some who trusted in themselves that they were righteous and regarded others with contempt: "Two men went up to the temple to pray, one a Pharisee and the other a tax collector. The Pharisee, standing by himself, was praying thus, 'God, I thank you that I am not like other people: thieves, rogues, adulterers, or even like this tax collector. I fast twice a week; I give a tenth of all my income [AG: all I get].' But the tax collector, standing far off, would not even look up to heaven, but was beating his breast and saying, 'God, be merciful to me, a sinner!' I tell you, this man went down to his home justified rather than the other; for all who exalt themselves will

be humbled, but all who humble themselves will be exalted."
(Luke 18:1-14)

Luke has taken over two parables, each focusing upon two well-known characters in the ancient Near East: an unscrupulous judge and a nagging widow (Luke 18:2-5), a Pharisee and a tax collector (18:10-14). He has placed them in a new framework (18:1, 9) and has added concluding comments to each parable (18:6-8, 14b) as he reapplies their teaching to the situation of his own community.

Luke wants to encourage his people not to lose heart (Luke 18:1) because of the seeming delay in the coming of the Son of Man (18:7). Rather, they should persist, confident that God will hear their prayer, so that when the Son of Man comes he will find many faithful followers upon the earth (18:8). This confidence, however, is to be placed in God, not in themselves (18:9). "All who exalt themselves will be humbled, but all who humble themselves will be exalted" (18:14b). Children find their place in the kingdom of God (18:15-17), but the rich, while they cling to their riches and oppress the poor, will never enter it (18:18-29).

You Can Rely on God

The first parable centers around an unscrupulous judge and an unprotected widow. They happen to live in the same town. The judge is bad through and through and possesses no conscience at all. He has been appointed to secure justice in the name of God, particularly for the weak and the unprotected, but he "neither feared God nor had respect for people" (Luke 18:2).

The widow, without her husband to protect her, is helpless and exploited. In a financial action (the only type of case heard before a single judge), justice is being withheld from her (18:3). It is certain that the widow will win the case if the action ever gets to court. Yet the judge, who has the power to fix the trial date whenever he likes, is not prepared to list the case for hearing. Her adversary apparently is a rich and powerful man in that region (18:4).

The action of the judge in failing to help a widow, of all

people, is ample demonstration of the fact that he neither feared God nor had respect for people. In the Old Testament, God is recognized as "Father of orphans and protector of widows" (Ps. 68:5) and is described as the one "who executes justice for the orphan and the widow and who loves the strangers, providing them food and clothing" (Deut. 10:18). The prophets attack the rulers, judges, and lawmakers of Israel who mistreated widows and orphans, the weakest members of the covenant community (Isa. 1:17, 23; 10:2). Already in Israel's earliest law code, the community is warned: "You shall not abuse any widow or orphan. If you do abuse them, when they cry out to me, I will surely heed their cry; my wrath will burn, and I will kill you with the sword" (Exod. 22:22-24).

Deuteronomy carries the constant refrain to care for "the strangers, the orphans, and the widows." These are in a vulnerable position without the normal protection of a Jewish male head of the household, and they are to receive special philanthropic treatment (Deut. 16:11, 14; 24:17, 19-21; 26:12-13; 27:19). If a judge refuses to assist a helpless petitioning widow, he does not have to tell the people of the first century that he "neither fears God nor respects people"—his actions speak even louder than his words. He is corrupt through and through. Josephus, the Jewish historian and contemporary of Luke, describes King Jehoiakim in similar words: "He proved to be unjust and wicked by nature, and was neither reverent toward God nor kind to man" (*Antiquities* 10.5.2).

Widows play a more significant role in Luke than in the other Gospels. They are not featured at all in Matthew and John. Mark has only the denunciation of the scribes, who "devour widows' houses" (Mark 12:40), in contrast to the positive example of the poor widow who gives everything she owns to the temple treasury (12:41-44).

Luke has both of these incidents (Luke 20:47; 21:1-4), plus four significant stories about widows found only in his Gospel: the prophetess Anna, though eighty-four years of age, "never left the temple but worshiped there with fasting and prayer night and day" (2:36-38); the widow of Sarephath in the days of Elijah (4:25-27); the raising of the son of the widow of Nain (7:11-17); and this parable about the widow and the ruthless judge (18:1-8). Luke's emphasis reflects the significant role played by the widows in the early church (Acts 6:1; 9:39-40; 1 Cor. 7:8; 1 Tim. 5:3-5, 9, 11, 14, 16) and accords with his overwhelming interest in the disadvantaged and oppressed sections of the population.

In our present parable, the woman is too poor to bribe the judge; persistence is her only weapon. Her continual visits and incessant nagging play on his nerves, she eventually wears him down, and justice is done (Luke 18:5). The teaching of this parable is to some extent parallel to that of the friend at midnight (11:5-13) who, in order to preserve his honor and to avoid shame, is only too willing to grant the request. Here, however, the sayings (18:6-8) attached to the original parable (18:2-5) go further and relate the teaching to justice and faith.

Learn from the story of the unjust judge, says the Lord of the church (Luke 18:6). Even an unscrupulous judge is prepared to accede to the wishes of a woman for whom he has nothing but contempt. How much more will God listen to the cry of the poor and the oppressed who have no alternative but to cry to him night and day. Justice will be done; those who rely on God may be sure that he will vindicate them (18:7-8). The real question, though, is not whether God will grant justice. That is certain. The real question, following the earlier teaching about the day of the Son of Man (17:22-37), is whether or not the Son of Man will find any faith on earth when he comes. We ask, "When will God reveal his justice?" But Luke asks, "When he does, will we be found faithful?"

God Is Merciful to Sinners

The second parable (Luke 18:9-14) centers on two persons well-known in religious circles in the ancient Near East: a Pharisee and a tax collector. The parable itself (18:10-14a) is in pure narrative form, with a setting (18:9) and a generalizing conclusion (18:14b) provided by the Evangelist. These additions enable Luke to direct the parable toward specific issues that have arisen in his community.

The Pharisee, as depicted here, is the ideal religious person. Certainly many of those who listened to the parable in the days of Jesus would have recognized him as such, and the same holds true of those who first read the story in the Gospel of Luke. His catalog of self-adulation begins with the negative but reaches its climax in his positive declaration of law-keeping. Although his prayer may seem rather crude, the Thanksgiving Hymn from Qumran contains one that is only slightly less so "[I give thank]s, O Adonai, for you have not cast my lot among the congregation of vanity and have not set my decree in the assembly of hypocrites" (Thanksgiving Hymn: 1QH 7.34).

The Pharisee has not committed any serious transgressions of the commandments (Luke 18:11) and has, in fact, been able to fulfill the Law completely (18:12). Indeed, he has determinedly managed to go beyond the Law's requirements. Instead of the annual fast on the Day of Atonement (Lev. 16:29-31), he fasts twice a week: no food or drink from sunrise to sunset twice a week (in a hot land!) as an act of atonement for the sins of his people.

Some well-known individuals in the Old Testament fasted on certain solemn occasions in addition to the Day of Atonement. David fasted in mourning over the death of his first son born to Bathsheba (2 Sam. 12:21). King Ahab fasted after Elijah pronounced God's judgment on him because of the murder of Naboth and the stealing of his vineyard (1 Kings 21:27). Ezra fasted in "mourning over the faithlessness of the exiles" (Ezra 10:6). Nehemiah did likewise in Babylon when he heard that the people of Jerusalem were demoralized and the city walls and gates were in a bad state of repair (Neh. 1:4). Daniel fasted as he counted the years that were to pass before the desolation of Jerusalem would come to an end (Dan. 9:3). Such fasts were connected with specific incidents, but the spirit of this passage suggests that the Pharisee sees himself engaged in regular meritorious acts of fasting for the salvation of Israel.

Luke tells us earlier that the Pharisees and the disciples of John the Baptist fast frequently (Luke 5:33). The Didache (about 120 C.E.) instructs Christians not to fast on Mondays and Thursdays "with the hypocrites" (the Jews), but on Wednesdays and Fridays! This, however, is a much later development in the Christian tradition (Didache 8).

The Pharisee also goes further than the Law requires in paying tithes of everything he buys (the stress is on "all"); he ensures that he uses nothing that has not been tithed. For some of the goods he purchases, the tithe is already paid by the producer (of corn, new wine, and oil), but he does not want to leave anything to chance. Perhaps the producer is an irreligious person and not diligent in paying the tithe; perhaps he is forgetful or lacking in concentration and inadvertently forgets to tithe something which the Pharisee purchases. Our hyperreligious person does not mind having to pay a little extra in order to maintain his religious purity and perfection. He does not fulfill the Law grudgingly, either; at the end of it all, he gives thanks to God (Luke 18:11).

In the first century our model religious person may well have been a Pharisee. As Josephus the Jewish historian says, they were "a body of Jews known for surpassing others in the observances of piety and exact interpretation of the laws" (*Jewish War* 1.5.2). We would be wrong, however, to restrict the reference to Pharisees, since here they represent a type of religious person known by various names and titles throughout the history of the Jewish faith and of the Christian church. They are the kind of people who, according to contemporary religious standards at whatever time, would be reckoned to find favor in the eyes of God.

The tax collector is something altogether different. If the Pharisee is the epitome of the righteous person, the tax collector is the epitome of the notorious sinner. He collaborates with the Roman occupation forces and manages to make handsome profits from oppressing his neighbor, defrauding him whenever possible. In contemporary literature we read not only of the combination tax collectors and sinners, but also of tax collectors and robbers, tax collectors and prostitutes, tax collectors and swindlers, tax collectors and adulterers, tax collectors and thieves, tax collectors and murderers. They are well-known by the company they keep! "They possessed no civil rights, and were shunned by all respectable persons" (Jeremias, *Parables,* 141). Their very occupation rendered them unclean, and "to obtain God's forgiveness was in the eyes of Jesus' contemporaries very nearly impossible for a tax collector" (Linnemann, 60).

Naturally, in contrast to the confident Pharisee, the tax collector stands at a distance, perhaps even in the outer court of the Gentiles, and cannot even bring himself to raise his eyes. He beats his breast in an act of contrition, and the only prayer he can offer is "God, be merciful to me, a sinner!" (Luke 18:13). His plea recalls the opening words of Psalm 51:1: "Have mercy on me, O God, according to your steadfast love; according to your abundant mercy blot out my transgressions."

This tax collector, says Jesus, goes down "to his home justified rather than the other," the Pharisee! Jesus' statement certainly shocks his hearers beyond measure! Impossible! Not so, says Jesus. Those who take a stand in their own strength, confident before God on the basis of their good works in fulfilling the Law, will not find acceptance with God. The ones who will be welcomed are those whose appeal is based solely on God's mercy. God welcomes the despairing sinners and rejects the self-righteous. For this reason, says Jesus elsewhere, "I have come to call not the righteous but sinners to repentance" (Luke 5:32).

Tax collectors play a strategic role in Luke's Gospel. Mark has one composite story involving tax collectors, with the call of Levi and the subsequent festival with many tax collectors and sinners in his house (Mark 2:15-17). Matthew has a number of references, in addition to those surrounding Matthew (Levi) and his friends, taken from Mark (Matt. 9:10-11; 10:3). Matthew shares with Luke three positive references (11:19; 21:31-32), but also has another two references which reflect the negative evaluation of tax collectors (and Gentiles) in contemporary Jewish society (5:46; 18:17). All the references in Luke, however, show the positive response of these "sinners" to John the Baptist and Jesus (3:12; 5:27-30; 7:29, 34; 15:1; 18:10-13; 19:2).

In both our present parable (Luke 18:9-14) and in the story of Zacchaeus (19:1-10), the tax collectors serve as models of discipleship. And in the Lucan setting of the three parables of the grace of God, they function programmatically as a picture of those who respond positively to Jesus' ministry: the lost sheep (15:4-7), the lost coin (15:8-10), and the lost son (15:11-32).

Just as Jesus responds to Zacchaeus by declaring, "Today salvation has come to this house, because he too is a son of Abraham" (Luke 19:9), so in our parable Jesus declares that the tax collector "went down to his home justified" (18:14). This is the only place in any of the Gospels where the term "justify" is used with such full theological meaning, known so well from the letters of Paul (Rom. 3:24-25 and many places). This does not mean that Luke has taken the idea from Paul, for the roots of the Pauline understanding are found already in the Old Testament and other Jewish writings (Ps. 51:19; Blessings: 1QSb 4.22; 4 Ezra 12:7). The parallel response to Zacchaeus, the arch tax collector, shows that Luke understands the parable as teaching that the tax collector experiences the justification of God which results in salvation. This tax collector, not that Pharisee, provides the appropriate picture for Christians. To be a Christian, says Luke, is to recognize that you are a sinner and dependent upon the mercy of God.

Keep on Praying

Luke has found two parables of assurance that God will answer the cry of the poor and the oppressed (Luke 18:2-8) and that God is merciful to sinners (18:10-14). He placed them together in a new setting to teach the community that their prayers should be persistent and humble. Luke was concerned that with the seeming delay in the coming of the Son of Man his people were beginning to lose heart and lack confidence in God. They might be a small downtrodden minority, but they were assured that God would answer their prayers.

Jesus gives a concluding statement: "All who exalt themselves will be humbled [by God], but all who humble themselves will be exalted [by God]" (Luke 18:14). This was probably an independent wisdom saying which Luke has added here, and also at the conclusion of the parable concerning

guests who choose places of honor at the wedding banquet
(Luke 14:11). The original saying may involve an allusion to
the prophetic denunciation of King Zedekiah: "Remove the
turban, take off the crown; things shall not remain as they
are. Exalt that which is low, abase that which is high. A ruin, a
ruin, a ruin—I will make it! (Such has never occurred.) Until
he comes whose right it is; to him I will give it" (Ezek. 21:26-
27). Readers of the Gospel of Luke, however, would probably have made an even more immediate reference to Mary's
Song: "He has brought down the powerful from their
thrones, and lifted up the lowly; he has filled the hungry with
good things, and sent the rich away empty" (Luke 1:52-53).

As in other sections of the Gospel of Luke, the parables of
assurance and promise to the poor and the outcasts have at
the same time become words of warning and exhortation to
the church: an exhortation to continue praying and to walk
humbly before their God, and a warning never to trust in
their own righteousness and nor to despise others. The gospel is good news of grace and love which knows no limits
save our willingness to receive it as a gift.

Strength for a Messianic Lifestyle

Although each of the Evangelists obviously believes in
prayer, there are remarkably different emphases in what they
have to say on the subject. Indeed, the differences are so
great that if we do not take into account the differing church
situations for which they were writing, we might be tempted
to think that they provide quite contradictory teaching on
this central aspect of the Christian faith.

Once Mark has written the dramatic description of Jesus
praying after his first day of ministry (Mark 1:35), he places
surprisingly little emphasis on prayer. In fact, he records only
one of Jesus' prayers (14:36). There is no record of Jesus
teaching his disciples to pray, and he gives only two brief
rules about praying (11:24-25). Like all of the stories about
Jesus praying (6:41, 46; 8:6; 14:22-23, 32-42), they have come
to Mark from the early church, and he places no real stress
upon them. Clearly, the subject of prayer did not present any
serious problem in the Marcan church.

In the teaching on discipleship, however, this Evangelist has retold the story of the epileptic boy (Mark 9:14-29) in such a way as to emphasize the dynamic nature of faith and the essential nature of prayer as dependence upon God. It appears, then, that as far as Mark is concerned, prayer is not a matter for theoretical speculation or internalized pietism. For him, prayer never exists alone. It can only be understood and practiced within the context of missionary struggle in the world. That is why, in this Gospel, Jesus prays at the end of his opening day's ministry in Capernaum (1:35).

Matthew did not have to encourage his people to pray because he was in a Jewish-Christian community where the members were heirs of the rich spiritual tradition of Israel. However, being so conscious of their need to maintain a right relationship with God, they were apparently in danger of overlooking the importance of their relationship with their neighbors. In the Sermon on the Mount (Matt. 5—7) and the sermon on communal relationships (Matt. 18), Matthew's teaching on prayer is directed to the Christian community rather than to individual Christians. He repeatedly stresses that it is within the communal context where prayer takes on its real meaning.

Characteristic of the First Gospel is the recurring theme that the love of God and the love of neighbor must always accompany one another (Matt. 5:23-24; 6:14-15; 7:12; 22:34-40). He uses the Lord's Prayer (6:7-15) as an example of a brief, trusting prayer of a faithful community which is prepared to bring their requests before God and to have the faith to leave them with our loving Father who "knows what you need before you ask him" (6:7-8).

Luke was facing quite a different situation again; he was writing to a Gentile church struggling to maintain faith in the face of Christ's delay in returning. Without a long background of prayer and worship, many lacked the sustaining power for the long haul through history. Luke had to encourage his church to pray and to keep on praying, so that when the Son of Man comes he will still find many believers upon earth (Luke 18:1, 8).

Thus all of the key people in Luke and Acts are described

as people of prayer (Zechariah, Anna, Simeon, Mary, Peter, James, John, Cornelius, and Paul, among many others). All of the important moments in the ministry of Jesus are associated with prayer (e.g., Luke 3:21; 5:16; 6:12; 9:18, 28-29; 22:39-45; 23:34, 46). Through the parable of the unscrupulous judge and the nagging widow (18:2-5), Luke encourages his church to keep on praying. In the parable of the Pharisee and the tax collector (18:9-14), Luke assures readers that God is merciful to sinners.

Our situations are no doubt quite different from those encountered by the Evangelists. Yet with the renewed interest in prayer and spirituality that is so evident at present, we ought not to neglect their insights. Western Protestants, even in times of spiritual renewal, are often in danger of reducing prayer to the level of privatized piety unrelated to the struggles of the world, with the corporate dimension relegated to the ranks of an unnecessary optional extra. Western radicals, even in times of great social upheaval and political change, are often in danger of turning their backs on the divine dimension, seeking to accomplish reforms, even revolutions, through their own strength. Little do they realize the enormous spiritual energy required for such sustained activity.

The fight for justice will not be won overnight. It is a long hard struggle, and those involved may not live to see the fruit of their labors, let alone that day when "justice [shall] roll down like waters, and righteousness like an everflowing stream" (Amos 5:24). In the early seventies, the opportunity for justice seemed to have dawned. Many committed themselves to work for the poor, and it seemed that substantial victories were won. Today, under the power of transnational wealth and the military-industrial complex, the possibility for justice seems as far removed as ever. Not surprisingly, some have given up the fight. Others have learned from bitter experience that those who wish to continue in the struggle must be prepared to pay a heavy price, both in their own lives and in the lives of their families and friends. There is no doubt that they are en route to the Promised Land, but the journey through the wilderness is long.

God provides streams of prayer and communal spirituality in the desert. But the mistake of some is to anticipate finding a shortcut across the wilderness and saving time by not stopping at the streams. While continuing to be involved in God's mission of justice in the world, the worshiping community finds strength for the messianic lifestyle as its members come before God with empty hands and broken hearts and rediscover the crucified and risen Jesus in their midst. Strength is renewed and hope is rekindled in the presence of the one who suffered and died for his convictions and was raised for the liberation of the world.

Questions for Discussion

1. How can we learn to trust God today?

2. What do we mean when we say that faith is a dynamic day-to-day reality influencing the whole of life?

3. Has your road to the Promised Land passed through the wilderness? Why did you keep going?

4. Do you find it hard to pray for your daily bread when the freezer is full and the refrigerator overflowing?

5. How can we forgive and forget?

6. Is prayer a reality? Or is it just an escape for people who find life too hard?

7. How does prayer relate to the struggle for justice?

8. Do you find prayer difficult? What might make it easier for you? Could your present group help you?

8

Shade Along the Roadside

Discipleship and Grace

A Remarkably Open Person

Throughout this book we see the central feature of the teaching of Jesus: in his words and works the kingly reign of God has drawn near. The reign of grace, the time of joy for the downtrodden, the sinners, and the outcasts, the era of good news to the poor—all this has begun to break into human history. The gospel, preached and lived out by Jesus, is good news of grace and love, costly grace and sacrificial love. The required response is a radical reorientation of life, a life lived out in believing obedience. In the Gospels this life of repentance and continuing faith is set forth as the life of discipleship, life on the road, following Jesus.

The radical reorientation of life in following Jesus has to do with specific acts of self-sacrifice in concrete situations. It means, among other things, that a person is to be no longer enslaved by material possessions. As a follower of Jesus, one resolutely refuses to attempt the impossibility of serving God and money at the same time. But the disciples' detachment from material possessions stands in stark contrast to their concern for the well-being of the people of God. Following Jesus, disciples are being liberated from themselves and their own selfish desires and ambitions. Through their openness toward God in Jesus, they are in the process of being liberated toward their sisters and brothers, who are also seeking to do the will of God. A radical detachment from the ways of the world and a corresponding commitment to the community of the new people of God—these are integral to the life of those who are following Jesus.

Yet the call of Jesus which brings the disciples together as a community of the people of God distinct from the world is also the call which thrusts them out to a life of obedience in the world. Life on the road involves mission, and in following Jesus, the early church was a community on a mission of all-embracing grace and love in the world. It was this that gave the very reason for their existence—it gave meaning to life as they dedicated themselves to embrace especially the poor and oppressed, the outcasts and notorious sinners, all those traditionally excluded from the people of God.

This life of community and mission also involved a voluntary renunciation of traditional ideas of power and privilege, and the acceptance of a new role as servants of Jesus and of humankind. The kingdom, whose imminent arrival they proclaimed, does not depend on their prestige, power, and authority; it is the work of a gracious and loving God, who has revealed himself in humility and powerlessness in Jesus of Nazareth, born in a stable and crucified on a cross. In their role as servants of Jesus and of humanity, they were involved in the battle with the demonic, the struggle against personal and social evil in which there can be no neutrality and in which there will be no easy victories. The defeat of the demonic, however, is a sign to those who have faith that God's kingly reign of grace was and is breaking into history and liberating the victims of oppression.

Believers are involved in the mission of God in the world, in the battle against the domination of evil. They have voluntarily renounced traditional ways of power and status. Through Jesus they are, however, made aware of a new status they have before God, and they are conscious of a new power which is available to them from God. The outward journey in the mission of grace and love has as its necessary counterpart the inward journey of prayer and dependence upon God, the source of grace and love. Here again, though, disciples are never alone; they are conscious of the needs of their brothers and sisters and of the necessity of being in a right relationship with them. They are also aware that the battle will be long and hard; they continually need access to strength beyond their own. Apart from the grace of God, they might not survive the pressures of their own lives, let alone participate in the liberation of the oppressed.

It is now time to return to the point from which we began to look at the whole question of life on the road: the inbreaking of God's kingly reign as a time of grace and love for all humanity—all, without distinction! We have noticed that the Gospels frequently speak about the nature of the response required by the grace of God, the *cost* of being on the road with Jesus. But they always do this on the basis of the *call* to the life on the road, the fundamental revelation of the grace of God in Jesus of Nazareth. From a New Testament standpoint, the *call* to discipleship always precedes the discussion of the *cost* of discipleship. Both are to be understood as acts of "costly grace," since both have been made possible by the self-giving love of Jesus.

At the time of their call, the earliest disciples are not involved in a devout life of prayer and meditation, temple attendance, or religious observance (Mark 1:16-20; 2:14). Instead, they are fishing, mending nets, and collecting taxes. The call comes to them not because of who they are or what they are doing. It comes to them because of who Jesus is and what he is doing: Jesus is the grace of God incarnate, intimately involved in bringing God's love to the world.

Traveling the length and breadth of Palestine with Jesus, a group of very different people from quite different backgrounds becomes a community of grace (Mark 3:13-19). They are related to one another not because of a common ideology, but because of a common relationship to Jesus. As an extension of the messianic mission of Jesus, they are sent out on a mission of continuing grace in the world, preaching, teaching, and healing the sick (6:7-31). Aware of the motherly and fatherly care of God, their natural concern for material security is in the process of being broken (Matt. 6:14-34). Their obsession for power and prestige is gradually being overcome (20:25-28; 21:5, 16). In prayer and thanksgiving, they return to the source of grace and love (6:5-15).

Indeed, precisely this belief in the overflowing love of God that knows no boundaries is the distinctive emphasis of the ministry of Jesus, and therefore of the life of discipleship. The rabbis taught that the blind and the lame could not even participate in the public worship of God. The devout monks of Qumran stated quite categorically: "No madman, or lunatic, or simpleton, or fool, no blind man, or maimed, or lame, or deaf man, and no minor, shall enter the Community, for the Angels of Holiness are with them" (Messianic Rule: 1QSa 2.3-10). But when John the Baptist expresses his doubts about the messianic ministry of Jesus, he is told: "The blind receive their sight, the lame walk, the lepers are cleansed, the deaf hear, the dead are raised, and the poor have good news brought to them" (Matt. 11:5).

The marginalized people of society, the ones so often pushed to the periphery and forgotten—these become the center of attention with Jesus, the Savior who comes not to invite the righteous to share in salvation, but the notorious sinners (Mark 2:17). Jesus singles out for special attention the lepers, required to live outside the camp, regarded as "unclean," and denied fellowship with others; Gentiles, who have no share in the privileges of Israel; women and children, who have no status within the community; notorious sinners, despised tax collectors, drunkards, and prostitutes. "Amongst the most certain elements of the tradition in any case is the fact that Jesus displayed a provocative partiality for sinners and identified himself with people who had neither religion nor morals. . . . It cannot be denied that Jesus was 'in bad company.' Dubious characters, delinquents, are continually turning up in the Gospels" (Küng, 272).

This understanding of God offering undeserved love and all-embracing acceptance did not go unchallenged, however. It struck at the basis of traditional Jewish religion and culture of the first century. This fresh insight into the being of God destroyed the exclusive claims of the temple, the Law, the cult, all that the religious leaders and pious people considered sacred. It threatened the entire religious world of the first century and of traditional religiosity throughout all of history.

Mark's arrangement of the material following the call of Levi graphically portrays a situation which must have happened many times in the life of Jesus: he calls a notorious tax collector to follow him, he enjoys table fellowship with a large number of tax collectors and notorious sinners, the religious leaders challenge the disciples about his heretical behavior, and Jesus declares that he has come to call sinners to salvation (Mark 2:14-17). That simple Gospel narrative displays most clearly the dividing line between the religion of good works and respectability on one hand, and the way of grace and love on the other hand. Grace must always remain the first and the last word of Christian discipleship. It is grace which provides the welcome shade from the burning heat that so often threatens life on the road.

Matthew and Mark, however, never use the word *grace*. Luke uses the Greek word for *grace* exclusively of Jesus (2:40, 52; 4:22) and of the angel's message to Mary (1:30), except for the secular uses of the term (Luke 6:32-34; 17:9). At no stage do they make the word into a technical theological term, as in the Pauline writings. Rather than concentrating upon heavily weighted words, the Evangelists retell stories from the life of Jesus in such a way that their meaning is immediately transparent. Thereby they call on their readers to appropriate those stories into their own experience.

In this final chapter we will explore three such stories: the healing of two blind men, which stresses that discipleship is a miracle of divine grace (Mark); Peter's attempt to walk on the water, which underlines the fact that the grace which begins the life of discipleship sustains it through even the most difficult of adventures (Matthew); and the parable of the prodigal son and his elder brother, which indicates that there are no acceptable limits to the overflowing grace of God (Luke).

It Takes a Miracle or Two (Mark 8:22-26; 10:46-52)

Throughout the first part of the Gospel of Mark (1:14—8:26), Jesus reveals his authority in word and action only to be greeted by the increasing darkness of the world. First, the religious and political leaders plot to kill him (3:1-6), then his own townspeople at Nazareth reject him (6:1-6a), and finally even his disciples fail to understand him (8:4-21). In words reminiscent of the fearful prophecy of Isaiah 6:9-10, Jesus has to ask them, "Do you still not perceive or understand? Are your hearts hardened? Do you have eyes, and fail to see? Do you have ears, and fail to hear? And do you not remember?" (8:17-21). Such is the blindness of the world, which threatens to engulf even those nearest to Jesus.

With the incident at Caesarea Philippi (Mark 8:27—9:1), there is a distinct change in Mark's presentation. Until this point Jesus has revealed himself only in a veiled way, and those who perceive his true identity are not permitted to reveal it to others (3:11-12 and many places). But now Jesus speaks openly to his disciples about the suffering Son of Man, who must go the way of the cross (8:31; 9:31; 10:33-34). Up to this time, Mark gave indirect clues to the cost involved in following Jesus (6:1-6, 14-31), but now Jesus makes it the subject of explicit and extended teaching (8:34—9:1; 9:35—10:31; 10:38-45). The disciples, however, repeatedly fail to understand.

On the first occasion when Jesus predicts that the Son of Man will be rejected and killed (Mark 8:31), Peter is incensed and rebukes Jesus for speaking in such despicable terms (8:32). Jesus will not be so easily turned aside, and he goes on to teach the disciples, and the crowd, that those who follow him must do so by way of the cross (8:34—9:1). When the message of Jesus is confirmed by the divine voice on the Mount of Transfiguration (9:2-8), the three disciples with him do not understand his teaching on the death and resurrection of the Son of Man (9:8-13). Thereafter Jesus teaches all the disciples about discipleship as dependence upon God (9:14-29).

Jesus tells of his death a second time (Mark 9:31), but when they reach Capernaum he asks them what they have been speaking about on the way. They have been discussing who is the greatest. Clearly they do not understand. So Jesus places a child in their midst and instructs them at length on the true meaning of discipleship (9:35-50). A third time Jesus speaks on his impending death (10:33-34), but immediately James and John ask for positions of honor and glory in the kingdom of God. They still do not yet understood, so Jesus teaches them about discipleship as sacrificial service (10:38-45).

So that we might not mistake his intentions, Mark has placed his teaching on discipleship within the theological framework of two miracle stories. The healing of the blind man at Bethsaida (Mark 8:22-26) concludes the first half of the ministry of Jesus with its emphasis on the blindness of the world (3:1-6; 6:1-16; 8:14-21). That miracle anticipates the second stage of Jesus' ministry, with his repeated attempt to open the eyes of the disciples. The healing of Bartimaeus, the blind man of Jericho (10:46-52), concludes the teaching on discipleship, indicating what happens once the eyes of the blind have been opened. This story looks forward to the passion narrative, where the miracle of grace takes place (11:1—16:8).

> They came to Bethsaida. Some people brought a blind man to [Jesus] and begged him to touch him. He took the blind man by the hand and led him out of the village; and when he had put saliva on his eyes and laid his hands on him, he asked him, "Can you see anything?" And the man looked up and said, "I can see people, but they look like trees, walking." Then Jesus laid his hands on his eyes again; and he looked intently and his sight was restored, and he saw everything clearly. Then he sent him away to his home, saying, "Do not even go into the village."
> (Mark 8:22-26)

> They came to Jericho. As he and his disciples and a large crowd were leaving Jericho, Bartimaeus son of Timaeus, a blind beg-

gar, was sitting by the roadside. When he heard it was Jesus of Nazareth, he began to shout out and say, "Jesus, Son of David, have mercy on me!" Many sternly ordered him to be quiet, but he cried out even more loudly, "Son of David, have mercy on me!" Jesus stood still and said, "Call him here." And they called the blind man, saying to him, "Take heart; get up, he is calling you." So throwing off his cloak, he sprang up and came to Jesus. Then Jesus said to him, "What do you want me to do for you?" The blind man said to him, "My teacher, let me see again." Jesus said to him, "Go; your faith has made you well." Immediately he regained his sight and followed him on the way. (Mark 10:46-52)

Mark has placed these two miracle stories in a strategic manner in the construction of his Gospel narrative. They are the only miracles involving the healing of blind people in the Gospel of Mark, but that is almost all they have in common. The first is styled after a typical miracle story, while the second seems almost to have been a miracle story in the process of being refashioned as a discipleship call narrative. Their distinctiveness allows one story to provide the introduction and the other story the conclusion to Mark's central teaching on the life of discipleship. Their positions could not have been reversed. The first describes the miracle of grace which must precede discipleship; the second depicts the appropriate discipleship response to that miracle.

Discipleship Is a Miracle of Divine Grace

Immediately prior to the commencement of their fateful journey to Jerusalem, Jesus and his disciples arrive at Bethsaida, a bustling town on the northern shore of the Sea of Galilee. There some people bring a blind man to Jesus so that he might lay his hands on him and heal him (Mark 8:22-26). For a long time now, Jesus has been well-known as a miracle worker (1:21-27 and many places). But the time of miracles is almost over; the time of teaching on discipleship is about to begin (8:27—10:52). Jesus has no desire to attract supporters by miraculous healings, for they simply cannot understand their real significance (8:14-21), so he leads the man out of the village.

The countryside is the favorite location of the ministry of Jesus in Mark's Gospel (1:35, 45; 3:13; 6:31-32; 8:4, 27; and many other places), but here Mark is probably seeking to stress again his theme of "the messianic secret." Thus Jesus frequently commands the unclean spirits or those who have been cured to say nothing to others (1:34, 44; 3:11-12; and other places), for his true identity can only be understood in the light of the cross. As Mark is about to begin his major section of teaching regarding discipleship as the way of the cross, he does not wish to be distracted by the crowd's enchantment with the way of glory. Suffering discipleship is the very concept with which the disciples themselves are experiencing so much difficulty; they will repeatedly misunderstand it (8:27—10:52).

As in many of the miracle stories of the ancient world, Jesus uses spittle and the laying on of hands to affect the cure. The first attempt, however, is only partially successful. While the blind man can now identify certain indistinct shapes as people, they look more like trees walking about. With the second attempt, the man is completely cured. He is told to keep away from the village. Again, Jesus does not want people flocking to him as to a popular miracle worker.

In many ways, the present story is similar to the earlier account of the healing of the deaf mute in the region of the Decapolis (Mark 7:31-37): some people bring the person to Jesus so that he might lay hands on him, Jesus takes the person aside privately, he uses spittle and touch to effect the cure, and he wants the miracle kept secret. But there are important differences as well: in the earlier story the emphasis is on the effect of the miracle, with the man talking about it everywhere, to the astonishment of all the people (Mark 7:36-37). Here there is no mention of the effect of the miracle, and the emphasis is on the gradual nature of the cure, especially the difficulty which Jesus experiences in healing the blind man (8:25).

This unique difficulty Jesus experiences is the greatest problem when this story is read from a simple historical perspective. It suggests that the miracle-working Messiah had an off day. Such a misunderstanding is almost certainly why

Matthew and Luke both omit the story—the only Marcan miracle skipped by both of the later Evangelists. For the same reason, few sermons are heard on this text even today. Mark, however, is not concerned about possible historical difficulties; his interest, as always, is theological. For him, this is not just a story which happened once upon a time at Bethsaida in Galilee. It is a story which embodies gospel truth: opening the eyes of the blind is so difficult that it is impossible apart from the grace and power of God. But with God all things are possible—even the eyes of the blind can be opened.

As we have observed, Jesus explains to his disciples the meaning of his impending death, but each time they fail to understand the implications of what he is talking about. Hence, he is forced to give further extended teaching on the meaning of discipleship. Not once, not twice, but three times! How hard it is to open the eyes of the blind! So often we see only the shadowy blur of images, like trees walking about. Even when the teaching is clear, we have difficulty in bringing it into contemporary focus, and our vision and lifestyle are frequently distorted. Nothing short of a divine miracle will open their eyes, and nothing short of a similar miracle will open ours. Thanks be to God for his grace and for the power in the call of Jesus which perseveres until we are able to see clearly and to follow him!

Again, it must be obvious that this is not mere history, as though history were simply the retelling of facts from an almost forgotten past. This story is continually contemporary. It is gospel. Mark has included it at this particular point in his account of the ministry of Jesus because he realizes that the idea of a rejected and suffering Messiah will always be a stumbling block. Jesus' followers will always find difficulty in understanding and appropriating his teaching on costly discipleship. The opening of the eyes of the blind is always difficult. It is possible only through the grace and power of God, for discipleship is nothing less than a miracle of divine grace.

The Divine Grace of Discipleship Is Costly Grace

At the beginning of the second story (Mark 10:46-52), we are told that Jesus and his disciples have now arrived at Jericho, the last stop before Jerusalem, on their journey to that city of rejection, suffering, and death. Jericho, with ancient and noble traditions, was Herod's rich and expansive winter capital. The narrative starts as Jesus is leaving the town and going out into the countryside, the favorite location for the ministry of Jesus in this rural Gospel (in Luke 18:35 the story begins as Jesus is entering the city). The disciples and a large crowd are said to be accompanying him.

The disciples have been present with Jesus throughout the entire preceding section (Mark 8:27—10:45), for it is to them that he was directing his teaching. On two occasions when the crowd was present, Jesus went into the house to instruct the disciples privately (9:28-29; 10:10-12). The only time Jesus addressed the crowd directly in this section was at the beginning of the journey, near Caesarea Philippi, when he said to the disciples *and* to the crowd, "If any want to become my followers, let them deny themselves and take up their cross and follow me" (8:34). As Jesus leaves Jericho, it is important that the crowd is accompanying him in large numbers, for in the encounter with Bartimaeus they will at last see a person who is prepared to follow in the way of Jesus (10:52). What was declared in theory at the beginning of the journey is demonstrated in practice as the journey to Jerusalem reaches its climax.

Bartimaeus (an Aramaic name meaning "the son of Timaeus"), a blind man, is sitting by the side of the road. He already knows about Jesus: who he is (the merciful "Son of David"), his name ("Jesus"), where he comes from ("of Nazareth"), and what he can do ("let me see again"). When he ascertains that the great crowd is there because of Jesus, he cries out, "Jesus, Son of David, have mercy on me!"

The crowd tries to silence Bartimaeus. Despite all the miracles they have seen and heard about, they can hardly believe that Jesus would be concerned about a blind man relegated to the edge of society. Their protests only serve to increase his enthusiasm. Yet again he makes his confession of faith and his appeal. Contrary to the onlookers' expectation, Jesus calls the blind man. Now those who earlier tried to suppress him, pass on the message and say, "Courage!" "Cheer up!" Bartimaeus jumps for joy, throws off his coat, and comes to Jesus. His appeal succeeds. Because of his faith, his sight is restored, and he follows on the way.

As always in Mark's miracle stories and discipleship stories, Jesus occupies the center of the stage. Yet there is a tremendous christological concentration in these eight verses. This is the only time so many names and titles are used of Jesus in one story: "Jesus" (Mark 10:47, 49-50, 52), "Jesus of Nazareth" (10:47), "Son of David" (10:47-48), "Master/Rabbi/Teacher" (10:51). The significance of this list becomes even clearer when we observe that five of Mark's sixteen miracle stories have no names or titles at all: Peter's mother-in-law (1:29-31), man with a withered hand (3:1-6), feeding of the 5,000 (6:32-44), walking on the water (6:45-52), and feeding of the 4,000 (8:1-10). The majority of Mark's miracle stories have just one title: a leper (1:40-45), stilling the storm (4:35-41), Syrophoenician woman (7:24-30), a deaf mute (7:31-37), and blind man of Bethsaida (8:22-26). Some have two titles: exorcism at Capernaum (1:21-28), a paralytic (2:1-12), and cursing of the fig tree (11:12-14, 20-25).

The only miracle stories which come anywhere near our present one in the use of christological names and titles are much longer accounts: the healing of the Gadarene demoniac (Mark 5:1-20, where the name "Jesus" occurs five times and the title "Son of the Most High God" once); the combined story of the woman with a hemorrhage and of the daughter of Jairus (5:21-43, with "Jesus" five times and "the Teacher" once in twenty-three verses); and the healing of the epileptic boy (9:14-29, with "Jesus" four times and "Teacher" once in sixteen verses).

One title is of particular interest in the midst of all of this christological concentration in the story of blind Bartimaeus: "Jesus of Nazareth" (Mark 10:47), used by Mark to signify authority and crucifixion. In the opening miracle story, where the stress is on the authority of Jesus, the demoniac in Capernaum shouted, "What have you to do with us, Jesus of Nazareth? Have you come to destroy us? I know who you are, the Holy One of God" (1:24). At the end of the Gospel when the young man dressed in white meets the women at the empty tomb, he says "You are looking for Jesus of Nazareth, who was crucified" (16:6). Authority and crucifixion are the twin christological themes of our present story as well.

The role ascribed to Bartimaeus in this story is particularly significant. If Jesus occupies center stage, he certainly has to share it with the blind man from Jericho. This is the only time we are given the name of a person healed by Jesus (the nearest we have elsewhere would be Simon's mother-in-law or Jairus's daughter). His name is given in both Aramaic (Bartimaeus) and Greek (son of Timaeus). Note the parallel naming of Simon of Cyrene, where the Gospel says he is "the father of Alexander and Rufus" (Mark 15:21). It is virtually certain that Mark wants us to understand that both Bartimaeus and Simon became Christians and perhaps were known to the people of his church. Certainly their parallel experience of discipleship is stressed by Mark: Bartimaeus followed Jesus on the way to Jerusalem and the cross, and Simon carried the cross behind Jesus on his way to crucifixion.

Much has to happen, however, before Bartimaeus can serve as a model of discipleship. He has to overcome, first of all, the prejudice of the crowd, which does not understand the grace of God and seeks to silence the blind beggar crying to Jesus for mercy (Mark 10:48). However, the blind man can see what is apparently still hidden from both the crowds and the disciples, who had earlier tried to stop the people bringing children to Jesus (10:13-16). Bartimaeus knows that his one hope of salvation is in Jesus, and because of this, he will not be silenced. Indeed, he cries out all the louder.

In the earlier discipleship call narratives in the Gospel of Mark, we are told what the people are doing at the time of their call: two were fishing (Mark 1:16-18, Simon and Andrew), two were overhauling their nets (1:19-20, James and John), and one was collecting taxes (2:14, Levi). So here, Bartimaeus is described not simply as a blind man, as in the case of the man at Bethsaida; instead, he is "a blind *beggar*." Mark reports that he "was sitting by the roadside" carrying on his work of begging just as Levi was "sitting at the tax office," carrying on his work of collecting taxes.

Apparently it was a standard custom for oriental beggars to spread their coats out along the road so people going by might throw alms onto them. If Mark has this practice in mind, he could well be stressing that when Jesus called Bartimaeus, he throws aside his cloak, abandoning his tools of trade to follow Jesus, as did Simon and Andrew, James and John, and Levi. If Mark does not have this particular custom in mind, then he indicates in more general terms that Bartimaeus joyfully throws away the one thing he owns, all that he has for protection, to follow Jesus.

When confronted earlier by a rich man seeking eternal life, Jesus tells him, "You lack one thing; go, sell what you own, and give the money to the poor, and you will have treasure in heaven; then come, follow me" (Mark 10:21). The irony is that the rich man is not prepared to part with his possessions. He goes away sad, having rejected the way to eternal life. But the poor man readily abandons the one thing he possesses and runs to Jesus! Here Mark uses two Greek words with double meanings. One word, *sōzō*, means both "heal" and "save"; the other, *hodos*, means both "road" and "way." Mark intends his readers to understand thus: Jesus told Bartimaeus that his faith had both saved and healed him, and Bartimaeus, in turn, followed Jesus on the way to the cross.

The statement "your faith has saved you" or "made you well" (Mark 10:52), given also to the woman who had experienced hemorrhaging for twelve years (5:34), has the sound of a liturgical declaration of absolution. Its use in connection with a miracle story is made possible by the double meaning and is a reminder of the holistic view of salvation espoused in the New Testament. Salvation includes not simply the saving of the soul but also the healing of the body—that is, the salvation of the whole person.

The opening Scripture quotation of the Gospel of Mark declares that John the Baptist, as the forerunner of Jesus, will "prepare the way of the Lord" (Mark 1:2-3). The central discipleship section (8:27—10:52) is also held together by the theme of "the way" (8:27; 9:33-34; 10:17, 32, 46, 52). This always carries with it the theological significance that "the way to Jerusalem" (10:32), the way of suffering and death, is "the way of the Lord" (1:2-3); that way is to be followed by all Christians (8:34). Bartimaeus is the first to understand the truth of the teaching of Jesus and follow on the way (10:52). In the early church, according to the book of Acts, Christians were known as followers of "the Way" (Acts 9:2; also 18:25-26; 19:9, 23; 22:4; 24:14, 22).

As always, of course, Mark is writing theology in the story of Bartimaeus. Those who cry out to Jesus for mercy and healing, who have received the grace of God and experienced the power of God in their lives, and who have been saved by faith—those are the ones who abandon their professions and profits to become joyful followers of Jesus on the way to Jerusalem, the way of crucifixion and resurrection. Here, at last, in the person of a blind beggar relegated to the margins of society and reduced to penury, is a person who understands that to be a follower of Jesus, you have to take up the cross and follow him (Mark 8:34).

It is difficult to open the eyes of the blind (Mark 8:22-26). But once the grace and power of God have permeated the deepest recesses of our being, we cannot but joyfully follow Jesus on the way to Jerusalem, even though we know it is the way of rejection and suffering, of death and resurrection (10:46-52). Discipleship is costly grace. It is grace, but it is costly because it leads to Jerusalem. It is costly, but it is grace because it is the result of the continuing work of God in our lives.

Have You Tried Walking on Water? (Matthew 14:22-33)

Matthew was writing for a Jewish-Christian church clearly prone to legalism and judgmental attitudes. Throughout his Gospel, Matthew seeks to engender a more open and generous spirit by presenting Jesus as the merciful Christian Messiah whose example is to be followed, and by calling for a greater degree of acceptance among Jesus' followers.

The legalistic approach was particularly manifested in an eagerness to develop "a pure church" which excluded those who failed to maintain the "high standards." This we observed in chapter four, on Matthew's understanding of community (Friends for the Journey). The parable of the tares in the field and its explanation (Matt. 13:24-30, 36-43) are, in fact, a veiled attack on this kind of Christianity. The parable of the lost sheep (18:10-14) and of the unforgiving servant (18:21-35) are also attempts to encourage a more gracious and forgiving pastoral attitude. We want to interpret the story of Peter's rescue within this context of a church which needs to develop a fresh understanding of the concept of grace in the life of discipleship. Matthew underlines the fact that the grace which begins the life of discipleship sustains it throughout even the most difficult adventures.

> Immediately [Jesus] made the disciples get into the boat and go on ahead to the other side, while he dismissed the crowds. And after he had dismissed the crowds, he went up the mountain by himself to pray. When evening came, he was there alone, but by this time the boat, battered by the waves, was far from the land, for the wind was against them. And early in the morning he came walking toward them on the sea. But when the disciples saw him walking on the sea, they were terrified, saying, "It is a ghost!" And they cried out in fear. But immediately Jesus spoke to them and said, "Take heart, it is I; do not be afraid."
>
> Peter answered him, "Lord, if it is you, command me to come to you on the water." He said, "Come." So Peter got out of the boat, started walking on the water, and came toward Jesus. But when he noticed the strong wind, he became frightened, and beginning to sink, he cried out, "Lord, save me!" Jesus immediately reached out his hand and caught him, saying to him, "You of little faith, why did you doubt?" When they got into the boat, the wind ceased. And those in the boat worshiped him, saying, "Truly you are the Son of God."
>
> (Matt. 14:22-33)

Peter plays a particularly important role in the Gospel of Matthew, where he is presented in a much more positive light than in Mark. Yet Peter has traditionally been associated with Mark. The popular view from the time of Papias, Bishop of Hierapolis about 140 C.E., has been that "Mark was Peter's interpreter" (in Eusebius, *Ecclesiastical History* 3.39). In each of the synoptic Gospels, the call of Peter takes priority over the other disciples (Mark 1:16-20; Matt. 4:18-22; Luke 5:1-11). In the Gospel of John, the first thing Andrew does after meeting Jesus is find Peter and bring him to Jesus, who immediately gives him his new name "Rocky" (John 1:40-42). The list of the twelve disciples varies somewhat in names and order, but Peter is always at the head of the list (Mark 3:13-19; 10:1-4; Luke 6:12-16; Acts 1:12-14). Only in Matthew is it emphasized that Peter is "first" (Matt. 10:2; note that there is no "second"!). Peter is the rock on which the church is built (Matt. 16:18, NRSV notes), with power to bind and loose (16:19; compare 18:18, where the same authority is given to all the disciples).

In many places some of the harshness of Mark's portrayal of Peter is diminished. On the Mount of Transfiguration, for example, Peter says to Jesus in the Marcan account, "It is good for us to be here; let us make three dwellings, one for you, one for Moses, and one for Elijah." The Evangelist adds, "He did not know what to say, for they were terrified" (Mark 9:5-6). Matthew omits the reference to Peter not knowing what to say and changes the tone of Peter's statement completely: "Lord, it is good for us to be here; if you wish, I will make three dwellings here, one for you, one for Moses, and one for Elijah" (Matt. 17:4). Likewise, when Jesus first predicts his death, the bald statement of Peter's rebuke of Jesus (Mark 8:33) is changed: "God forbid it, Lord! This must never happen to you" (Matt. 16:22). Yet in Matthew, Peter is still sternly rebuked as being on the side of Satan.

Already in Mark, Peter is pictured as the spokesman for the disciples (Mark 8:29; 9:5; 10:28; 11:21). But Matthew particularly accentuates this in portraying Peter as the one who initiates the occasion for Jesus to explain things to his disciples (Matt. 15:15; 16:16; 17:24; 18:21). In Matthew, Peter is the one (not the disciples as in Mark) who asks Jesus to explain to the disciples, and thereby to the church, the meaning of his teaching on clean and unclean food (Matt. 15:15). Even more strikingly, the tax collectors ask Peter whether or not Jesus pays the half-shekel tax. Jesus' explanation is finally given by Jesus, through Peter, to the church (17:24-27).

In the discourse on relationships within the Christian

community, Peter asks Jesus the vital question, "Lord, if another member of the church sins against me, how often should I forgive? As many as seven times?" And Peter receives the answer for the church, "Not seven, but . . . seventy times seven!" (Matt. 18:21-22). In the story of the rich young ruler in Matthew, Peter not only says "Look, we have left everything and followed you" (as in Mark), but goes on to ask the question, "What then will we have?" (19:27). In the Gospel of Matthew, Peter is depicted as the leader through whom Jesus teaches the church.

But was not Peter the very one who denied Jesus? How then could he possibly be the one through whom Jesus teaches his church? We read the story of Peter with his boastful profession of faith (Matt. 26:31-35), shameful denial (26:69-75), and subsequent restoration to leadership (16:18-19; cf. Luke 22:32; John 21:15-19). This is one of the most striking illustrations of the continuing grace of discipleship to be found anywhere in the New Testament. Peter's attempt at walking on the water reads like a sermon on the career of Peter, an eloquent example for the Matthaean church. That very church held Peter in high esteem as a leader, but it was tempted to take a legalistic approach to others who, in their opinion, had fallen from grace (Matt. 18:15-17).

Peter's Enthusiastic Confession

In the Gospels, particularly in Mark, the basis of Matthew, Peter appears as the most impetuously outspoken of the disciples. He is the one who knows that Jesus is the Messiah (Mark 8:29), brashly tries to prevent Jesus going the way of the cross (8:32-33), wants to stay on the mountain and enjoy the glory forever (9:5), and boasts that they have left everything to follow Jesus (10:28). At the Mount of Olives, Jesus quotes from Zechariah 13:7 to reinforce his belief that all of the disciples will forsake him and flee when the pressure mounts against them. Peter is not at all sure about the others, but he is certain that he will stand firm, no matter what happens. Then Jesus emphatically and solemnly predicts that Peter will deny him three times before the night is out (an "amen" saying). Again, Peter remonstrates all the more vigorously: "Even though I must die with you, I will not deny you!" (Mark 14:27-31). We will meet this same brash and courageous Peter in our present story from Matthew's Gospel.

As we observed in the story of the stilling of the storm (Matt. 8:23-27), the early church recognized in the image of the boat a symbol of the church. In the stormy waters, they recognized the chaos of the world which threatened its very existence. Once again, Matthew is writing on two levels as he tells the story of the disciples on the lake. He describes the dilemma of the disciples on the Sea of Galilee and at the same time describes the situation confronting his church. At the command of Jesus, they have launched out into the deep and are now a long way from the security of the shore. There can be no turning back, for Jesus has sent them to the other side; but they are taking a severe battering, with mountainous seas and a strong head wind.

Matthew's persecuted church would have recognized themselves in the story. And Matthew strengthens the corporate image by saying that "the boat was battling with a heavy sea" or "being swamped by the waves" (Matt. 14:24, AG), rather than that "they were distressed in their rowing." He naturally omits Mark's difficult statement that "he intended to pass them by" (Mark 6:48), for its application to the contemporary church situation would not have been immediately apparent. The Evangelists agree, however, that Jesus comes to them walking on the water, and that when they see him coming in the half-light of the early morning, they are terrified, thinking it is a ghost. Jesus calls on them to be courageous and to forget their fear.

Up to this point, Matthew has been basically retelling the story as he found it in the Gospel of Mark, adapting it to his own situation. Now he continues with a story found only in his Gospel: Peter's attempt to walk on the water (Matt. 14:28-33). With the rest of the disciples cowering in the boat, Peter makes his response: "Lord, if it is you, command me to come to you on the water!" (14:28). This is the typical Peter of the Gospel tradition: brash, courageous, outspoken. While the others are trembling in fear, Peter is ready to move. He recognizes Jesus as "Lord," but he has no doubts about his own ability. He throws down the challenge. All he needs is a word from Jesus. If Jesus can do it, so can he!

This is so much like the Peter we meet on the Mount of Olives: even if he would have to die with Jesus, he will never deny him (Matt. 26:35)! "Captain Courageous" has great confidence in his ability to withstand the pressure of any situation, no matter how challenging.

Peter's Sinking Doubts

Peter ought to know better than to challenge Jesus. His command to Peter consists of one word, "Come!" That simple command is sufficient for Peter, for he has recognized Jesus as his "Lord" (Matt. 14:28), and he is his obedient disciple. A one-word command, and Peter is over the side of the boat, walking on the sea toward Jesus. But then he realizes the strength of the wind blowing in his hair and the instability of the water under his feet. He sees the strength of the opposition, and he too is afraid and begins to sink.

A similar event takes place when Jesus is betrayed by Judas and arrested on the Mount of Olives by "a large crowd with swords and clubs." All of the other disciples leave Jesus (Matt. 26:47-56). But as Jesus is being led off to the high priest's house, Peter courageously follows, even though at a distance, right into the house of the high priest, to see the end (26:57-58). He makes a brave start, and perhaps he will, after all, disprove Jesus' prediction that before the rooster crows twice, he will deny Jesus three times. Once Peter enters the courtyard of the high priest's house, however, he begins to "sink." It only takes one of the young servant girls to confront him, and he denies all knowledge of Jesus. When the bystanders join in, he denies it again and again (26:69-75). Matthew stresses, "He denied it before all of them" (26:70, added to Mark).

The story of Peter's failure is one of the few stories told in all four Gospels (Mark 14:66-72; Matt. 26:69-75; Luke 22:54-62; John 18:15-18, 25-27). Hence, all of the churches knew that, despite his enthusiastic and courageous confessions of loyalty, Peter had denied Jesus the night before he had been crucified; and not just once, but three times! This was a truth which couldn't be covered up. This was no rumor. The facts were too well known.

Jesus' Gracious Rescue

When Peter begins to sink in the stormy sea under the weight of his own doubts, all he can do is make a last desperate plea, "Lord, save me!" (Matt. 14:30). That is enough. Jesus immediately reaches out, catches hold of him, and puts him back in the boat (14:31). The wind drops, and the disciples worship Jesus as "the Son of God" (14:32). The early church, on hearing the story told to them over and over again, may well have recalled the cry of the persecuted psalmist's cry and also his thanksgiving:

> Stretch out your hand from on high;
>> set me free and rescue me from the mighty waters,
>> from the hand of aliens,
> whose mouths speak lies,
>> and whose right hands are false.   (Ps. 144:7-8)

> He reached down from on high,
>> he took me;
> he drew me out of mighty waters.
> He delivered me from my strong enemy,
>> and from those who hated me;
>> for they were too mighty for me.   (Ps. 18:16-17)

Peter's urgent cry reminds us of the plea of the group of disciples on the stormy sea on another occasion, "Lord, save us! We are perishing!" (Matt. 8:25). Even in their most desperate moments, they remember and acknowledge that Jesus is the Lord of the church. He is the only one who can be depended upon to rescue them from their distress. This earlier story of the disciples on the stormy sea ends, however, with the question: "What sort of man is this, that even the winds and the sea obey him?" (8:27). The answer is given in the following story, when the two Gadarene demoniacs acknowledge Jesus as "Son of God" (8:29).

Here, however, following the rescue of Peter, those in the

boat fall down at his feet in worship and confess, "Truly you are the Son of God" (Matt. 14:33). In Mark this supreme christological statement of faith is offered by the Gentile centurion at the foot of the cross. But in Matthew, the response, "Truly this man was God's Son!" is made by "the centurion and those with him, who were keeping watch over Jesus, [and] saw the earthquake and what took place" (27:54). Their statement is strikingly anticipated here by the disciples in the boat (14:33).

It seems highly unlikely that the disciples recognize and confess Jesus as the Son of God simply on account of the miracle of walking on the water. After all, they have already seen him still the storm (Matt. 8:23-27), cleanse a leper (8:1-4), heal the sick (8:14-17 and many places), feed five thousand men plus women and children (14:13-21), and even raise the dead (9:18-26). Yet here for the first time, the disciples recognize his divine sonship as the community bows in worship. They have, at last, witnessed a real gospel miracle.

There have always been arguments about whether or not Jesus could have walked on the water, and certainly there are many who doubt that Peter could have managed even a few faltering steps. But that is not the point—at least not according to Matthew. For the Evangelist, the real miracle is to be seen in the fact that when a disciple makes an enthusiastic confession only to follow it with such abysmal doubts, Jesus does not let that one fall. The doubter has only to cry out for help to the Lord of the church, and he will reach out and rescue the one sinking. This is gospel truth, for it happens over and over again in the history of the church and in the life of every disciple.

After Peter's miserable performance in the courtyard of the high priest, we might well expect to hear nothing further about him. Certainly, we would never expect to see him emerge again as the leader of the early church. But there he is, the chosen preacher on the day of Pentecost (Acts 2:14-36). Indeed, even before that he is a recognized leader in the apostolic community, making arrangements for the replacement of Judas (1:15-26). What has happened between the night of denial and the day of Pentecost that Peter should be able so readily to assume his role of leadership in the Christian community?

The answer lies right at the end of Mark's Gospel: the young man at the empty tomb tells the women that Jesus has risen. They must give a message to the disciples "and [especially] Peter" that he has gone on to Galilee; there they will see him, even as he promised (Mark 16:7). The later account in the Gospel of John tells of Jesus' gracious appearance to Peter (John 21:15-19) and explains his ability to rise from a night of failure.

It is important to recognize that discipleship is a miracle of grace (Mark 8:22-26; 10:46-52). But it is even more important for the Christian community to recognize that it is a miracle of *continuing* grace (Matt. 14:22-33). Faith does not exhaust itself in the initial response to the call to follow Jesus, and grace does not restrict itself to the initial call. The grace of God comes to us afresh every morning, as is most readily apparent in our times of difficulty and doubt.

There's Always a Welcome (Luke 15:11-32)

It is certain that Jesus was frequently in bad company. It is equally certain that this is one aspect of the ministry of Jesus which Luke delights to highlight. There are no acceptable limits to the overflowing grace of God. Those considered to have no hope in this world are singled out by Luke as the special recipients of God's grace. Luke more frequently than any other Gospel shows Jesus' concern for Samaritans (Luke 10:33; 17:16), Gentiles (7:2), widows (4:25; 7:12), women (4:38; 7:37; and many places), children (8:41; 18:15), lepers (7:22; 17:12), the demon-possessed (4:41; 8:27), the sick (5:17; 4:38, 40; 6:6; and many places), the poor (16:20; 21:3), tax collectors (5:30; 19:2), and notorious sinners (15:1; 19:7). God's welcome is open to all, and therefore it is especially important for Luke that, at the beginning of his ministry in Nazareth, Jesus applies to himself the words of the prophet Isaiah:

> The Spirit of the Lord is upon me
> because he has anointed me

> to bring good news to the poor.
> He has sent me to proclaim release for the captives
>   and recovery of sight to the blind,
>   to let the oppressed go free,
> to proclaim the year of the Lord's favor.   (Luke 4:18-19)

It is not surprising, then, that Luke was well aware of accusations brought against Jesus by religious leaders. They were shocked by his irreligious association with outcasts and his free offer of forgiveness to notorious sinners. Luke's clearest defense of the gospel for the outcast is to be seen in a series of parables (Luke 15:1-31) which he has collected and placed within the journey to Jerusalem. On this trek Jesus repeatedly instructs his disciples on the meaning of life on the road (9:51—19:48). The opening verses (15:1-3) set the scene by stating that one day when many tax collectors and outcasts are listening to Jesus, the religious leaders take umbrage at the way he welcomes them. Jesus responds with three parables: the lost sheep (15:4-7), the lost coin (15:8-10), and the lost son (15:11-32).

All three of these parables in Luke 15 stress the joy which is experienced when someone regains something which has been lost. Luke makes it quite clear that his human joy is but a pale reflection of the joy which God experiences when he recovers what has been lost (15:7, 10, 24, 32). The longer third parable broadens the perspective, however, so that it now includes the attitude of those who are not able to share the joy and take part in the festivals celebrating the return of the prodigals (15:11-32).

> Then Jesus said, "There was a man who had two sons. The younger of them said to his father, 'Father, give me the share of the property that will belong to me.' So he divided his property between them. A few days later the younger son gathered all he had and traveled to a distant country, and there he squandered his property in dissolute living. When he had spent everything, a severe famine took place throughout that country, and he began to be in need. So he went and hired himself out to one of the citizens of that country, who sent him to his fields to feed the pigs. He would gladly have filled himself

with the pods that the pigs were eating; and no one gave him anything. But when he came to himself he said, 'How many of my father's hired hands have bread enough and to spare, but here I am dying of hunger! I will get up and go to my father, and I will say to him, "Father, I have sinned against heaven and before you; I am no longer worthy to be called your son; treat me like one of your hired hands." ' So he set off and went to his father. But while he was still far off, his father saw him and was filled with compassion; he ran and put his arms around him and kissed him. Then the son said to him, 'Father, I have sinned against heaven and before you; I am no longer worthy to be called your son.' But the father said to his slaves, 'Quickly, bring out a robe—the best one—and put it on him; put a ring on his finger and sandals on his feet. And get the fatted calf and kill it, and let us eat and celebrate; for this son of mine was dead and is alive again; he was lost and is found!' And they began to celebrate.

"Now his elder son was in the field; and when he came and approached the house, he heard music and dancing. He called one of the slaves and asked what was going on. He replied, 'Your brother has come, and your father has killed the fatted calf, because he has got him back safe and sound.' Then he became angry and refused to go in. His father came out and began to plead with him. But he answered his father, 'Listen! For all these years I have been working like a slave for you, and I have never disobeyed your command; yet you have never given me even a young goat so that I might celebrate with my friends. But when this son of yours came back, who has devoured your property with prostitutes, you killed the fatted calf for him!' Then the father said to him, 'Son, you are always with me, and all that is mine is yours. But we had to celebrate and rejoice, because this brother of yours was dead and has come to life; he was lost and has been found.' "

(Luke 15:11-32)

This story has variously been called the parable of the prodigal son, the elder brother, or the father and the two lost sons. It is a beautiful double parable with a clearly defined literary structure in two parts. The first section on the younger brother uses inverted parallelism of twelve ideas, the second six reversing the first six:

1 A son is lost—"Give me my share"
  2 Goods wasted in extravagant living
    3 Everything lost—"he spent everything—
      he began to want"
      4 The great sin—"feeding pigs for Gentiles"
        5 Total rejection—"no one gave him anything"
          6 A change of mind—"he came to himself—
          I perish here"
          6^1 An initial repentance—"make me a servant
          [I will pay it back]"
        5^1 Total acceptance—"his father ran
        and kissed him"
      4^1 The great repentance—"I am not worthy
      to be called your son"
    3^1 Everything gained—a robe, ring, and shoes
    [restoration to sonship]
  2^1 Goods used in joyful celebration
1^1 A son is found—"My son was dead and is alive,
  was lost and is found."   (Bailey, 160)

In the structure of the section of the parable relating to the younger brother (Luke 15:11-24), the focal point is at the center where the change takes place. The younger brother comes to himself and begins to take the necessary action of reconciliation with his father.

A similar, though naturally simpler, structure is to be found in the story of the older brother (15:25-32):

1 He comes—"as he came and drew near to the house"
  2 Your brother is safe—a feast—"your father has killed
  the fatted calf"
    3 A father comes to reconcile—"so his father came
    out entreating him"
      4 Complaint # 1—How you treat me—"you never
      gave me a kid"
      4^1 Complaint # 2—How you treat him—"you killed
      for him the fattened calf"
    3^1 A father tries to reconcile—"Beloved son . . .
    all that is mine is yours"
  2^1 Your brother is safe—a feast—"It was fitting
  to make merry"
$[1^1$ is missing.]   (based on Bailey, 191)

The center point of this section of the parable is the ego-centric complaining of the elder brother. But the structure is incomplete (with 1^1 missing), and the major emphasis comes upon that which is missing at the end of the story. If the literary structure were complete, it would tell how the elder brother comes into the house, joins in the celebrations, and is reconciled to the other members of his family. Alas, that does not happen. The older son remains forever outside the family of grace.

The loving father's attitude and action remains consistently gracious throughout both sections of parable, and the literary structure draws attention to the crucial difference between the two brothers. The younger son who is lost repents, and the family rejoices; the elder son refuses reconciliation and is lost.

A Son Is Lost to His Family and His Community

As with many of the parables of Jesus, this one begins quite naturally with a series of events which are immediately intelligible to his hearers. Under first-century law, the farm and all that belong to it, plus two-thirds of the disposable property, go to the elder son. The younger son receives one-third of the disposable property. This transfer of property, however, takes place only on the death of the father. For a younger brother to ask for his share while his father is still alive—this is virtually to wish for his father's death. It is an act of total rejection of the father and of family relationships. Should such a thing occur in that culture, the father would undoubtedly refuse the request and beat the son.

But in this story, the father accepts the rejection and "demonstrates an almost unbelievable love by granting the request" (Bailey, 161). He loves his son to such an extent that he is prepared to absorb his humiliating rejection and grant him his freedom—a radical act of love.

The younger son's rejection does not stop there, however. To turn the property into cash and to head to another country involves a similar rejection of the communal life of the village. Away from home, the young man continues the series of selfish mistakes which will lead him deeper and deeper into trouble. He squanders his inheritance in reckless living, and later in the story the elder brother will claim that his younger brother wasted his money in immorality (Luke 15:30, with a derogatory reference to "prostitutes").

The younger son is unfortunate enough to run out of money just when a severe famine hit that country, and he can not find work. The hearers of the story would be able to identify with the latter part of the young man's experience. There were ten major famines in and around Jerusalem in the 250 years between the capture of the city by the Greeks and its destruction by the Romans in 70 C.E., plus disasters which were a direct result of war (Jeremias, *Jerusalem*, 140-144). Still, the younger son's basic problems are of his own making. He rejected his family and his community, and before he is through, he rejects his religion and culture as well.

Instead of seeking assistance from the nearest Jewish community, which would gladly offer help, the younger son attaches himself to a Gentile. He must realize that this will eventually lead him to a wholesale denial of his Jewish faith—Sabbath observance and food laws will be only the first to go. Worse than that, the text certainly suggests that his services are not requested; he is not responding to an advertisement in the local paper. Instead, he is pictured as forcing himself on the generosity of a wealthy Gentile landowner: he selects a patron and goes and hires himself out (Luke 15:15).

That citizen politely tries to get rid of him by giving him a job which he reckons a Jew would never accept. The younger son shows how desperate he has become and how far he has wandered from the Law when he goes to care for the farmer's pigs. There is a Jewish saying: "Cursed is the man who keeps pigs." He has, in fact, stooped so low and his condition has become so wretched that he even contemplates table fellowship with the pigs, even though they have only the dry husks of the wild carob bean to share with him. He misses out again, however, for no one gives him anything to eat.

A Son Is Found and a Community Celebrates

In his misery, the prodigal finally comes to his senses. He recognizes that even the lowest of his father's laborers is better off than he is; he also realizes that the way he has been living is an affront to God and a disgrace to his father. He formulates his plan: he will head for home, confess his sin, and see if his father will give him a job.

It may well be that the motivation for the prodigal's repentance is less than what we might consider satisfactory. His motivation is very basic: hunger and hardship. He recognizes, however, that he has no valid claim on his family. His hope is to become a day laborer, the lowest and most vulnerable social and economic position. Such a worker does not even live on the property and is granted employment only as it is available on a day-to-day basis.

The prodigal can look forward to only one thing when he returns to the village that he has rejected: humiliation and shame. He insulted them all and went off to make his own way in the world. He is returning a miserable failure.

The father's welcome, however, surpasses all possible expectations. It is always considered beneath the dignity of an aged oriental gentleman to run. But when the father sees his son in the distance, he runs to greet him, throws his arms about his neck so that he cannot go down on his knees before him, and kisses him on the cheek as an equal.

The son is not even able to finish his carefully rehearsed confession. The father interrupts and orders one lot of servants to bring the ceremonial robe (a mark of high distinction), the ring (a symbol of authority), and the shoes (a luxury which distinguishes the free man from the slave). He calls on another lot of servants to kill the prize calf which they have been fattening for a special occasion. A kid or a lamb would have been sufficient for a family celebration, but no, the father wants the whole village to celebrate. The son that was lost has now been found. So the fattened calf it is!

A Son Refuses to Join the Communal Celebrations and Is Lost

By now the listeners would begin to realize why Jesus is telling them this particular story. They have attacked him because he is so often in the company of sinners. He has told them the story of a sinner who repents and is immediately welcomed back as an honored member of the family and of the community. Before they can object, Jesus continues with the story of the elder brother, and as in all double parables, the emphasis is on the second half.

The elder son has been working out on the farm and reaches home only after the loud, joyous celebrations are well underway. It is strange that he has not been notified beforehand, but perhaps the father is well aware that the elder son would be upset and that he may even try to stop the celebrations before they begin. Since most of the village would have heard and been invited, it is strange that he has not heard before he nears home. Whatever has happened, the sound of music means that the feast is already well underway by the time the elder brother arrives. The rhythm of the music would tell him that it is a joyful occasion—certainly not a funeral!

However, the elder son is so suspicious that he does not rush in to find out what the good news is that they are celebrating. Instead, he sends in one of the young boys hanging around in the street. This is not what we expect in a normal family situation. Thus it is not surprising that, when the elder brother finds out what it is all about, he refuses to go inside and join in the festivities.

The father again takes the initiative. He "goes out to the elder brother even as he ran to meet the younger" (Linnemann, 79). He begs him to come in, but to no avail. The elder brother reproaches his father and disowns his brother: "this son of yours." "Middle Eastern customs and the Oriental high regard for the authority of the father make the elder son's actions extremely insulting. . . . There is now a break in relationship between the elder son and his father that is nearly as radical as the break between the father and the younger son at the beginning of the parable" (Bailey, 195).

The father, despite everything, is still the loving father, even of his angry, reproachful elder son. The onlookers would surely expect the father to rebuke such a disrespectful and ungracious son who brings public shame upon his father. But he doesn't. The father does not attack his son and does not defend his own action. He shows his love and compassion for his elder son—the same love and compassion which he shows for his younger son. The father speaks to him with particular affection ("my dear son") and reminds him of the unbroken fellowship which they have enjoyed all these years (has it only been years of drudgery—was there never any joy?). He rightly points out that all he owns belongs to him since the younger son has already received his share of the estate. He gently reminds him of their family relationship. It is, after all, his *brother* who has just returned from the dead.

The elder son has shown an incredibly selfish attitude. His idea of a good time is to celebrate with his friends, away from his family. He cares nothing about a brother who has come back from the dead. Indeed, he does not even acknowledge him as a member of the family. He does not know the meaning of "family" and does not know how to respond to a loving father. Nothing will soften his heart. Not surprisingly, he knows nothing about true happiness. He wants a party to make himself happy; he can't understand that *because* they are happy, they are having a party. When a lost son comes home, the community has no alternative but to rejoice. They are so happy that community relationships are restored, they can't help themselves; they have to kill the calf they have been fattening for a special occasion. There can be no happier occasion for a community to celebrate. What a pity that one member of the community can not join the party!

The parable is addressed to religious people, to those who above all others are in danger of adopting the stance of the elder brother. In the time of Jesus they may well have been the "Pharisees and the scribes" (Luke 15:2). But all who are zealous for God are in danger of allowing their religious zeal to restrict God's grace to those who, like them, have continued loyally in his service for years. For this reason Luke has placed these parables within the framework of the journey to Jerusalem (9:51—19:48), during which Jesus is instructing his followers in the way of discipleship. The church in all ages faces the danger of limiting the overflowing love of God so as to exclude the prodigals and notorious sinners. Thereby they convert the way of grace into a religion of good works in which there is little cause for celebration. With Jesus, however, there is always the chance for the prodigal to come home. He will always be welcome.

A Remarkably Open Community

We have repeatedly observed the openness of Jesus of Nazareth, who crossed the boundaries to welcome the despised and oppressed groups of Palestinian society. Those who had been pushed to margins and deprived of their status found themselves singled out for special attention. The Nazarene was so partial to these groups that he even went as far as promising the kingdom to the poor (Matt. 5:3; Luke 6:20), the powerless (Mark 10:15), and the persecuted (Matt. 5:11-12; Luke 6:22-23). Among his disciples, he even numbered fishermen (Mark 1:16-20), tax collectors (2:14), and freedom fighters (Luke 6:15). There doesn't seem to have been a "religious person" among them. Indeed, the religious community of the day was almost totally opposed to Jesus.

The radical openness of Jesus challenged the dominant understanding of God among his contemporaries. But by the time the Gospels came to be written, the traditional religious perspective was threatening to take over again. We can see this most clearly in Matthew's community, which was prone to legalism and judgmental attitudes. The members sought to develop a "pure church" (Matt. 13:24-30, 36-43) by excluding all those who failed to maintain high standards (18:10-14, 21-35). However, as the Evangelist emphasizes, if these rules were applied across the board, the apostle Peter would have been one of the first to be thrown out!

Despite Peter's enthusiastic confessions of faith, he failed miserably—even to the point of denying Jesus (Matt. 26:69-75). The story of his attempt to walk on the water (14:22-33) is presented as a parable of divine forgiveness extended to a loudmouth failure who had been given every opportunity to succeed. If the one who had denied Jesus could go on to lead the church, there must be room for anyone who wants to join! As Matthew stresses, grace is not only available at the beginning of the Christian life, it is there throughout—if we are prepared to extend the same grace to others (6:14-15), no matter how many times they might fail (18:21-22).

The dominant problem confronting Mark's church in this regard was power rather than purity. Thus, throughout his Gospel he stresses that discipleship is not a human achievement; it is possible only through a divine miracle of grace (Mark 8:22-26; 10:23-27; 14:26-42). The grace of discipleship, however, is costly grace. Those who have been graciously called to follow Jesus must walk the way of the cross. On that road, life and liberation will be found (10:46-52).

Luke is determined to extend the social and political parameters of his community. More than any other Evangelist, he stresses the positive role played in the ministry of Jesus by the marginalized and outcast people of Galilee. This is the Gospel where the Samaritans, the lepers, the widows, and the despised tax collectors come into their own. In Luke, Jesus defends most clearly his call for a community without protective walls and fences. Welcome the lost; celebrate when they are found (Luke 15:1-31 and many places). Kill the fatted calf; call the community together to rejoice whenever the lost return. Even those who have lived with the pigs are to receive the royal robe and the ring of authority.

Yet today people are calling for homogeneous churches! Welcoming the prodigals and embracing the notorious sinners of our world may not lead to magnificent manses and crystal cathedrals, but it will lead us to Jesus, the incarnate grace and love of God. There we will find liberation and hope for humanity—and for ourselves.

Traveling with Jesus sets us free from the mad craving to succeed and allows us to be real people again. We can live with our disappointments and face our failures because we know that, among the lepers, Jesus always encounters us as grace and love. This grace and love liberates us and allows us to celebrate God's presence in the midst of our broken humanity. To celebrate with Jesus, however, we must be willing to welcome all those whom he has invited to join with him in life on the road. The wretched of the earth and the failures in the church are among the first to be invited.

Questions for Discussion

1. What does it mean to say discipleship is a miracle of divine grace?

2. Is it still hard to open the eyes of the blind?

3. Have you ever tried walking on water? What happened?

4. With whom do you identify in the parable of the prodigal son? Why?

5. How can the church welcome the prodigals and embrace the sinners in our day? What will happen to our standards if we do?

6. Have you experienced the grace of God lately? How? Did it make any difference in the way you live?

7. How is the grace of God working in your church, community, or group?

8. What are your hopes for the future?

The Road from Nazareth Leads into the Future

Although I naturally was not aware of it at the time, I was already taking the first faltering steps in a life on the road with Jesus on that first morning when I went to Sunday school in Wauchope. There I heard the story of Jesus calling disciples to follow him and felt the magnetic attraction of the stranger from Galilee. In those early years everything was focused on the present. The past, insofar as I was aware of it, was made up mostly of pleasant memories of the last couple of days, and the future was mainly dreams of what we would be doing down by the river next week. Any thoughts of life on the road with Jesus had to fit into that sort of framework.

The process of growing up added new dimensions. The study of history and culture, anthropology and sociology, brought fresh insights into the meaning of life on the road. I have spent years in reading the story of Jesus and analyzing the Gospels. This reinforced my understanding of how Jesus meets us as a stranger from another world and yet leads us on as our companion for the journey and our friend for the future. The stories come from an age almost lost in the mists of time and from a culture separated from us by the revolutionary advances of history. Yet as we hear the stories and sing the songs, the road that started in Nazareth leads us into the future. The risen Lord goes before his people, calling us to follow, challenging us to new heights of apostolic daring, and comforting us when we stumble and fall. The road goes on. The same Jesus who called the first four fishermen in Galilee calls us to the journey of faith on the road which leads into the future.

The Road Begins in Nazareth with Jesus and the Disciples

Jesus came preaching and teaching that the time of fulfillment had drawn near, that God's kingly reign was about to
break into human history. Through his ministry Satan was
being defeated, the blind were receiving their sight, the lame
were walking, the lepers were being cleansed, the deaf were
hearing, the dead were being raised, and the good news was
being preached to the poor.

Many of the religious and political leaders were unable to
understand his teaching, and they were indignant at the way
he behaved. As a wandering charismatic preacher, he associated with the riffraff of society, and that invited both the
wrath of God and the condemnation of the authorities. The
little people of society, however, recognized in the stranger
from Nazareth the fulfillment of their desires and ambitions.
Wherever he went in Galilee, the poor and the outcasts, the
women and the children, the sick and the demon-
possessed—all these flocked to greet him. When they arrived, they found that he had a special place for them.

Jesus proclaimed and lived out the good news of the
kingdom, and he invited people to a life of discipleship on
the road with him. The invitation was a call of grace, thoroughly undeserved, motivated entirely by the love of God in
Jesus Christ. It offered liberation and fulfillment, a life of celebration with God and of service with brothers and sisters.

Like prodigal children who had experienced the forgiveness of the waiting parent, they were delighted at the opportunity of participating in God's heavenly banquet. Like
spurned tax collectors and notorious sinners who suddenly
found themselves invited to the carnival of God's grace, they
joyfully abandoned their boats and their books and went off
after Jesus with scarcely a care about tomorrow and the trouble it might bring. As far as they were concerned, the cares of
the world were passing away, the carnival of heaven had already begun!

But it was often costly to accept his invitation to discipleship, for life on the road was not only exciting, it was also
challenging and dangerous. Jesus reminded one of the doc-
tors of the Law who wished to follow him, "Foxes have holes,

birds of the air have nests; but the Son of Man has nowhere to lay his head" (Matt. 8:20). He warned the disciple who wanted first to go off and bury his father, "Follow me, and let the dead bury their own dead" (8:22). The one who wished to say good-bye to those at home was told, "No one who puts a hand to the plow and looks back is fit for the kingdom of God" (Luke 9:62). Jesus was on his way in the pilgrimage of life, and those who wanted to enter into life "must take up their cross and follow" him (Mark 8:34), giving absolute allegiance to the kingdom of God and to the service of humanity.

The ethical demands of the kingdom, preached and lived out by Jesus, always touched the point at which the person was enslaved to the powers of the old age and was thus unable to respond to God's gracious invitation. Since this invitation was to liberation and new life in the kingdom, the message of Jesus challenged those areas and aspects of life which held people in chains, so bound by the past and the present that the future was no longer open to them. Yet when people experienced the reality of the kingdom breaking into the world, it was like joy overwhelming their total existence, penetrating every area of their lives. By comparison, nothing else in life mattered, and no price was too great to pay. They gladly surrendered everything they owned, so that they might have that which was of ultimate worth.

In order to follow Jesus on his preaching missions throughout Palestine, the first disciples had to leave their possessions behind. They had to say good-bye to their families and their friends, their professions, and their profits, because they were following the wandering preacher of Galilee. He was in Capernaum one day and in Cana the next.

As they traveled, they heard Jesus commend the poor widow who gave away all her money, and they witnessed his emphatic approval of the woman who squandered her money in a dramatic act of single-minded devotion. He taught them that they must resolutely refuse to attempt the impossibility of seeking to serve God and money at the same time. And he encouraged them to learn from the birds of the air and the flowers of the field that God could be trusted to care for them. Jesus pronounced God's blessing on the poor and declared that their place in the kingdom of God was secure. He denounced the rich as having already received the only reward that belonged to them. A new value system was beginning to emerge.

As they lived with Jesus on the road, the disciples became a new community of the people of God. They learned by bitter experience and delightful pleasure that their day-to-day existence was no longer totally under their control. What happened in their lives was now determined by their relationship to Jesus Christ. When he was invited to a wedding feast in Cana of Galilee, they were also invited. But when the Son of Man had nowhere to lay his head, they had nowhere to lay theirs. When he was received into a house, they were also received into the house; when he was rejected, they were rejected. What happened to him, happened to them because they belonged to him.

Jesus had become the center of their existence, and his grace bound them together. But it was to be an open community based on grace and love, not a closed enclave determined by rites and respectability. The tax collector and the freedom fighter were equally welcome, and they were included simply because Jesus, in his grace, had called them. No group had a franchise on the friendship of Jesus.

As the disciples traveled with Jesus, they heard him teach on the necessity of being concerned for their brothers and sisters, their neighbors, and even those who were persecuting them. He taught that they were to love God with all their heart and soul and mind and strength, and they were to love their neighbors as themselves. He emphasized that this loving concern was to be shown in forgiveness, in doing for others what they expected others to do for them, and in caring for the hungry, the thirsty, and the naked. The community of the new people of God was bound together by its allegiance to Jesus, and it knew no borders.

The call of Jesus which brought the disciples together as a community of the people of God also led them out on mission in the world. As they traveled, they noticed that while Jesus' mission was directed towards all Israel—the rich and the poor, the learned and the illiterate. He seemed to show a particular partiality for the outcasts of society—lepers, notorious sinners, despised tax collectors, drunkards and prostitutes, women and children. They saw that Jesus offered hospitality to society's nobodies, joined in their festivals, and promised them places of honor at the messianic meal of the people of God. His mission was one of all-embracing grace and love.

In preparation for their later worldwide mission, Jesus sent them out in pairs, preaching the gospel, healing the sick, and casting out demons. Their mission, like his, consisted in persuading people to change their way of living. They taught them how they might live in a proper relationship with God and with each other, healed the lives of individuals, and changed or destroyed the demonic forces that hold people captive. It was an urgent and costly mission, with severe restrictions on what they might take on the journey. It was fraught with danger, but it met with considerable success.

The mission of the disciples, as a continuation of Jesus' messianic mission, involved a voluntary renunciation of traditional ideas of power and privilege. It meant the acceptance of a new role as servants of God and of humanity. Born in a stable and raised in the obscure and despised village of Nazareth, Jesus took his stand with the despised and dispossessed people of Galilee. He claimed authority to forgive sins, to exercise lordship over the Sabbath, and to ignore their stringent food regulations. He cured the sick, cast out demons, cleansed lepers, and expelled traders and pilgrims from the temple in Jerusalem.

Jesus had the power to defeat the forces of evil, yet he was crucified "outside the camp" (Heb. 13:13), rejected by the power elite of his day. Even in his death, Jesus was found in the company of the despised, the rejected, and the tortured outcasts of society. His contemporaries looked for a messianic leader of great power and glory who would restore the political fortunes of Israel, but Jesus refused to fulfill these hopes and ambitions as he deliberately identified with the plight of the powerless.

The disciples traveled with Jesus and heard him promise the inheritance of God's kingly reign to the poor, the persecuted, and the powerless. They witnessed the way he took his stand against oppressors seeking to exploit the law to their own advantage, while at the same time he welcomed the weak and powerless. Repeatedly, Jesus sought to teach them that the way to greatness was to be found in humble service.

The disciples were struggling to understand that involvement in God's mission of grace and love in the world required the renunciation of traditional concepts of power and status. At the same time, Jesus was seeking to make them aware of their new status before God and of a new power available to them from God. As they traveled, they had to learn that their outward journey of mission was to have its necessary counterpart in the inward journey of prayer and dependence upon God, the source of grace and love. On the road with Jesus, they saw that during his own ministry Jesus retreated to the wilderness for times of prayer, and they heard the way he spoke to God as a child spoke to his father. He taught them to pray to his Father in the same way, seeking the inbreaking of his kingdom and confidently asking him to supply all their needs. This was to be their privilege and their power, though they were to recognize that it was a privilege and a power available to everyone.

At the time of their call, the earliest disciples were not involved in a devout life of prayer and meditation, temple attendance, and religious devotion. Instead, they were fishing, mending nets, and even collecting taxes. The call to follow Jesus came to them not because of who they were or even who they were to become. It came to them because of who Jesus was—the incarnate grace and love of God. As they traveled the length and breadth of Palestine following Jesus, this group of very diverse people became a community of grace, relating to one another because of their relationship to him.

These disciples were sent out on a mission of continuing grace in the world as an extension of the messianic mission of Jesus—preaching, teaching, and healing. Because of their awareness of the loving grace of God, their natural concern for material security was conquered and their obsession for power, privilege and prestige was finally overcome. They frequently returned to the source of grace and love in prayer and thanksgiving. They often struggled, and sometimes they tripped and fell. But, in Jesus, God repeatedly met them in grace and love, always inviting them to continue their journey with him.

The Road Leads On Through History with Jesus and the Early Churches

When the first disciples responded to the call of Jesus, their lifestyle was radically transformed as they followed him on his preaching missions throughout Galilee, later journeying with him as far away as Jerusalem. The Gospels, however, were written long after Jesus ceased his ministry as a wandering charismatic prophet. And as the Evangelists reinterpreted the stories of Jesus and the disciples, they developed lifestyle principles for the later churches to which they were writing.

It is clear from the Gospels that not all who responded positively to Jesus' proclamation of God's rule of grace actually accompanied him on his journeys through Palestine. Not all abandoned parents and profits to follow him. Simon's mother-in-law served Jesus in her home. The paralytic and his friends returned home after Jesus had healed him and forgiven his sins; the woman with a hemorrhage, though told that her faith had saved her, was healed and told, "Go in peace." When the Gadarene demoniac was healed, he wanted to travel with Jesus, but Jesus sent him home to tell his family and friends of his experience.

On the other hand, there were often many others beside the disciples accompanying Jesus on his journeys. Mostly, the Gospel writers simply refer to this group as "the crowd," an anonymous collection of people from all over Galilee. But at times we learn more about them. On one occasion, for instance, we are told that one of the large groups of people who "followed him" were tax collectors and notorious sinners. On another, we find that the women at the foot of the cross "used to follow him and provided for him when he was in Galilee" (Mark 15:41). Groups like these may have accompanied Jesus for longer or shorter periods of time. In the story of the feeding of the four thousand, we are told that they had been with him for "three days," and the passion account says that many other women "had come up with him to Jerusalem" (15:41), a long journey in the time of Jesus.

Not all who accepted Jesus' message were called to follow him. And not all of those who followed him at various times were called in a special way to be his disciples. However, we often overlook a significant fact when we study the Gospels: when the Evangelists came to develop their presentations of the contemporary significance of Jesus, they used the stories about the disciples as models, or paradigms, for Christian life within their churches. These stories were never allowed to become mere recitations of events and happenings from the life of Jesus and his friends. They were never reduced to the level of yarns about the good old days. They were always regarded as lessons in contemporary Christian living, told in storybook fashion.

It is a remarkable thing that after the resurrection of Jesus, as Christianity was spreading throughout the Empire, the early Christians continued to tell the stories of the way Jesus called his disciples to follow him through Palestine. Even when they lived in communities scattered throughout the Mediterranean world, they remembered them and reinterpreted them as the call of Christ to themselves. Many Christians had never seen the Sea of Galilee and knew nothing about tax collecting, much less about fishing. Yet even they saw in these stories definitive examples of the way God works in the world. As these stories were recounted, the early church continued to hear Jesus calling people to faith, bringing them together as his people, and leading them out to continue his mission in the world. They described a new way of living and called many to faith again and again.

Long after Jesus had disappeared from the face of the earth, the picture of him moving through Palestine continued as a primary Gospel image. The stories about the disciples and others were retold, not as isolated encounters, but as a new way of living for those who would respond positively to the call to follow Jesus. Each Gospel, however, has its own particular emphasis, its own particular theology, its own particular ethos and lifestyle. Each was written in an attempt to meet the challenge facing a particular congregation in a particular situation at a particular point in history. What might be regarded as an appropriate response at one time, might be considered as quite inadequate at another. A lifestyle commended in one situation might be quite detrimental in another.

This plurality of approach can be clearly seen, for example, by the differing ways in which Matthew and Luke incorporate such an important piece of tradition as the Lord's Prayer. Both use the prayer as an incentive for the development of a more meaningful spirituality, but they do so in very different ways. Writing for Jewish Christians who liked to pray and pray and pray, Matthew uses the Lord's Prayer as an example of true prayer, which is both brief and confident. There is no need to keep on badgering God; instead, make your requests known and have enough faith to leave the matter with him. Don't keep prattling on like the heathen, who think that they will be heard because of their many words.

On the other hand, Luke was writing for Gentile Christians who seemed to know very little about the life of prayer and who were apparently tempted to give up praying altogether. He says that here in the Lord's Prayer is a model that can be followed by anyone. Through repeatedly praying this short prayer, they will be encouraged to keep on praying and not lose heart. Luke reminds those who wanted to give up that the life of prayer requires persistence.

A similar diversity can be seen in the attitudes of Matthew and Luke toward material possessions. Matthew was writing in a middle-class urban situation where his readers were facing the danger of trying to find their security in material possessions. He was primarily concerned that they should learn to trust God for the future, and that in the present they should give priority to the service of the kingdom. One simply cannot serve God and mammon. Luke, however, came to write to a church which had long been poor but had recently seen the emergence of a rich group within its membership. He states quite bluntly and categorically that none can be a disciple of Jesus unless they first give up all their possessions. Thus Luke describes incidents from Christ's early ministry in Jerusalem to illustrate how he thinks this should happen in his own community.

Even on matters where the Evangelists are essentially in agreement, there is a considerable divergence in direction and emphasis. Both Matthew and Luke, in opposition to situations which had developed in their respective communities, stress the need for the church to be understood as an open community of grace. Matthew, however, was facing a church which tended towards legalism in its community relationships. They had taken over from the synagogue the rule concerning the proper method of handling cases of discipline which inevitably arose from time to time.

While restating the regulation for discipline, Matthew takes the opportunity to teach his church that there is no limit to God's grace nor to the forgiveness offered within the community of his people. The regulation was that first a disciple should discuss a fellow member's sin with that one privately. If the offender does not listen, a group of two or three should speak to the erring one officially. If the offender still will not listen, the matter is to be taken to the church. And finally, if the straying member will not listen to the church, that one should be excommunicated.

This procedure seems eminently reasonable, for the person has at least three opportunities for repentance. Yet grace is never so reasonable, and it is grace that must moderate the danger of a legalistic interpretation of such a regulation. So, immediately after giving this regulation, which was obviously being followed in the Matthaean church and so could not be ignored, Matthew has Peter ask Jesus how many times he should forgive his brother who sins against him—as many as seven times? The answer of Jesus—until seventy times seven—means that the church will think seriously before using the rule of excommunication again. Forgiveness must be an ongoing principle of the life of the church, for it is to be an open community of grace.

The Lucan church, on the other hand, was facing the danger of respectability. Many of its members had begun to forget the poverty of their past and to move upward in the social scale. Confronted with this danger of imminent elitism, Luke delights in telling stories of how the most disreputable of people came to Jesus and found a ready welcome in his community. Samaritans and sinners, women and lepers, and tax collectors abound in this Gospel. And if anyone should object, there are all of the distinctive parables Luke presents, justifying Jesus' action and showing the way the community must always be open to the people who need it most.

There are important differences between Gospels. Nonetheless, the Evangelists are united in their belief that discipleship must always be related to the concrete issues of life. Indeed, the primary reason for the existence of four very different Gospels is this insistence that the gospel must be related to the specific situations in which they find themselves. If it were not for this belief, the Gospel of Mark could have simply been taken over by the Matthaean and Lucan churches, or by the Johannine churches, for that matter. But we have the four Gospels, for the good news must always be reinterpreted.

The Road Leads into the Future with Jesus and with the Churches of Today and Tomorrow

We stand at quite a distance both from the origin of the Christian tradition and from its early reinterpretations in the Gospels. This means that our process of reinterpretation is both more complicated and more necessary than that undertaken by the Evangelists. While we are nonetheless called on to reinterpret it for our own situations, the life and ministry of Jesus remains normative. And the Gospel accounts indicate ways in which the principles may be reapplied to varying situations.

The process of reinterpretation requires an understanding of the tradition and of the contemporary situation. Therefore, the Christian church, as a community of faith, has an important prophetic function. This is a function of the whole community of faith and of those who are called to a pastoral, priestly, and teaching office within the church. Neither the church nor its leaders can adopt a neutral stance toward either the Jesus tradition or the cultural context. The faith cannot be lived in a vacuum removed from the religious, social, and political realities which determine the contours of life.

In the Western world, we have been much influenced by the tradition of individualism which has its roots in Greek philosophy and in the spirit of the Renaissance. Our Protestant churches have mediated the faith to us through an excessively individualistic understanding of the Bible and of the Reformation. With an emphasis on privatized spirituality and individual decision making, fueled by the competitive spirit of consumerism, we have come to see the Christian faith as predominantly concerned with the relationship of an individual to God. The community dimension has been reduced to the level of an optional extra, suggested perhaps for those not strong enough to make it on their own.

This situation of excessive individualism is rapidly reaching crisis proportions with the emergence of the alienated society. Increasingly, we are experiencing the sense of being shut off, guarded, overprotective of ourselves, and unsure of our neighbors. In its most acute form, this alienation is displaying itself in the rapidly increasing suicide rate among young people, in the alarming spread of drug abuse among middle-aged housewives, in the frantic pace of modern cities, and in the appalling loneliness of the elderly. But it is there just as surely in humanity's race against itself, which is pushing technological development at an exponential pace. This is depriving us of the time and opportunity for authentic human living.

One of the issues which needs to be near the top of the agenda in our churches is the question of how, once again, the church may become the church—a community of people bound by the grace and love of God, supporting one another and embracing humanity in a mission of liberation and reconciliation. We need space in which we can learn to be human again. We need time so that we may learn again to worship God, love one another, and celebrate the life which is ours through Jesus Christ. In some situations this is beginning to happen through small groups, in other places through house churches, and in others through the development of intentional Christian communities. My own convic-

tion is that it is the latter option which offers greatest possibilities for a new way of living, but I recognize that it is not
the only option.

Whichever way we seek to recover the corporate dimension of faith, it is clear that we may not restrict the Christian
lifestyle to Sunday morning worship and an occasional meeting during the week. It needs to be corporate, therapeutic,
and evangelistic—to embrace all of life and to be open to all
of God's people. For too long we have been molded by the
dictates and desires of our consumer society. The time has
come to say no to these destructive forces so that we might
again embrace life with enthusiasm and energy.

On the basis of what we have seen in the life of Jesus and
in the lifestyle of the early churches, here is the possibility for
us to rediscover the meaning of Christian family, community,
and people of God; to find our interrelatedness in a lifestyle
of support and service. Together in Christ we have the basis
for responsible relationships covering all areas of our living.
This is the exciting possibility of life together on the road
with Jesus Christ. It is a difficult possibility, but it is this very
difficulty which makes it such an important and urgent undertaking.

Already in the earliest of churches, and throughout much
of church history since, the issue of material possessions has
posed serious challenges and questions relating both to the
lifestyle of the rich and the suffering of the poor. The acute-
ness of the problem at the present time arises from the stag-
gering disparity between the two groups and the demonstra-
ble relationship between them. The poor are getting poorer
in many parts of the world because the rich are getting richer.
We have been preoccupied with East-West issues of communism versus capitalism. But now there is a shift, and we are
learning that the major political problem at present is the
North-South reality of the way wealthy countries are oppressing their poorer trading partners. The church is at the
center of the debate and discussion because of our wealth in
the North and our involvement with the poor in the South.

We like to talk about "the global village" for it has something of a romantic ring about it. That village, however, is

anything but romantic, with almost 70 percent of the inhabitants living in poverty, 25 percent in varying degrees of middle class, and only 5 percent wealthy. Yet that 5 percent probably spends half the money and controls prices and production for almost all commodities in half the world. The statistics are appalling. Two-thirds of the people of the world have inadequate diets, and 400 million are so badly undernourished that they are incapable of physical or mental work. Ten thousand people die of starvation every day!

Australians, like North Americans, live in one of the wealthiest countries of the world. Yet we live in close proximity to a vast sea of poverty in the world. For too long we have allowed the economists and politicians to develop our fiscal policies, even when we have realized that they are so often acting under pressure of powerful interest groups representing the military-industrial complex and large financial institutions. These pressures often do not even arise in Australia in the first instance, but have their origin in the board rooms of the large transnational companies and organizations. The interests of these groups are patently not those of the majority of the population, much less those of the suffering people of the world.

We Christians are a people striving to develop a responsible lifestyle based on the life and ministry of Jesus and yet related to the concrete issues of today. Thus we want to work for a new international economic order and for a new system of trade agreements based on justice for all, rather than systems formulated to further the interests of the rich and powerful. At the same time, we want to bring our own lives, and the lives of the Christian communities of which we are a part, more and more in line with the ways of the kingdom of God. One of the marks of the new responsible church will be a simpler lifestyle and a more just sharing of resources among the whole community, with particular concern for those who are presently suffering through institutionalized discrimination.

In this book I have repeatedly suggested that the key to understanding the significance of the life and ministry of Jesus for the twentieth-century church is to be found in the fact that he lived on the underside of history, among the marginalized and outcast people of society. He may have been born in Bethlehem, but he made the despised village of Nazareth his home, living on the other side of the tracks and working for a new community of liberation and justice.

As in North America and Europe, Australian society has produced a long list of outcasts. We have women and men who have yet to receive full acceptance into the "okker society," the great Australian myth. Most notable are the Aboriginal people and Torres Strait Islanders, especially those of mixed descent who have been deprived of their tribal lands and have drifted to become displaced and deprived persons in the cities. In our own city of Melbourne, not to mention the other major cities of the Commonwealth, the ethnic groups still struggle against prejudice in many areas. We have the largest Jewish school outside of Israel, we are the third largest Greek city in the world, and we have more Irish than Dublin itself. However, prejudice and discrimination have yet to be eliminated.

In the first generations after immigrating here, the majority of these people live in closed communities, frequently in the depressed areas of the city, often in dehumanizing high-rise apartment buildings. In many places they find acceptance only to the degree that they are prepared to divest themselves of their own national heritage and become anonymous citizens in a basically Anglo-Saxon society. The Jews, Italians, Greeks, and Irish may now have been absorbed, but the problem has simply been transferred to those who have arrived more recently, the Turks and the refugees from Southeast Asia.

As elsewhere, there is the community of the poor and the downtrodden, a community which the Australian Government Commission of Inquiry into Poverty showed was much larger and growing more rapidly than anyone imagined. There are those who have been ostracized through alcohol and drug dependence. There are the prostitutes and those regarded as social deviants. There are the members of the various subcultures, all of whom are struggling for acceptance in Australian society.

Yet as in North America, in all the major cities of our country, the churches are flourishing in the respectable middle-class and upper-middle-class suburbs. In the depressed areas and institutionalized areas of the cities, where many of the marginalized people are to be found, the churches are languishing. This is a situation which will have to be remedied if we are to live a responsible Christian lifestyle which has its roots in the life and ministry of Jesus of Nazareth. The good news in Jesus is based on grace and love rather than on works and respectability. It calls us to live and to view society from the underside of history. As we can learn to live from this perspective, our attitudes toward the world around us will be radically transformed, and we will find ourselves venturing further into a new way of living, the way of discipleship, following Jesus Christ.

Life on the road may be difficult for some of us, especially if we have been brought up on a privatized Christianity which has avoided the hard socioeconomic decisions inevitably part of a responsible Christian lifestyle. However, it will never be boring. With each new challenge that comes to us in the community of God's new people, there also comes a new opportunity to follow Jesus, and with that opportunity comes the promise of grace. The Jesus who graciously calls us to a new lifestyle on the road is the same one who accompanies us as we journey into the future.

This life of discipleship is essentially a pilgrimage in the company of all others who are being led by the one who first set his face toward Jerusalem. The road to Jerusalem leads to the cross and travels on to the resurrection. The crucified and risen one calls and empowers his followers as they journey toward that day when his kingdom will be revealed in all its glory, as his will is accomplished on earth as in heaven, and as all his people live together in justice and peace.

Palestine in New Testament Times

Map by Paula Johnson, Merrill R. Miller, and Jan Gleysteen

+ Means city has uncertain location

Leader's Guide

Aim for a ninety-minute session to handle each chapter. If more time is needed, the group could spend more than one session on a chapter.

Here is a basic outline for each session:

- *Beforehand:* Read the chapter yourself and ask each group member to read it.
- *Starting Out:* A warm-up activity introducing a central idea or theme of the session.
- *Reading the Map:* Look together at the three Bible passages used in the chapter. Grasp what the Bible says about the topic.
- *Pondering the Route Choices:* Compare the Gospel accounts with the stories of the group members. Let the Questions for Discussion stimulate the group to ponder applications for Christian discipleship today.
- *The Way Ahead:* Gather up response to what has been studied, discussed, and learned. List suggestions for prayer and action.

Here is a sample of a Starting-Out exercise for chapter 3: Be yourself. Spend a few moments thinking of as many advantages as you can for not having one specific material possession. For example, not owning a car could mean: I walk more, am healthier, meet more people outside my immediate circle of friends and family, have more opportunities to share the gospel, am more open to receive and give, have freedom from worries about the upkeep of my car and the stresses of driving, have more money to use in other ways in God's service. . . . In pairs, share your ideas.

This activity will lead into the Bible stories.

(Based on a forthcoming Australian discussion guide for this book.)

Bibliography

Anderson, Hugh. *The Gospel of Mark.* London: Oliphants, 1976.

Apostolic Fathers, The. Ed. by Michael W. Holmes. Tr. by J. B. Lightfoot and J. R. Harmer. 2d ed. Grand Rapids: Baker Book House, 1990.

Bailey, Kenneth E. *Poet and Peasant: A Literary-Cultural Approach to the Parables in Luke.* Grand Rapids: Eerdmans, 1976.

Behm, Johannes. "Noeō." In *Theological Dictionary of the New Testament,* vol. 4, ed. by G. Kittel, Grand Rapids: Eerdmans, 1967:948-1022.

Best, Ernest. *Following Jesus: Discipleship in the Gospel of Mark.* Sheffield: JSOT Press, 1981.

Bonhoeffer, Dietrich. *The Cost of Discipleship.* London: SCM Press, 1974 (=1948).

Bornkamm, Günther. *Jesus of Nazareth.* London: Hodder & Stoughton, 1963.

Bornkamm, Günther, Gerhard Barth, and **Heinz Joachim Held.** *Tradition and Interpretation in Matthew.* London: SCM Press, 1963.

Brown, Raymond E. *The Gospel According to John.* 2 vols. Garden City: Doubleday, 1966, 1970.

Brunner, Emil. *The Word and the World.* London: SCM Press, 1931.

Camara, Dom Helder. *The Desert Is Fertile.* London: Sheed & Ward, 1974.

_____. *Hoping Against All Hope.* Maryknoll: Orbis, 1984.

Cranfield, C. E. B. *The Gospel According to St. Mark.* Cambridge: University Press, 1959.

Crossan, John Dominic. *The Historical Jesus: The Life of a Mediterranean Jewish Peasant.* San Francisco: Harper San Francisco, 1991.

Crowe, Jerome. *The Acts.* Dublin: Veritas Publications, 1979.

Dead Sea Scrolls in English, The. Tr. by G. Vermes. 3d ed. New York: Penguin Books, 1987.

Ellis, E. Earle. *The Gospel of Luke.* London: Nelson, 1966.

Ewald, George R. *Jesus and Divorce,* Scottdale, Pa.: Herald Press, 1991.

Fiorenza, Elisabeth Schussler. *In Memory of Her: A Feminist Theological Reconstruction of Christian Origins.* London: SCM Press, 1983.

Fitzmyer, Joseph A. *The Gospel According to Luke.* 2 vols. Garden City: Doubleday, 1981, 1985.

Ford, J. Massyngbaerde. *My Enemy Is My Guest: Jesus and Violence in Luke.* Maryknoll: Orbis, 1984.

Fromm, Erich. *To Have or To Be?* London: Jonathan Cape, 1978.

Galilea, Segundo. *Following Jesus.* Maryknoll: Orbis Press, 1983.

Gardner, Richard B. *Matthew.* Believers Church Bible Commentary. Scottdale, Pa.: Herald Press, 1991.

Geldenhuys, J. Norval. *Commentary on the Gospel of Luke.* London: Marshall, Morgan & Scott, 1956.

Gundry, Robert H. *Matthew: A Commentary on His Literary and Theological Art.* Grand Rapids: Eerdmans, 1982.

Gutiérrez, Gustavo. *The Power of the Poor in History.* London: SCM Press, 1983.

_____. *We Drink from Our Own Wells: The Spiritual Journey of a People.* Maryknoll: Orbis Books, 1984.

Haenchen, Ernst. *The Acts of the Apostles.* Oxford: Basil Blackwell, 1971.

Hahn, Ferdinand. *Mission in the New Testament.* London: SCM Press, 1965.

_____, **August Strobel,** and **Eduard Schweizer.** *The Beginning of the Church in the New Testament.* Edinburgh: Saint Andrew Press, 1970.

Hengel, Martin. *The Charismatic Leader and His Followers.* London: T. & T. Clark, 1981.

_____. *The Crucifixion in the Ancient World and the Folly of the Message of the Cross.* London: SCM Press, 1977.

Holl, Adolf. *Jesus in Bad Company.* London, Collins, 1972.

Jeremias, Joachim. *Jerusalem in the Time of Jesus.* London: SCM Press, 1969.

_____. *The Lord's Prayer.* Philadelphia: Fortress Press, 1974.

_____. *The Parables of Jesus.* London: SCM Press, 1963.

_____. *The Prayers of Jesus.* London: SCM Press, 1967.

_____. *Theology of the New Testament.* London: SCM Press, 1971.

Josephus. *Works of Josephus.* 10 vols. Tr. by H. St. J. Thackeray et al. Loeb Classical Library. Cambridge: Harvard University Press, 1926-1965.

Kee, Howard C. *Community of the New Age: Studies in Mark's Gospel.* London: SCM Press, 1977.

Kelber, Werner. *Mark's Story of Jesus.* Philadelphia: Fortress Press, 1979.

Kraybill, Donald B. *The Upside-Down Kingdom.* Scottdale, Pa.: Herald Press, 1978, 1990.

Küng, Hans. *On Being a Christian.* London: Collins, 1978.

Linnemann, Eta. *Parables of Jesus: Introduction and Exposition.* London: S.P.C.K., 1966.

Lorenz, Konrad. *Civilized Man's Eight Deadly Sins.* London: Methuen, 1974.

M'Neile, Alan H. *The Gospel According to St. Matthew.* London: Macmillan, 1961 (=1915).

Manson, T. W. *The Church's Ministry.* London: Hodder and Stoughton, 1948.

_____. *The Sayings of Jesus.* London: SCM Press, 1949.

Marshall, I. H. *The Gospel of Luke: A Commentary on the Greek Text.* Exeter: Paternoster Press, 1978.

Metz, Johann Baptist. *The Emergent Church: The Future of Christianity in a Postbourgeois World.* London: SCM Press, 1981.

Mishnah, The. Tr. by H. Danby. London: Oxford University Press, 1933.

Moltmann, Jürgen. *The Church in the Power of the Spirit.* London: SCM Press, 1977.

_____. *The Open Church: Invitation to a Messianic Lifestyle.* London: SCM Press, 1978.

New Testament Apocrypha. Ed. by Wilhelm Schneemelcher. Vol. 1, *Gospels and Related Writings.* Tr. by R. M. Wilson. Louisville, Ky.: Westminster John Knox, 1963, 1990.

Old Testament Pseudepigrapha, The. Ed. by James H. Charlesworth. 2 vols. Garden City, N.Y.: Doubleday, 1983, 1985.

Padilla, René. "Evangelism and the World." In *Let the Earth Hear His Voice*, ed. by J. D. Douglas, Minneapolis: World Wide Publications, 1975:116-146.

Qumran. See *Dead Sea Scrolls*.

Reumann, John. "Introduction." In Joachim Jeremias, *The Lord's Prayer*, Philadelphia: Fortress Press, 1964:v-xiii.

Schnackenburg, Rudolf. *The Gospel According to St. John*. Vol. 1. New York: Herder & Herder, 1968.

Schutz, Roger. *This Day Belongs to God*. London: Faith Press, 1961.

_____. *Struggle and Contemplation*. New York: Seabury Press, 1974.

Schweizer, Eduard. *The Good News According to Luke*. Atlanta: John Knox Press, 1984.

_____. *The Good News According to Mark*. Richmond: John Knox Press, 1970.

_____. *The Good News According to Matthew*. London: S. P. C. K., 1976.

_____. *Jesus*. London: SCM Press, 1971.

Senior, Donald, and **Carroll Stuhlmueller**. *The Biblical Foundations for Mission*. London: SCM Press, 1983.

Soelle, Dorothee, and **Fulbert Steffensky**. *Not Just Yes & Amen: Christians with a Cause*. Philadelphia: Fortress Press, 1985.

Taylor, Vincent. *The Gospel According to St. Mark*. London: Macmillan, 1959.

Theissen, Gerd. *The First Followers of Jesus: A Sociological Analysis of Earliest Christianity*. London: SCM Press, 1978.

Thielicke, Helmut. *The Prayer That Spans the World*. Cambridge: James Clark, 1965.

Index of Ancient Sources

Author Index

Subject Index

The Author

Born in a small country town in Australia, Athol Gill first studied agriculture. After a short career in business, he began to train for the Baptist ministry. He studied in Sydney, London, and Zurich, where he earned a doctor of theology degree under Eduard Schweizer. For the past twenty years he has been teaching New Testament in Australia.

Gill founded the House of Freedom Christian Community in Brisbane in 1972 and the House of the Gentle Bunyip Christian Community in Melbourne in 1974. With his family he lived as an extended household which is part of the House of the Gentle Bunyip. This is an inner-city community working with people suffering schizophrenia, with students, and in advocacy for people suffering from human rights abuses in Central America.

Gill worked with Central American Mission Partners and the Salvadorian support network, groups acting as advocates for the oppressed and persecuted. He has served on the Baptist World Alliance Commission on Human Rights. All these involvements add credibility to the message of *Life on the Road*. He was a strong advocate of the gospel for the poor.

Gill has served as visiting professor at the Matija Vlacic Illiric Theological Seminary in Zagreb (Yugoslavia, now Croatia), the Baptist Theological Seminary in Rüschlikon (Switzerland), the American Baptist Seminary of the West in Berkeley, and Central Baptist Theological Seminary in Kansas City. He has lectured in Australia and New Zealand, Eastern and Western Europe, and the United States.

Athol Gill was dean of Whitley (Baptist) College, University of Melbourne, 1975-79, and then professor of New Testament there, until his sudden death on March 9, 1992, at the age of 54, just one month before his first doctoral students graduated. He attracted many students to his courses and was widely known and respected for the quality of his academic work, for his deep commitment to living the faith he taught, and for his warm humanity. His influence extended across denominational barriers and embraced an extraordinary range of people.

David Batstone commends Gill's discipleship in his article "A Follower of Jesus: The Living Legacy of Athol Gill—1937-1992," published by *Sojourners*, June 1992, 23-26.

In addition to this book, Gill has published *The Call to Discipleship, Good News to the Poor, Fringes of Freedom*, and many articles, pamphlets, and chapters. He was preparing two other books for publication: *Interpreting the New Testament*, and *Theirs Is the Kingdom: The Place of the Poor in Scripture*. His presentations are polished through his frequent speaking engagements at conferences throughout Australia, New Zealand, and Southeast Asia.

Athol is survived by his wife, Judith Ann Prior, and two adult children, Jonathan and Kirsten. He was a member of the Clifton Hill Baptist Church and chaired the pastoral committee there.